P9-CRB-582

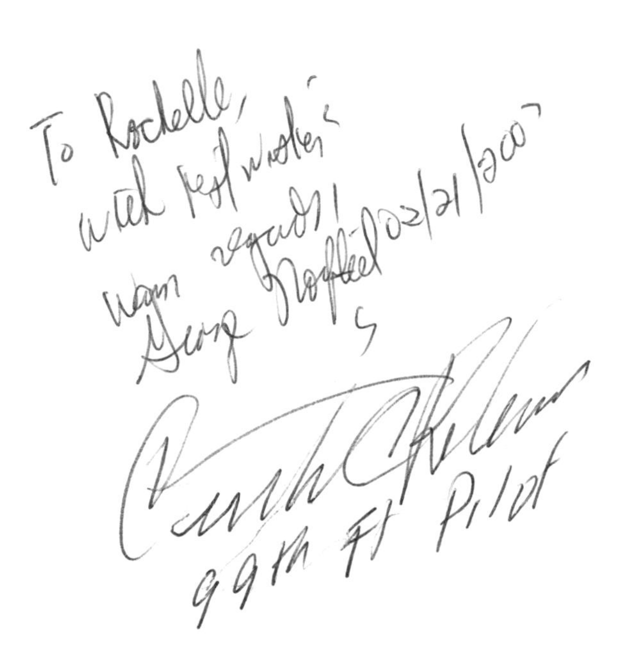

A Pilot's Journey

A Pilot's Journey

Memoirs of a Tuskegee Airman
Curtis Christopher Robinson

George Norfleet

Robnor Publishing, LLC

The author would like to thank Joan Pierotti, the late George Lowell Robinson, Faye Norfleet and staff members of The Library of Congress, and U.S. National Archives in Washington, D.C., and Greenbelt, Maryland, for their assistance and support in creating this book.

Robnor Publishing, LLC
Washington, D.C.

Article for The Washington Post printed with permission
Cover from Parade Magazine printed with permission

Library of Congress Control Number: 2005937869

ISBN 0-9776192-0-6

Photo Credits: Unless otherwise credited, all photos are from the collection of Curtis Christopher Robinson. Every effort has been made to identify copyright holders.

This book is dedicated to Lawrence A. Tyler, Jr., a young man with great potential for excellence in whatever endeavor he chooses. He just needs to have confidence in himself and his abilities. I hope this book inspires him to reach for the brass ring and to take all that comes with it.

Curtis Christopher Robinson

Contents

Preface

By George Norfleet
March 25, 2006

In June of 2003, Curtis Robinson and I began a series of interviews with the goal of writing his memoirs. As I listened to his life's story, I was taken by the rich, broad, and engaged life he had lived. The more I heard, the more aware I became of the fundamental basis of his success. Much of it is due to the family's patriarch, Thomas G. Robinson, his grandfather, who was born a slave, but became a minister, a teacher, and was elected the postmaster of Bamberg in the county of Barnwell, South Carolina in 1883. He was a man who so valued an education that he purchased land near Claflin College soon after it was established on which to build his house so that his children would have an opportunity to get an education. This he did after he completed his college education there around 1872. This patriarch imbued the family with timeless values for success and accomplishment.

Curtis Robinson's was born in Orangeburg, S.C., in 1919. His hometown provided a community environment that re-enforced the values taught in his home. By 1940, he had earned a degree in chemistry from Claflin College during a time when even a high school education was not available to black Americans in his hometown unless they paid for it. And this is what many did. Claflin College and South Carolina State College were both located across the street from his home. Their professors, instructors and teachers lived in his neighborhood. And those institution's graduates accounted for many of the town's tradesmen, artisans, and business people, who were also his neighbors. He was a son of the burgeoning black middle class, two generations removed from slavery.

In April, 2004, I was made aware of the location of a Tuskegee Airman's gravesite in my hometown in Gates County, N.C. I visited the site which is listed with the National Register of Historic Places as Buckland. The location of the gravesite is on the grounds of a 1795 colonial house originally owned by William Baker, the state official who introduced the bill in the North Carolina State House that created Gates County. Locally the site is called "the old Smith home." The late Reginald V. Smith is the Tuskegee Airman buried there. His brother Graham Smith was also a Tuskegee Airman. The site derived its local name ("old Smith home") from their grandfather, Charles E. Smith (1857-1951), himself a former slave who had worked there when it was a plantation, bought the farm in 1914, and hence its local name.

I found the story of the Smiths' grandfather as remarkable as that of Curtis Robinson's grandfather. It became apparent that the Tuskegee Airmen's success was not accidental, nor was it just the sons of the black upper class who succeeded. Apparently it wasn't just the training program that made them aviation standouts. These young men were the first products of the black middle class that were being allowed an opportunity to compete in American society in a meaningful way commensurate with their ability. They were the black community's leaders-in-waiting making a debut in 1942. For some, their grandfathers, first generation freemen, embodied a mindset very influential in its own way to the success of their grandsons. It wasn't the Tuskegee Airman Program that made them great. It was who they were along with their prior preparation provided by their families, institutions, and communities that equipped them individually and collectively to succeed.

Many of his fellow pilots became nationally renowned – generals, U.S. cabinet secretaries, college presidents, mayors of large cites and so on. After World War II, Robinson married his college sweetheart, Florie Frederick, started a family, valiantly battled all the problems and heartaches attendant with having a desperately sick child, graduated from pharmacy school, opened six pharmacies in Washington, D.C., and started a surgical supply company. He has been a pharmacist and entrepreneur for 54 years. C.C. Robinson is a modest but outgoing Tuskegee Airman whose life has been an extraordinary journey. Moreover, his life's story is part of a longer and equally remarkable Robinson family history whose origins are traced from the 1730s in Augsburg, Germany, and the west coast of Africa near Liberia, to South Carolina in the 1760s. His story and his family's are slices of the development and evolution of the black middle class. It's a story of struggle, success, hard work and, sometimes, tragic loss. Throughout life, his guiding force has been his faith in God and himself to lead him in the right direction, combined with a simple philosophy of the Golden Rule and loving his neighbor that he acquired from his community. He always had a knack for knowing what to do next in life, and more importantly, he did it! He managed to position himself one step ahead of the obstacles society presented him almost all of the time.

But this story is not one of bitterness or complaints. It is an extraordinary story of the life of one Tuskegee Airman from the 1920s through 2004, a story of individual success nestled within the story of the success and lifestyle of the early-striving black middle class. Today Robinson can be found running his remaining pharmacy five and a half days a week in Washington, D.C. He has known his customers for so long that they're not his customers anymore; they're his friends. And after 53 years in the business, why wouldn't they be -- especially considering the fact that at 86 years old he still delivers.

Introduction

Work on this book began in July of 2003 at the age 83. I wanted to share my experiences and observations and shed some light on the times in which I have lived. There is more to know about the Tuskegee Airmen than the portion of our lives spent as fighter pilots. Tuskegee Airmen were the product of the forebears and communities that illuminated the paths we would tread in life and showed us the way.

My life's story and family history provide some insights into this country's relationship with me during my 86 years and for generations of my family before me. It provides some insights into the relationships we sought to maintain with this country. It also details the manner in which I lived, values I embraced, the circumstances under which I became a fighter pilot during World War II, and the story of the life I lived thereafter.

A Pilot's Journey is representative of many Tuskegee Airmen. It is a recollection of events in my life from 1924, when I could first recall the stories in my favorite school book, through 2004, an eighty-year slice of twentieth century American life. My memoirs have been told from memory, recalled as accurately as an 86-year-old memory permits. If anyone familiar with Tuskegee Airmen history should find a discrepancy, I trust it will be insignificantly minor. Please attribute it to the passage of time and its tendency to obscure details. Rest assured, however, that all the events that follow are true, the circumstances are accurate and documented in other works. Hopefully, you will enjoy reading about the story of my life almost as much as I have enjoyed living it.

Curtis C. Robinson - 99th Fighter Squadron

Family Tree

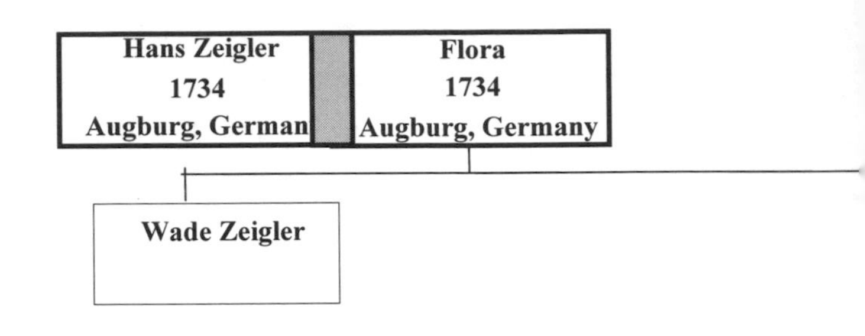

Hans Zeigler
1734
Augburg, German
Flora
1734
Augburg, Germany
Wade Zeigler

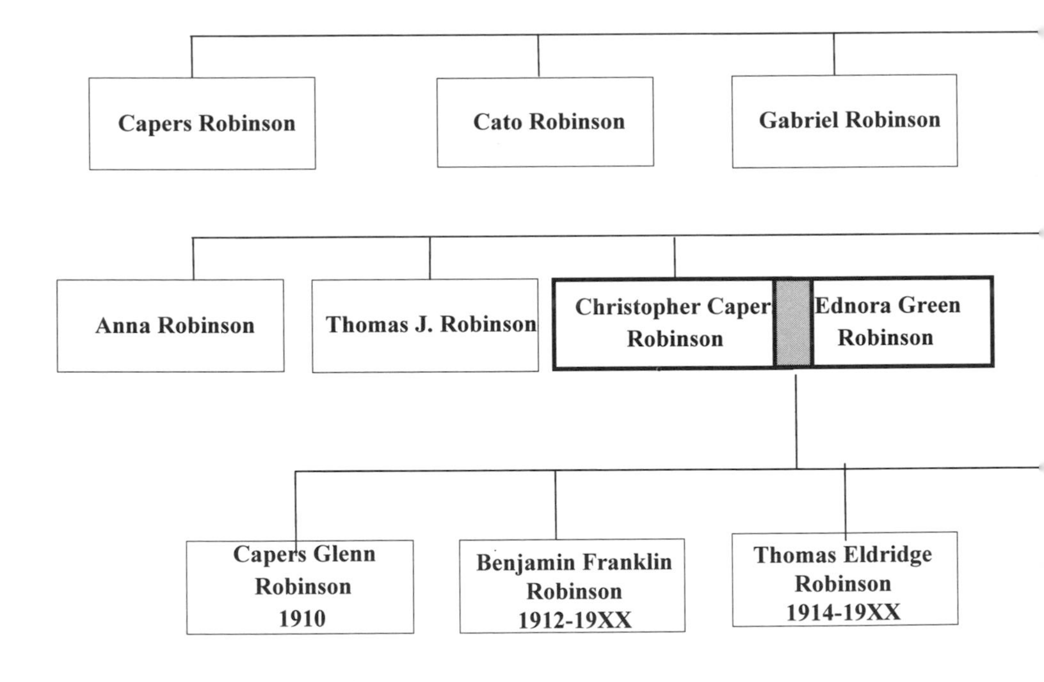

Capers Robinson
Cato Robinson
Gabriel Robinson
Anna Robinson
Thomas J. Robinson
Christopher Caper Robinson
Ednora Green Robinson
Capers Glenn Robinson 1910
Benjamin Franklin Robinson 1912-19XX
Thomas Eldridge Robinson 1914-19XX

Curtis Christopher Robinson

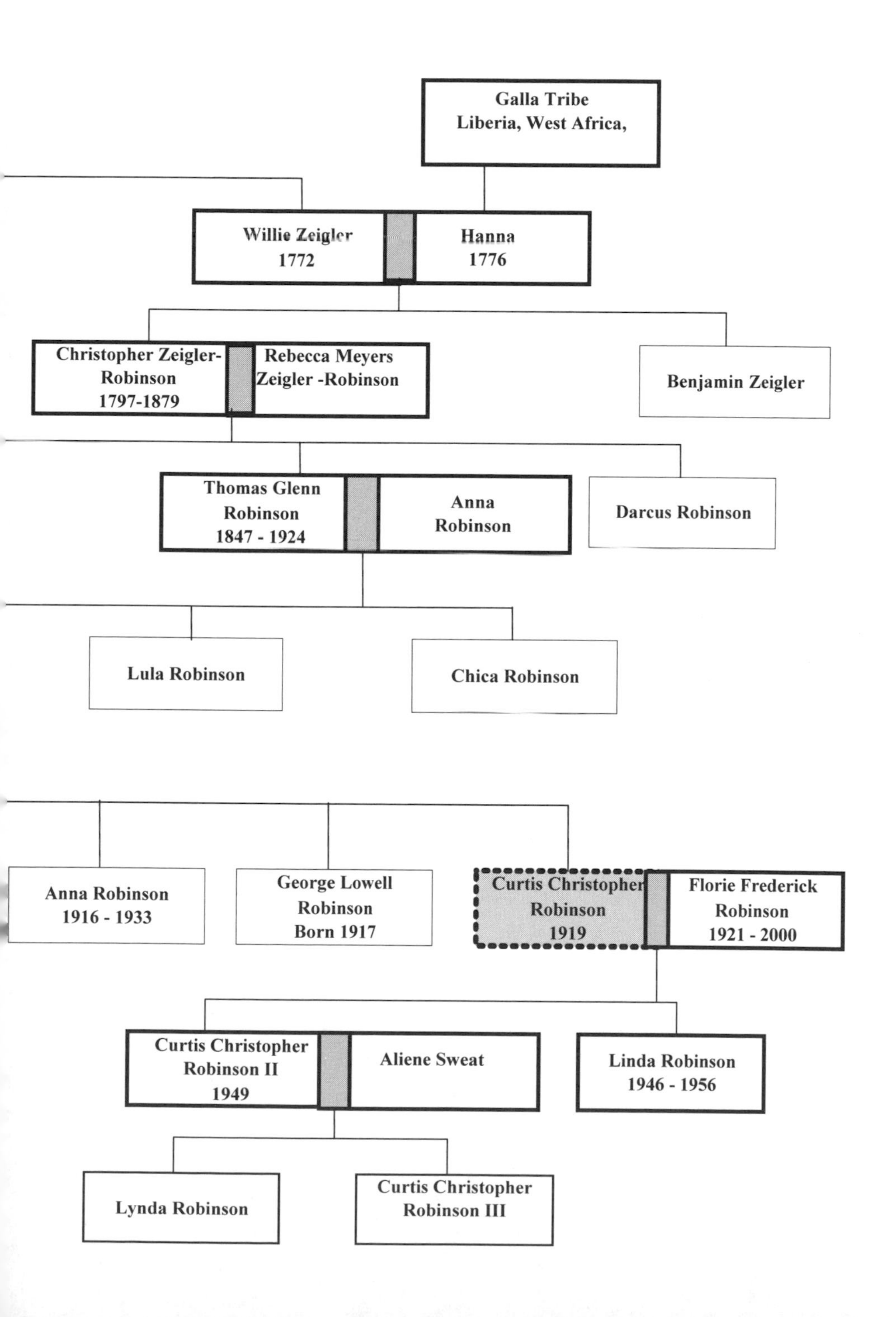

PART 1
THE EARLY DAYS

In The Beginning

"Red Shirts! "Red Shirts headed this way!" shouted a poll watcher in the South Carolina elections of 1876. Cato Robinson stopped his conversation with the poll supervisor and looked off in the distance. The men riding furiously his way were barely perceptible from the specks of red, the red jackets draping them. They created an enormous cloud of dust as their horses' hooves thundered against the earth and swirled particles of dust about them creating an affect that was both eerie and menacing. Cato observant and alert stood transfixed as he tried to estimate their numbers. "We better get out of here!" declared Thomas Glenn Robinson to his brother Cato as the mounted group of "Red Shirts" could be seen closing the distance between its ranks and their polling station where the brothers had been counting votes and monitoring voting boxes.

Fear of harassment, bodily harm, and death kept newly emancipated blacks hiding, retreating, and running for their lives as Congressional Reconstruction petered out. As soon as the federal government adopted a laissez-faire attitude towards the treatment of blacks by whites in the South after the Civil War, organized groups of white marauders roamed southern states intimidating black men, women, and children, destroying property, attacking, and sometimes killing blacks. The Redshirts organization had been formed in South Carolina around the same time that one of its sister organizations, the Ku Klux Klan, was being formed by former Confederate Tennesseans. Among Redshirts' requirements were, "Feel honor bound to control the vote of at least one Negro, by intimidation, purchase, keeping [him] away, or as each individual may determine how best to accomplish it." They were advised to deceive or attack blacks by the edict to "go in as large numbers as you can get together, well armed, and behave at first with great courtesy and assure the ignorant Negroes that you mean them no harm, and as soon as their leaders..." As for their clothing choice, "Every club must be uniformed in a red shirt, and they must be sure to wear it upon all public meetings and particularly on the day of election."

Redshirts were former Confederate soldiers who adopted their color in defiance of "scalawags," or natives of the area who cooperated with federal troops and "carpetbaggers," those deemed outsiders who either sought to exploit conditions that existed in the aftermath of war or idealists who cared about blacks. The Redshirts were actively seeking to subvert the elections of 1876. If Thomas and Cato Robinson were caught by these men, they would be lynched.

They ran around to the back of the building which was their area's polling headquarters and with the building as cover, they fled across the twenty yards or so of clearing into a cornfield. After going more than twenty rows in and being well hidden by the corn, Cato told his brother, "follow me!"

Cutting immediately to the right and running at full speed parallel with the rows until they reached the end at a ditch, they jumped over it and sped into the adjoining forest.

Youth and speed were on the side of 29-year-old Thomas Robinson and 27-year-old Cato. Cato, keen and attuned to nature was about 5 feet 11 inches tall and weighed about 170 pounds. With his long legs and fleet-footedness, Cato led their sprint as they raced through the forest past oaks and maples breathtaking in mid-autumn brilliance of oranges, yellows and red sprinkled with pines whose cones they crushed as they ran for dear life. After about fifteen minutes they emerged into a clearing that was the property tended by the Halls, black share-croppers who lived about a mile back, off a path at the far end of the clearing. Another path about a half mile up branched off of it to farmland worked by the Saunders. But first, there was a canal to cross used mostly for irrigation and drainage; the locals even fished there. It was probably thirty feet wide. They decided to catch their breath before approaching and trying to cross the bridge in the event they had to flee from trouble on the other side or were spotted otherwise.

The Robinson brothers were involved in the campaign of Robert Smalls who served in both the South Carolina Senate as a state legislator from 1868 until 1870 and as a U.S. Congressman from South Carolina from 1875 to 1885. Thomas and Cato greatly admired the legendary Smalls, a runaway slave who had escaped on a Confederate ship, the *Planter,* on May 12, 1862. He had commandeered the ship out of the Charleston harbor himself, right under the noses of Confederate soldiers and their cannons, all the while flying the Confederate flag and after having donned the captain's uniform. Once he was out of the range of Confederate cannons, he raised a white flag. He, a ship steer-man for his master, had guided many ships in and out of the harbor and knew it well, and knew all the signals to use to get past Fort Sumter. After the war ended, he bought his former master's house and lived there until he died. He was an intelligent man, one who knew how to get things done.

Although they worked on the Smalls' campaign, the Robinsons were not looking for trouble. Voting, reading, and writing were things that it struck them as perfectly sensible for free men and women to do. It was incomprehensible to them that they would be chased, threatened, and beleaguered like this as poll workers, particularly after the war and Reconstruction. They thought issues of their rights and freedom had been settled. It was also difficult to reconcile the animus of whites towards them, particularly since some of their ancestors were white. Their paternal grandfather, Willie Zeigler, and great-grandfather Hans Zeigler were white men. Hans had been born near Augsburg, Germany in Bavaria in 1734, married a woman named Flora and sired two sons, Wade and Willie. Willie, born in 1772, immigrated to America with his brother Wade and settled in the British Colony of South Carolina in the latter part of the 1700s.

Having caught their breath, Thomas and Cato decided it was time to move on. There along the bank of the canal they crouched in the brush remaining hidden as they moved towards the bridge. Hearing approaching horses, Cato motioned to his brother and they stood perfectly still. "It's Tobin!" Cato told his brother as their friend Tobin of the Saunders family approached in his road cart and pair of horses. They ran to the bridge, crossed it, and hurried towards him. Jumping into the cart, they told him that they all needed to clear out of the area quickly because they'd just barely escaped the dangerous Redshirts who were at the polling station. "Get up!" Tobin ordered his horses after he turned them around and they raced away, putting as much distance as possible between them, the voting station and the Red-Shirts. The Robinson brothers made it home safely.

Whites in the state of South Carolina were more bitter, hateful, dangerous, and violent towards blacks in the wake of the South's Civil War defeat than during Reconstruction. Sherman's troops had wreaked complete devastation on the entire state leaving many white South Carolinians enraged. Sherman considered the state to be the "cradle of secession" with South Carolina having been the first state to secede and having started the war by firing on Fort Sumter. And after having been overheard saying someone needed to "show South Carolina for the first time in her existence, she cannot do as she pleases," he pummeled, burned, and destroyed much of the state. "South Carolina is reaping at last the consequence of her treason…" he would say after the destruction of the state capitol. This left whites seething at having had their property destroyed, their state capitol Columbia burned, their way of life vanquished. To make matters worse, they witnessed the sight of northerners encouraging and helping blacks to participate in the political process during the 1870s and Reconstruction. In their minds the War hadn't changed the relationship between blacks and whites, and ex-slaves were a constant, visual reminder to whites of their defeat.

But in many cases, newly freed men and women found themselves penniless, without property, without friends, and without support from the federal government. Blacks were free but not equal. As quickly as they could, many southern states passed "black codes" or laws that severely limited the liberties of blacks. In South Carolina, black codes were instituted by the legislature in 1865. They were meant to control blacks and return them to their pre-Civil War status. The codes restricted movement by blacks into the state, required "servants" to protect the property of whites, required them to have permission from whites to leave the property, and prevented blacks from having skilled jobs as artisans, mechanics or shopkeepers without going before a district court judge and paying $100. Yet if they resided in the state, blacks were required to have jobs or face being arrested.

To exacerbate the work dilemma, some Southern states also prohibited blacks from owning farmland, creating an environment specifically meant to exploit blacks and steer them back into a climate of servitude. Any white person could arrest a black person upon his or her view that a black had committed a misdemeanor, but only a magistrate could issue arrest warrants for whites. Many blacks who were well trained in agriculture and farming techniques and were skilled craftsmen - carpenters, bricklayers, blacksmiths, shoemakers, and the like - were effectively barred from their professions by the establishment of various new license requirements soon after the war.

These hellish codes and practices would remain the social and economic conventions of the South well into the 1960s. They would sear and stain the soul of the South more than a hundred generations after the one most Southerners called their Savior had been sacrificed for sins like it hosted, they would malign a race well into the third millennium A.D. and invalidate the credibility of a nation supposedly committed to freedom.

Thomas and Cato Robinson's presence became particularly provocative and troublesome to whites while living in Bamberg County, South Carolina where Thomas ran for and was elected to the position of postmaster in 1883, and in Denmark, South Carolina, where Cato was elected to the same position six years after the end of Reconstruction. This was still a time of considerable political activity among blacks in South Carolina. Soon after he assumed the position of postmaster of Bamberg County, Thomas would be visited frequently by mounted marauders. For a while each night for several weeks, he braced himself for gun fights with local whites he believed to be Redshirts in what became a recurring, nightly, gun fighting affair. The house was really a log cabin covered by clapboards with only doors and shutters, so few bullets came through. He would put a trunk across the front door, position his guns on top of the trunk, and return gun-fire. All the while, his wife and children took cover as whites circled and fired on the house, reminiscent of Indians circling wagons in old cowboy movies.

Thomas Robinson would not be intimidated nor would he be deterred. He remained in his position and in his home, and served his entire term as postmaster of Bamberg County in spite of threats, gun fire directed at his home, and persistent attempts of mob violence. He held the position for four years. But efforts to get him would not cease. In one instance, a white citizen accused Thomas of having sworn at him and attempted to make a citizen's arrest under South Carolina's black codes. Thomas struck the fellow for having assaulted a public official. Local attempts to prosecute him failed. Near the end of his term, horse-mounted, white marauders burned down his home, setting it afire while he and his family slept. The family managed to survive the ordeal unharmed.

As he watched the burning logs that had been his home, Thomas G. Robinson was thinking beyond the moment. He began to reflect upon his family's history almost as if it were flashing in front of him.

Thomas and Cato's grandmother's life's story was a different matter than that of Willie Zeigler, their grandfather. Around the same time that their grandfather Willie was born, a female child, who would later be known as Hannah, was born in 1776 to the chieftain of the Galla tribe located off the coast of West Africa near Liberia. Her story has been passed on in the family for many generations and researched by family members who visited both places – Germany and Liberia. At some undetermined time, this African female of royal parentage was captured by slave traders and shipped to the New World off the coast of South Carolina.

During the slave trade period, the custom was that slave traders were to take no members of royal tribal families since many chieftains supplied the slave traders with slaves. If this mistakenly occurred, the chieftain would be allowed to exchange three to five slaves for the stolen family member. Though no proof exists, it is believed by family members and it is their family's oral history that the Galla chieftain sent the required number of slaves to redeem his daughter. According to family lore, the ship's captain died en-route to South Carolina and his successor sold not only the redemptive slaves but the chieftain's daughter as well. Thus Hannah, as she came to be known, was unable to gain her freedom.

A small framed woman with beautiful features, Hannah was purchased by Willie Zeigler in 1795, and he later married Hannah. While marriage between different races was not common in 1795, there were no laws forbidding interracial marriages in South Carolina at that time. However, unless they were overcome by moral or religious qualms, which was unlikely under the circumstances of time, geography and regional proclivity, most slave owners simply owned female slaves as personal property and could do with them as they pleased. So it is also a possibility that Hannah and Willie lived together but not as husband and wife, an assessment shared by some family members.

Willie and Hannah had two sons, Christopher Zeigler -

Thomas and Cato's father - and Benjamin Zeigler – their uncle. Christopher, who later changed his surname to Robinson, was born in 1797 and died in 1879. And regardless of his parents' marital status, by law Christopher and Benjamin were still considered slaves and they remained so until Emancipation, as did their descendants. They lived with their parents and their Uncle Wade on a plantation the Zeigler brothers established near the South Edisto River in the center of the state of South Carolina. Wade married an English woman and, like Willie, had children; however Wade's children were free. The two families lived together without any significant friction.

This living arrangement meant that Thomas and Cato's father Christopher and his brother Benjamin did not feel the harsher effects of slavery during these early years. As children, Christopher and Benjamin interacted and played regularly with their first cousins, Wade Zeigler's children, who were not of mixed parentage. In fact, Christopher learned to read with help from his white cousins; Thomas learned to read with the help of his father and his white cousins, too. Christopher married the former Rebecca Myers in 1845, and they had five children: Capers, Thomas, Cato, Darcus (the only girl), and Gabriel, whom the family called "Cutter." The siblings lived together on the Zeigler farm until Wade's death around 1858.

From the time his grandfather, Willie, and Uncle Wade died, his family experienced unending hell visited upon them by whites. First it had been the white members of his own family, then his community, and his state. He just didn't know what to make of the irrational hatred and hostility they bore towards blacks. The most striking blow to him in the course of his family's history had been the separation of his family.

Hannah, his grandmother, died as a fairly young woman for reasons not known. Willie, his grandfather, asked Wade to purchase his children, Christopher and Benjamin, and to look after them – nobody knows why. Maybe it was to protect them in the event something happened to Willie, who as a relatively new emigrant may not have had the resources to send his sons out of the area. Or perhaps the issues of the slave-states and free-states were not clearly delineated at that time. History tells us that during the early period of slavery, northern states (New York for an example) had slaves for a short time. In any event, Wade bought Willie's children. Subsequently, upon the death of their Uncle Wade, his property was divided among his white heirs in Val Dosta, Georgia. That could have been their end as a family.

His brother Gabriel was inherited by family members who lived in West Palm Beach, Florida. Gabriel was a slightly darker but nearly perfect facsimile of Willie Zeigler and the Zeiglers, in particular, with angular facial features. "How," Thomas wondered, "was it possible that Willie's family members, who were also Gabriel's family members, not see the family resemblance in him?" Sadly he acknowledged they must; they just didn't care. Thomas would learn later that after having been separated from his kin, lonely and angry with nothing to lose, Gabriel fled. He escaped through the swamps of Florida and ended up living with the Indians. This was about 1858 or 1859. The family didn't see him again until well after the Civil War. He came back to South Carolina and stayed a month or so and then went back to join his family; he had married an Indian woman and was living with her tribe.

The family lost track of Darcus, Thomas Robinson's sister and the only girl among his siblings. She was inherited by relatives in Val Dosta, Georgia, and never saw her family again. No one in the family knows what became of her. "Poor Darcus," Thomas thought, "beautiful Darcus." In the end it was possible, if not likely, that her beauty was her curse.

Separated from her family, crossing the path of ungodly men in the hell of the ungodly South, their beloved Darcy vanished and was lost forevermore.

Christopher Zeigler, his wife Rebecca and sons Thomas, Cato, and Capers remained in South Carolina after Willie Zeigler's death. In 1861, Civil War was declared and many blacks were freed as the Union swept through the South. Christopher and his sons were freed in 1865 by General Sherman. A company of Sherman's Army and many followers camped near a place called Midway and the South Edisto River and, while there, spread the news to the slaves that they were free. A census of the freed slaves was taken. Union forces told the newly freed slaves that they could choose surnames that would be theirs permanently.

This is when Christopher Zeigler told his wife and children that they were no longer Zeiglers, but they and their offspring would be Robinsons henceforth and forevermore. For in reality, to all in their Zeigler family, except Willie and Wade, they were never Zeiglers, never human, but family property. So now it was officially time to cut their ties with the Zeiglers, to part and set upon a different destiny. Thomas Glenn Robinson was seventeen years old when that happened. He joined the Union Forces as a water-boy and followed them as far as Columbia, S.C. He was with the Yankees when they burned the State House and destroyed Columbia.

Under the Andrew Johnson administration, nothing was done to accommodate the new status of freedmen and many had nowhere to turn. But even this plight was an improvement over past conditions. Soon after the war, Christopher Robinson began to transport logs down the Edisto River on a raft to Charleston, South Carolina, in order to provide food, clothing, and shelter for himself and his family. He acquired a bit of land, about eighty acres, and also farmed. It was less than five years after the war that Claflin College was established. Since Christopher, the ex-slave, was eager to give his oldest son, also an ex-slave, the chance for an education, the elder Robinson accumulated a little money by sacrificial savings to finance the project. And thus it happened that Thomas Glenn Robinson entered Claflin College and attended long enough to be considered qualified to teach school in Bamberg County. He was an entering member of the second class in September 1870. After marriage, he acquired a few acres of land in his county, farmed, taught school to support a growing family, and got involved in politics.

Now, Thomas Glenn Robinson stared at the ambers from the remnants of clapboards still simmering in the night that had once covered his home and tried to understand the level of hatred that would drive men to terrorize him in the night and try to kill his entire family. How could it have come to this? He could not bring himself to hate, but he was not beyond self defense and at this moment perhaps even taking the offensive. Robinson did not fear whites in Bamberg, South Carolina; he thought them insane and used that assessment as his frame of reference in taking actions to preserve his own life when he dealt with them. But this situation was different; they were trying to kill his wife, his babies. He realized that these were the type of men who, if successful in their murderous projects, would after the bodies were found, figuratively pick the bones and flesh as this seemed to be the nourishment, the soul food by which their culture lived, fodder for their way of life.

"Why not teach them a lesson?" he thought. He had seen how easily they fell individually and collectively while with Sherman's troops as they soundly registered victories. He remembered how quickly they fled when he had fired at them with his shotgun those nights when they attacked his home.

They really weren't nearly as frightening or tough when you gave them their own medicine, he thought. Then he dismissed those thoughts for he would not be transformed into a man of that type. Besides, God had set him free, and Sherman had been an effective executor of punishment in lieu of his own rage. He vowed to stand with dignity, understanding at that moment that hatred was morally corrosive and had no real value.

He embraced his wife, Anna, and they hugged each other. She was frightened and shaking but they felt blessed to be alive with their seven children. Anna lent him strength. She was a smart, strong, and supportive woman. And while she had feared for the safety of her children during nightly raids and gunfire, she stood firmly behind Thomas Robinson and his approach to life. She was almost like a career woman of her time, given her involvement in his churches. She, too, was literate although she wasn't as educated as her husband. It's not known how far she went with her education, but she had to have learned a lot because she organized and managed study activities for the numerous children who lived in their home to attend school, and she was very involved in teaching children to play the piano, organizing events, and managing church affairs for her husband.

Thomas Glenn Robinson was a powerful man of conviction who stood 5 feet 6 and weighed 145 pounds during his prime. He had a booming voice, a preacher's voice, and was a man of faith, vision, strength, determination, and love. At the end of his tenure as postmaster and after being burned out of his home in Bamberg, South Carolina, it was time for reflection and serious soul searching. He decided that it was time to leave Bamberg County. After many years of political activity he got out of politics. But he continued to pursue ways to find meaning in his newfound freedom. Education and religion became the means by which he would seek to provide meaning to his family's existence. He joined the South Carolina Conference of the Methodist Episcopal Church, and preached, farmed, and taught school until he had accumulated sufficient money to purchase land and build a home in Orangeburg, S.C. His primary purpose in locating there was to be close to Claflin College where his own children could get an education.

A Methodist minister, the Reverend Abram Middleton, who was a trustee and founder of Claflin College, ordained Thomas Robinson as a minister in 1870. Thomas Robinson preached from that day on until his death in 1924. After becoming an established minister, he relinquished his farming and teaching interests and devoted his life exclusively to the Christian ministry. He had a parish in Bamberg, S.C., and one other ministry in Orangeburg and would rotate between them, preaching at one church on one Sunday and the other church the next Sunday. He believed in education so much that he would bring in members of his congregation to live in his home and send them to school at no charge to them if he thought they showed promise.

And what is more, Curtis Robinson, the Tuskegee Airman remembers, "My grandfather was the head of the family, no doubt about it! And everybody knew it. Even though my father had six children, he was just like a boy to my grandfather." Cato Robinson became a minister, also. He had two boys and both of them became ministers. Thomas Robinson's ambition to see his children educated at Claflin College was realized. Two of his sons and three daughters completed either a part or all of their formal education there. By 1940 ten grandchildren had done so, too.

Orangeburg, South Carolina

Thomas Robinson settled in Orangeburg, South Carolina, after leaving Bamberg County in the early part of the 1890s. Several years later, he gave his son, Christopher, three quarters of an acre of land on which to build a home for his wife and five children. Curtis Robinson and a sister five years his junior, who lived just three months before she died, were born there.

Orangeburg is a small town located near the center of the state of South Carolina, 45 miles south of Columbia, the capital, and 85 miles northwest of Charleston, the chief sea port. The overall area and Orangeburg itself were established near the north fork of the Edisto River in the 1730s, at which time Swiss and German farmers began settling in the area. Orangeburg is the county seat of Orangeburg County, S.C. The land was flat and good for farming, and by the early 1920s the city of Orangeburg had a population of about 11,000.

The city itself was divided by railroad tracks belonging to the Southern Railway Company that cut off a quarter of the eastern part of the city. That portion of Orangeburg was occupied by blacks and the western portion by whites with the exception of a small concentration of blacks along the railroad tracks on the west side where more profitable black businesses were located, along with a few of the nicer black homes and the handsome black Methodist church. Alongside the railroad on the east side is where blacks had their grocery stores, cleaners, barbershops, and other small businesses. Right around the corner was the largest grocery store in town. It was owned by the Maxwell family, a black family whose patrons, however, were almost exclusively white. Their prices were so high that black families like the Robinsons couldn't really afford them. There were several small stores in the community, also. They weren't called convenience stores then, but that's what they were, and they were all over the area.

On the western side of Orangeburg were large antebellum homes and the business district. The business district occupied about five blocks with businesses on the side streets, also. Blacks had a large church in this part of town, in the center of the town, near the courthouse during Robinson's early childhood and where his family worshiped.

Whites had large farms just outside of town that were tended by the black laborers who lived on the farms as tenant farmers, and as a result, the proportion of blacks in the county was much higher than the proportion of blacks in the city. Blacks made up approximately twenty-five percent of the city's population. In the county, however, they accounted for over half of the population. But contact between whites and blacks who lived in the city was limited. Only the maids, chauffeurs, and craftsmen had any real contact with whites who resided there.

Those blacks who lived on the farms owned by whites were located beyond the eastern edge of Orangeburg, beyond

Robinson's community. They were tenant farmers who accounted for a moderate amount of Orangeburg County's population. Traditional tenant farming or sharecropping arrangements were methods of land lease, a labor arrangement used by large farmers and landowners to produce crops. Tenant farmers consisted of two groups. There was a class known as "share tenants" who supplied capital - mules, plows, seeds, etc. - and kept a higher percentage of the crops they produced. And there was another group, traditional "sharecroppers" – the vast majority - who provided only labor. Typically, both groups were paid after the crops were harvested, net of the costs of seed, fertilizer, supplies, rent and other miscellaneous items and expenses the tenant farmer was deemed to have incurred. The landowner usually kept the books, and often the tenant farmer wasn't literate, which worked significantly to his detriment; but much the same if he were literate. And regardless of which type of tenant farmer they were, over half of the blacks in the country who sharecropped were in the lowest categories of poverty in the United States during the 1930s and 1940s.

The city limits stopped at Robinson's grandfather's house. Thomas Glenn Robinson's address was Route 1, Box 1; Orangeburg, South Carolina, and Curtis Robinson's family lived next door at Route 1, Box 3. The area where Robinson lived faced both Claflin College and South Carolina State College. Claflin is a privately funded university which was founded in 1869. In 1872 the state of South Carolina decided to provide public funds for a college for blacks. The State gave money to Claflin to include an agricultural and mechanical curriculum in their program. The state-funded curriculum was made up of mathematics, agriculture, mechanics, printing, bricklaying, ironworks, and carpentry. Several years later in 1876, South Carolina Agricultural and Mechanical Institute (later to become

South Carolina State College) was formed and separated from Claflin College. South Carolina State kept the agriculture, carpentry and bricklaying classes. Many of their graduates were the tradesmen of that era and built most of the houses in the area up until the end of World War II when white tradesmen came in and began building.

This was the profile of the hometown where Curtis Robinson was born on August 25, 1919, the sixth child of Christopher Capers Robinson and his wife Ednora Green Robinson. He was born about nine months after the end of World War I and was the fifth boy in the family. And for as long as he can remember, almost everyone in his family and school called him "CC." When he began school, parents didn't register children like today; on his first day of class his brother merely showed him his classroom and that's where he went. The teacher asked him his name and he said "CC Robinson." He was strictly known as CC Robinson for the first three years of school until his cousin, his fourth grade teacher, made him use his whole name. Other than that, he wrote his name as CC and everybody called him that.

During Robinson's elementary school days in the 1920s, South Carolina State College had a dairy and needed someone to bring the cows in from the pasture each morning, wait for them to be milked, and take them back out to pasture; for that you got two quarts of milk. That job started in Curtis Robinson's family with his oldest brother and worked its way down to him. In the winter months, Robinson remembers his mother's voice awakening him with, "CC, it's time to get up," as Ednora Robinson called out to her youngest child as dawn beckoned another day. Robinson would sit up, swing his legs over the edge of the bed that he shared with his brother George, rub his eyes, think about the day ahead, and get up and get prepared for his morning job. On those cold mornings after he arose and dressed, he would make a fire in the family's wood heater because there was no heat in the house at night. Then, he would get his pail and head out to bring in all the cows for milking. There were also college students in the dairy to help milk them; but South Carolina State didn't have any milking machines in those days and it was all done by hand. Once that was done, Robinson led the cows back out to pasture and received two quarts of milk. By the time he returned home, it was time for breakfast, and he would eat and head off to school. He was the last child in the family with that job and recalls, "I was glad to get rid of it."

Robinson's Orangeburg neighborhood was a very close-knit community. Nearly everyone there was of very modest means, many would be considered poor by today's standards, but people didn't consider themselves to be poor, and if in fact they were, it was not an impoverishment of the spirit. Every family in CC's community owned their home. For that era, they were the burgeoning black middle class in South Carolina. This was an area where the streets were named College Avenue and Gulf Avenue and ran parallel to a place called New Brooklyn, about eight or ten streets where you could go from one to the other without encountering obstructions or cutoff streets, all occupied by blacks. And they were from all walks of life.

There were teachers that lived around the corner from his home and all throughout the neighborhood, and his family knew many if not all of them. Robinson adds that, "When I was growing up near South Carolina State and Claflin, I knew a lot of the professors, several of whom lived in the neighborhood. And for the most part, they knew who a lot of us kids were, too. Other professional types - doctors, dentists, and several ministers - also lived in the neighborhood. The tradesmen, masons, and builders in the area were mostly black because South Carolina State College at one time had mechanical arts programs whose graduates became artisans in the area, and were my neighbors, too." South Carolina State's program was an important consideration for black tradesmen since the 'black codes' were meant to prevent blacks from having such trades; that training and education allowed them to address that portion of those barriers.

Adults, particularly the elders in Robinson's community, knew who all the children and their families were, and out of love, concern, or some other motivation, they provided constant oversight, observed children's behavior faithfully, and duly informed any misbehaving child's parents of all mischief. When he was in the fifth grade, Robinson and another boy had been chasing and frightening a school girl on the other side of town. They were chasing her home from school and he remembers, "She was screaming as she ran and we were right on her trail, but she was making such a fuss we soon stopped. Thereafter I headed home; I must have been seven or eight blocks from home. We didn't have many telephones in town. There were two doctors in the neighborhood with telephones, and I knew of two other people who had them, but as far as I know, that was it with telephones in my community. But somehow by the time I got home that day, my mother knew. How she found out things so quickly, I have never known to this day, but somehow she managed to find things out almost as soon as they happened." That's how it was in the Orangeburg, South Carolina, of CC Robinson's youth; the children belonged to the community and they behaved. And even with five boys in the family, they didn't really fight, not with each other nor with other boys in the neighborhood although his older brothers picked on him a bit.

Sundays in Orangeburg for the Robinson family revolved around the church. There were three black churches in the city of Robinson's youth: a Methodist Episcopal, an

A.M.E (African Methodist Episcopal) and a Baptist church. Later on there were many more; today there are more than ten Baptist churches alone. People would go to anybody's church, and of his Sundays Robinson adds, "I would get up on Sunday morning, have breakfast, go to Sunday school, and then regular service. After that, we'd return home and have dinner, but then there would be very little other activity. Sunday was treated like the Sabbath; we couldn't play sports or do any work, but we could listen to the radio, and I was allowed to work my hotel job."

The churches also had plenty of structured activities and organizations for youths; his had a Junior League for twelve and thirteen-year-olds and an Adult League for fourteen and fifteen year-olds. The churches stressed sharing and caring, and it was a close-knit neighborhood where people shared almost everything. And it had its impact on Robinson. "I have always believed that my Christian upbringing, plus my faith in God and myself would determine what I was going to do in life because I really had no plans for myself. I thought when I was very young that I would be a minister. Preaching was almost as important as education in my household; there were a lot of preachers in the family."

Sometimes as a child Robinson even practiced as though he were preparing for the ministry. "Moses said to Pharaoh, 'let, my people go,'" he would begin his sermon as a little boy, while standing behind a straight-back chair practicing his sermon. This was around the time that he was in the third grade. A new family had moved in across the street from his family. The father had tuberculosis so he was very sick. But they had four beautiful little girls, all of them as pretty as they could be. Every day the Robinson children would go over to their house, or they'd come over to the Robinsons, or the children would all meet out in the park and play, and they played with those girls all summer.

One day while Robinson and one of the little girls, the girl his age, were playing, he was preaching as he pushed her back and forth in the swing. He remembers, "She jumped off the swing, came around right to my face and said, 'I love you' and kissed me on the lips. I remember it as plain as if it was today; I tried to answer her back and I started stuttering, and I haven't stopped stuttering yet. I'm still stuttering. As an eight-year-old boy, I didn't know what to do and after that, she always wanted to play with me. So I gave up the idea of preaching. Her father died later on that summer, the family moved away, and I didn't see her again until she returned to Orangeburg to go to Claflin where we were freshmen together. But it was a different story when she came back to town. She no longer had eyes or time for me. She hardly even noticed me at all. I wanted her to notice me then."

Until CC Robinson was seven years old, his family worshipped at a beautiful church where the Orangeburg Courthouse now stands that had been built in 1891. The church – Trinity United Methodist Church, a Methodist Episcopal church at that time – was the sanctuary where the Robinson family had worshipped for many years and was one of three black churches in town. But this church was right in the center of town near the center square, a very desirable location on the western side of the city. The white "city fathers" condemned the church in 1926, put it up for sale, took the land, and built a county courthouse on that spot. A new sanctuary to replace the old wasn't completed until 1944. The congregation transitioned first to a tabernacle built in a week – a long structure with a row of seats on each side, a string of lights down the center, a sawdust floor, a big iron stove in the center for heat, a platform for the minister, and the old mourner's bench from the old church for communion. The new church was completed in phases because the congregation didn't want to incur a lot of debt. After about nine years, the congregation moved to the basement of the new structure. Then, nine years later they were able to move into their fully completed new church; they did it all on a "pay-as-you-go" basis.

Springtime in Orangeburg was the time for the Robinsons to dig up their garden and plant vegetables, and there would always be work to do in the garden in the afternoon after school. They had a lot, three-quarters of an acre in size. The family's small house sat on the front of the lot next to the street, and the garden was in the back. Usually CC's father, Christopher, planted a lot of vegetables: cabbages, beans, peas, carrots, and onions which supplied the family with a large variety and quantity of vegetables because the size of the garden was fairly large. The city and the county were also full of pecan trees, and the Robinsons had two large pecan trees in the back yard along with several peach trees, apple trees, pear trees, and grape arbors. So when the fruits and pecans were in-season, they ate very well thanks to the vegetables and other things the family grew. After hog killing time, everything was shared in the community. People who had lots of pecans shared them with people who didn't have pecan trees. "It was a neighborhood where everyone seemed to get along –as far as I knew as a child; there weren't many squabbles. It was a lovely community," recalls Robinson.

In the autumn months, the boys in the family picked cotton after the school day. Robinson's cotton-picking career, however, was short lived. He says, "After a couple of years I was excused from picking cotton because I wasn't very good at it." He had a cousin who would combine forces with his brothers George and Eldridge, and with him. The four of them would pick together going up and down the rows and every time they would empty their sacks, CC would empty his. At the end of the day his brother George would have about 97 pounds, his cousin about 115, his other brother would have about 110 pounds, and he would have 40; he wasn't fast at picking cotton no matter how hard he tried. The pay was fifty cents per hundred-pounds. And though working his best all day long, he would end up with just twenty cents bearing in mind that forty pounds was his high mark. Sometimes he would pick 35 pounds, sometimes 37. He wasn't making any money and concluded that he had better find something else to do besides pick cotton.

After his second season of picking cotton, the following spring he started going to some of the white homes asking for evening work and was able to find small jobs cutting grass. That was more profitable than picking cotton because he could earn fifty cents per day for cutting grass and trimming up. By the summer he had three yards that he would work, so he made a dollar and fifty cents per week which wasn't bad for a young boy during the late 1920s and early 1930s. Fifty cents a day was the amount a grown man would be paid for working as a laborer, and it was certainly more than he made picking cotton. While he was cutting grass, CC met a little fellow who had come to live with a lady who lived across the street from his family. She kept boarders - a lot of people kept boarders around there. Many boarders went to elementary school or high school at one of the area colleges because the public schools out in the county were extremely poor. However, not all boarders were necessarily going to school in the area. And it was through a boarder - a boy about his age - that Robinson began to interact with whites in Orangeburg.

Robinson had taken a pause from work while he wiped his brow as he was finishing some lawn work in his neighborhood. It seemed to him that he worked harder in his own neighborhood than he did on the west-side of town. Out of nowhere came a voice, "Hey, I can get you a job making more money than you're going to make cutting grass," the little fellow yelled to Robinson as he put the finishing touches on his neighbor's yard. "I don't know where he came from," Robinson says, "but he came to town to work, and he was a great tap dancer. He worked at the Edisto Hotel. The hotel had a section equivalent to a convenience store, a soda fountain, and they sold beer, patented medicine, ice cream and other miscellaneous hotel items. Well, this kid had a job there cleaning up, but he made most of his money by tap dancing. He was an excellent dancer and customers would give him tips. If a customer came in and bought something, he'd throw the kid a nickel, a dime or whatever, and the kid would tap-dance over to the coins like a pro and pick them up. Eventually, he got a better job some where else. He told me he would tell the owner of the hotel about me so that perhaps the owner would hire me for that job." Robinson was still cutting grass at the time, but the boy did as he promised, taking him down to the hotel and introducing him to the owner just before he left town.

The owner hired Robinson who was twelve or thirteen at the time. His two kids, who were about one or two years older than Robinson, worked there, too. Robinson was surprised when the fellow that got him the job introduced these kids to him. "He introduced them to me as "Mr." So-and-So and "Mr." So-and-So, whatever their first names were," he remembers. It was understood at that time in the South that black people never addressed white adults by their first names, but these two were kids Robinson's age so he went ahead and called them by their first names, anyway, which seemed normal to him. "But the funniest thing," he says, "was after I started working there, people used to come in and would throw dimes and nickels at me, and yell, 'dance, dance over there and pick them up,' but I didn't do it; I knew what was going on, and I couldn't dance, you know, so I would go on about my business. I guess the customers didn't know any better and thought that all blacks were great dancers. But not in my case, and the coin tossing soon stopped. I can only imagine the fortunes I might have made if I had known how to tap dance."

"One day a white guy came in the hotel. He was wearing white shoes and had a bottle of white shoe polish in his hand; he spotted me and said, 'I want you to polish my shoes.' I told him that I had never polished any white shoes before. The guy said, 'Oh yeah, you can do it; all you niggers know how to polish shoes.' Again I told him, 'I'm sorry, but I don't know how to polish white shoes.' He took me by the hand and led me out to his car. Then he sat down, and put his foot on the running-board. He handed me the bottle of white polish and told me to polish his shoes. So I opened the polish and poured the polish all over his shoes; it went "Glook, Glook, Glook." The gentleman snatched away the bottle of polish away and said, "You don't know how to polish any shoes!" I said, "I told you that." Robinson's shoe shining career ended up being shorter than his cotton-picking career.

"The owner of the hotel paid me $2.75 per week and wanted me to work seven days. I told him no because I had to be off at least a half day on Sunday to go to church, so I worked six and a half days a week." Even though he couldn't dance, and wasn't that great at polishing shoes, Robinson wanted to make more money on his new job and was enterprising about his strategy, "What I decided to do to make extra money at the hotel," he shares, "was to make a few deliveries; the other fellow had not been doing that; he was making money on the side dancing. So I began making deliveries - delivering beer here, or patented medicine somewhere else in town, or sometimes deliveries up to rooms in the hotel, itself. I had to convince the owner to buy a bike, however, which he did. It was his bike and when I left, I left it there."

The owner got to like Robinson quite well. Whenever he came to the store, he would frequently talk with him. Or he would take Robinson with him different places to do work more often than he took his own kids, and he would talk with him in a normal fashion, not a demeaning and condescending fashion as was typical of the way that whites talked to blacks at that time. When he got ready to go back to school, Robinson gave the owner two weeks' notice. The owner was shocked. He said, "You're going back to school?" And Robinson said, "Yeah." He said, "You don't have to do that. We like you, we really like you here and you've got a job with me for life." Mind you, this was 1931 or 1932. "He actually thought he was doing me a favor; he was serious," continues Robinson. "He thought that all blacks, if they had a little menial job like that, which was better than farm work, would be happy and could do all right. He thought that I would jump at the chance. But even after I had quit, he still seemed to like me. Later on, while in college, I joined a fraternity. Many of the guys who joined had to pay dues to join, and usually they received checks from their hometowns. I would take them to him, and he would cash their checks as a favor to me. He'd say, 'As long as you say it's O.K. I'll cash it.' It was one of those things. He thought highly enough of me that he wanted me to work for him for the rest of my life." Many of Robinson's classmates might likely have jumped at the chance. Most of them disappeared after the eighth grade. They moved away or took domestic jobs because after the eighth grade, educational opportunities were limited for blacks in Orangeburg at that time.

But in Robinson's own household and right next door at his grandfather's, the houses were full of black college graduates or students. He had two cousins from Florida living with his grandfather, attending school - his Uncle Thomas' daughter and his Aunt Lovey Mae's girls. There was also Mrs. Fredericks, the mother of two of his friends, and his uncle T.J.'s daughter, and a cousin, Philippine, who stayed there in high school. Robinson's grandfather hosted high school students because in some of the places in S.C., black schools were one or two-room schools with teachers who taught three or four grades, and school terms that lasted only four months. In these instances students had to go to school for two years to make one grade. So his grandfather brought some of them to Orangeburg. One cousin who lived with him, Agnes Edwards, who died in 2002 at 101, was the oldest of the grandchildren. Thomas G. Robinson sent her to Claflin for elementary school, high school, and college. She also earned a degree from Howard University around 1928 or 1930, then her master's degree at Columbia University three years later. Eventually she became the first black female high school principal in the state of Maryland at a school in Seat Pleasant in Prince George's County, Maryland.

Also of importance, the colleges' athletic fields were right across the street from the Robinsons, who were athletic young men. CC Robinson and all of his brothers played sports. The brothers would see the college teams' daily practices and would go over and play, too. Claflin had a nationally renowned black coach in 1929 by the name Brice Taylor. He had been the only black on the University of Southern California's football team when he played there and was their first football All America in 1925. He was inducted into their athletic hall of fame in 1995. He was Claflin's first nationally known coach. He was a big man though only about 5 feet 10 inches and had only a nub where a fully developed left hand should have been. He would catch a baseball, throw it up in the air, drop his glove, catch the ball with his right hand, and then he'd throw it. Taylor coached football, basketball and baseball. He held closed practice sessions, but he would allow Robinson, then just a young boy, to watch, and they became acquainted; he even used to play catch with him. In football, he coached the fundamentals, didn't have a passing game, but his Claflin team was one that moved three to four yards at a time with clouds of dust emitting from the field. He shared with Robinson his personal story that when the University of Southern California played teams that refused to compete against blacks during the 1920s, they would paint him to look white for those games. He seemed to like Robinson, tolerated all his questions, and taught him almost everything he knew about football. CC played football so much and learned enough about the game that by the time he got to high school, he was the high school football coach, a player–coach. He also played basketball as a forward and baseball where he played first base.

Even without those special circumstances, most children in the community went to college if their parents had any finances at all. If parents couldn't send all their children to college, they'd send at least one of them, and hopefully, each kid would help to send the next. And even if his family's relationship with Claflin was not enough, Robinson's relationship with coaches at Claflin and the schools athletic programs made him feel as if he were almost a part of the school setting before he started going there. Orangeburg was a progressive college town, especially for blacks, and because of that Robinson benefited and is still grateful.

Meet the Robinsons

Christopher Capers Robinson headed the Robinson family. He was a school teacher during the short school year of Robinson's youth and a house painter during the remainder of the year. "My father wasn't home that often unless he was sick," says Robinson, "because he taught school during the winter months and painted during the summer months." He taught all his sons how to paint. And he was a true gentleman. When he walked down the street, he always tipped his hat to the ladies, was nice to everyone, and he taught his children good manners. The elder Robinson sang in the choir, knew music, and he knew how to play the cornet. Although Robinson never heard him play it, the cornet was always lying around the house.

During one particular summer of painting Christopher Robinson, the family bread-winner, got lead poisoning through the paint he used and was sick for a whole year. His skin was broken out all over his body. Doctors would come to his home and put plaster sulfur all over his stomach, his back, and his legs, and Robinson remembers, "He appeared to almost be dying; he suffered so from his knees. He was a mess with sores which were just like Lazarus', and they lasted about a year. So between 1930 and 1931, my mother had to be the breadwinner. She was forced to leave South Carolina to find work as a maid in New York. She would be gone all spring and summer, would return during the fall and early winter months and then leave again in January or February." Even the local government was forced to take extreme measures during those times. When Christopher Robinson recovered from lead poisoning and went back to work teaching in Denmark, South Carolina, his pay was $27 a month. But the county had no money so they paid him in script, a paper substitute for money which could be redeemed for cash locally. He could take the script to local merchants and redeem it for goods at a charge of 5 percent. Merchants would hold the script until the county had the money to redeem them and then cash them in at their face value.

Ednora Green Robinson was a housewife who had met Christopher Robinson as a student at Claflin College where she earned a "normal degree." High percentages of Claflin students were marrying each other when Christopher and Ednora attended Claflin and that trend maintained itself well into the early 1940s. Around that time - years after Christopher and Ednora had married– seventeen percent of females, and twenty percent of males were marrying schoolmates there still.

She always cooked on a wooden stove. "But during the Depression, I can remember coming home and finding that the stove was cold which meant that my mother hadn't cooked because she had no food to cook," recalls Robinson of those dire times. "But there were always pecans, fruits, and things we could go out and get from the garden to fill our stomachs. My mother would can much of the fruits and vegetables taken from the garden for reserves."

Her family was from the upper part of South Carolina in

a place called Tatum, in Marlboro County and Bennettsville, over one hundred miles from where Robinson's family lived. Traveling during the early 1930s was so difficult that it would take the Robinsons all day to get to Tatum from Orangeburg. So CC didn't see an awful lot of his mother's family. But he was impressed by what he saw when he visited.

"I know that her grandfather owned a tremendous amount of land, two or three thousand acres," Robinson remembers. "He had houses on much of the land where his tenants lived, and he had a school built for them. I was there one summer when I was twelve or thirteen. There were several people cooking for everyone. At dinner time, they rang a large bell, and people came from all over to eat. There would be two or three tables twelve feet long, and the tenants would gather around. There was a lot of food, like they were feeding an army. I was impressed with a grape arbor that my great-grandfather had that was about a block long. Plus he had all types of fowl – turkey, geese, chickens and ducks – everything you could think of. It was a big operation." Robinson's paternal great-grandfather, Christopher Zeigler Robinson, had quite a bit of land, too, but nothing like this. Zeigler had about eighty acres, relatively small compared to the amount his maternal great-grandfather had.

Ednora's grandfather was married three times and had at least twelve children by each wife; one wife had twenty-two children. "The biggest problem associated with this," Robinson says, "was keeping up with all of them and finding them. Her grandfather built a large home with five bedrooms in Orangeburg, S.C. for his children and grandchildren for them to stay there to attend Claflin College. "That's how my mother met my father; her grandfather sent her down to Claflin to be educated," states Robinson.

The Robinsons lived in a small house consisting of two

bedrooms, a living room, a dining room, and a kitchen. The house had no electricity and no running water. "We read by lamp light fueled by kerosene, and we cooked on a wooden stove," explains Robinson. "The family ate our meals (always after prayer was said) in the dining room around a large round table." They had good books in the house. Christopher and Ednora Robinson saw to it that their children had good reference books such as works by Carter G. Woodson and Milton's *Paradise Lost.* They also had libraries nearby, and Robinson and his siblings were taught to use them. "That was one really good thing about Orangeburg;" Robinson says of his college hometown. "Anybody could use the college libraries, and both Claflin and South Carolina State had good ones. So when we were in school, we could check out books in the college library or sit in there and read even though we weren't enrolled there. The city had a library, but it was for whites, only. It wasn't much larger than my dining room, but blacks still couldn't go there. Fortunately, we didn't need to because we could go to the libraries at the colleges."

Family life revolved around the children. The oldest brother, Capers Glenn, was a loner whom the family called Glenn. He was very smart, bookish, and read all the time. He was born in 1910 and was the only one of the boys who did not go into the military.

Glenn made himself an office in his grandfather's barn in the loft where he built the first radio in the community. This was around 1923 and nobody else knew what a radio was. He subscribed to scientific journals and learned how to build a radio using what information he had read. His radio ran on batteries because the family had no electricity, and he ordered its parts. "To my knowledge," adds Robinson, "there were only about four radio stations that you could pick-up in town at this time– one from Cincinnati, one located in Pittsburgh, one based in NY, and one in Chicago." Those were the stations that he and his neighbors could get until later in the 1920s when Washington, Philadelphia, and all the other large cities began to have stations that would transmit that far. Glenn sprang it on the family one evening bringing this contraption into the dining room and turning it on. First it had earphones; later he equipped it with loudspeakers. Soon a trail of neighbors was coming to the house to hear this new thing.

Few blacks in town had automobiles at that time. But after Glenn graduated from college in 1930, he bought a 1931 Ford upon landing his first job. His Uncle T.J., another minister in the family, also had a car about that time, a 1926 E model Ford. He was the first in the Robinson family to own a car; Glenn was the second.

One evening after Glenn, his cousins, and some friends had been out partying in the country, they had a head-on collision with a truck as they were returning home. It was a terrible automobile accident that left him in a coma for close to a month. Somehow he managed to survive with a cracked neck, a fractured skull, a broken arm, a broken leg, and had a large piece of flesh taken out of his thigh. No one took him to the hospital because blacks in the Orangeburg area did not have access to hospitals during the early 1930s; they weren't allowed there. Instead, he was taken to a lady's house in a rural area of South Carolina, about 20 miles from Orangeburg where the accident happened. A doctor did visit him, stopped the bleeding and bandaged him up but didn't give him any medication at all, instead let him heal himself. The lady of the house let him recuperate there until he regained consciousness. Then the family took him home and nursed him back to good health. Had Glenn not been taken to that lady's house, he probably would have died waiting for an ambulance. Because of the injuries he received, he was the only one of the Robinson brothers who did not go into the military, but he continued to teach for the rest of his life.

Benjamin, born in 1912, was more the quiet, steady one and the second oldest child. He never had very much to say, but he was attentive and faithful. He majored in agriculture and was interested in farming, gardening, and agricultural issues. All the Robinson children graduated from Claflin College with the exception of Benjamin. During his junior year, he transferred from Claflin to South Carolina State College because they had an agricultural department. He majored in agriculture, graduated from South Carolina State, and became an agriculture teacher. He is the only one of the brothers who went into military service during World War II and did not become an officer.

Eldridge may have been the best and most knowledgeable athlete among the Robinson brothers. He played quarterback for Claflin College and enjoyed toying with his youngest brother. He was the one who always had some trick up his sleeve. Ever the gambler, he was funny, and he tried to get you one way or the other. Eldridge was the brother that the family called the "slick" one. "I never shall forget the county fair that would come by once a year," recounts Robinson. "My grandmother would get us all together and usually gave us 25 cents each to spend at the fair. On one occasion, about the first time I was allowed to accompany the older children, Eldridge got us all together. He knew we wanted to go on the rides which were a nickel each, so he explained to us that the rides were no different than riding in a wagon or anything else and weren't really that much fun. He talked us out of going on the rides so that he could get our money and go to one of the games-of-chance, claiming that he could win a lot of money. So we all listened to him and gave him our money. He didn't win anything. In fact, he lost all the money he had – ours included." Eldridge, born in 1914, was five years older than his brother CC, and graduated from Claflin College around 1935. After college he taught school; in 1941 he went into service. After serving his country, he taught high school psychology, and because he was very athletic, he also coached.

As the only girl, Anna slept in the living room on what was called the davenport, the five boys slept in one unheated room in two beds in the back of the house, and their parents in the other bedroom. "My sister Anna was quite talented," noted Robinson as he reminisced about her. "She was a highly skilled pianist, who took piano lessons from the time that she started school until the time she died at the age of seventeen during her last year in high school. She played for Sunday school, the church and many other occasions. She was a very sweet girl whom everybody loved, was quiet in her ways, and very musically inclined. I was the youngest child. She was between Eldridge and George and almost four years older than I. She was the only one of the children who ever babied me a bit. The rest of the boys would beat the hell out of me when they felt like it. But she was tender hearted. The doctors said that she had inflammation of the stomach. But in the past fifteen or twenty years, I've concluded that she had cancer of the stomach. The medicine that her doctor gave her never accomplished anything. She lay in bed about a year and kept getting smaller and smaller. Then she passed away. I still miss her very much."

George, born in 1917, was the brother that Robinson palled around with. He was two years older and Robinson describes him as, "George was my teacher. He taught me how to make many of our playthings: slingshots and a device we called a pluffer. A pluffer was made from a piece of cane; we would take a piece about a foot long and hollow it out. Next, we would get a dowel-like piece of wood or a long rod and braid the end so as to make it air tight when we put it in the hollowed cane. Then we would get a couple of china-berries, put one at one end, and one at the other end that would be pushed down a few inches. Then we would plummet the dowel by smacking the braided end inward, hard and fast, moving the dowel with the action of a piston; one berry would shoot out of it and the second one would now be in its place, and we'd just continue to add berries to keep shooting." He was the brother with an interest in airplanes. George had seen them in magazines, but neither he nor CC had ever seen a real one. He would cut out templates of model planes made of balsa wood and cardboard. Then they would assemble and fly them. He would show CC how to make boats with paddle wheels, wagons, skate mobiles, and those types of things. Over his lifetime he would prove to be extremely smart.

During the Great Depression when George was about fourteen years old, he had to quit school. Family finances were bad in the early thirties, and as there were five Robinsons enrolled at Claflin High School and College, somebody had to drop out. So, after finishing the first quarter of his second year in high school, George quit school. "It was a lucky thing that it occurred at that time," George would write later, "because our dear sister, Anna, took to bed with her final illness." They were only a year apart in age and George and Anna had become closer before she died. Because their mother needed to tend to her constantly, George had to take on all their mother's household duties. In those days that meant cooking, cleaning, and washing and ironing clothes. That's what he did for almost a year until the family could get its finances back together.

Curtis Robinson has the distinction of being the youngest child raised in the family – his baby sister's life having been just months long. As the baby boy, he remembers that he always followed his brothers' leads, always strived to keep-up with them, and to hold his own. One of his more vivid boyhood acts was one he never shared with his family. Up to the time that Robinson's father was painting the buildings on Claflin's campus, Claflin had had only three presidents, all white. The last one hired Christopher Robinson to paint for him. The president had a big silver server and a big bucket on a swing that was broken which he gave to Christopher Robinson. His son Curtis remembers them well, "I remember that one particular day my father happened to have the cornet and that bucket lying out on the back porch together. I was a little boy and was impressed by my newly acquired knowledge about how to dig a hole. I dug one and buried the cornet and the big silver server and bucket. I don't know why. I just did it to dig a hole, I guess. I didn't tell anybody, and I bet they're still there."

The Robinson family was very close-knit and holidays were about family. They were treasured and Robinson tells why, "The special thing about the holidays was that the family was together. During some Thanksgivings, things were tough and we didn't have a turkey. We raised chickens, and as I recall we'd have two or three chickens prepared for Thanksgiving as compared to Sundays when we'd customarily have just one. On Christmases our parents couldn't provide a lot. We had cousins who lived next door who were older than we. They'd give us toys like cap guns. I remember one particular Christmas (I never shall forget this one) the Christmas of 1929 or 1930. We hung our stockings up. The next morning we got up, and my father had put an apple in the bottom of each of the stockings and tied a knot; then he had put in an orange and tied a knot; then some raisins and tied a knot; and finally he put nuts in the stocking and tied a knot. We had a long stocking filled with fruits and nuts. My father couldn't afford to fill those stockings up with toys; he just couldn't afford it. But still we were happy and our spirits were nourished."

It was a happy childhood family environment led by parents who were protective and operated in a no-nonsense manner, parents who saw to it that their children were busy all the time. And if the children didn't have anything they could think of to do, their parents would find something for them to do. Robinson says, "What my parents said, they meant, and you didn't cross them. If you did something wrong, my mother would get you immediately. She was the real disciplinarian. My father would wait until after you had accumulated a few transgressions. Then, he would tell you, 'Remember when I told you not to do this and not to do that?' and he'd get you one day and go through all those things that had been piling up and then whip you; I hated that. But I loved him. Actually, he was a very gentle man; I guess I got some of that from him." If he saw one of his children having difficulty trying to do something, Christopher would go over and show them how to do it. Otherwise, he did not have a close relationship with any of his children. "I can remember very few times that I ever sat on his lap or anything like that," Robinson recalled. "He'd talk to me, try to guide me, and show me how to do things, but there was no showing of emotion. Neither was there from my mother. She would hug me occasionally, but there were few times that I ever heard her say, 'I love you.' But we knew that they loved us. They explained our relationships with whites to us and instilled in us the message that we had to be better than whites to succeed. They'd tell us that we were better, but that we had to prove it."

Christopher and Ednora Robinson were a civic minded couple whose contributions to their community and church were recognized in an article written about their family by Dean Horace Fitchett of Claflin College, in 1944. Dean Fitchett described the Robinson's raising of their children as, "a study in the development of family morale, based on a devotion to religion and spiritual values, a loyalty to school and community ideals and a common sharing in the successes and failures, the joys and the sorrows of the home." All of their children who lived to reach adulthood were college graduates. Of these, four graduated from Claflin College and one, Benjamin, from South Carolina State College. The Robinson family was at once typical and unusual for the times. They were a black family with ambitions, aspirations, worthy goals and ideals, people who drew strength from their faith and maintained persistent drive and inner resolve to succeed. They were one example of the striving, hard working, education acquiring, church-going, property-owning, patriotic, cooperative and burgeoning black middle class in Orangeburg, South Carolina. And one generation removed from slavery, the Robinsons were solidly established.

Days of Youth and Education

During the 1920s and 1930s, the state of South Carolina's approach to education for blacks in Orangeburg was caught in the void that existed during the time-span between the Plessy vs. Fergusson[i] court decision, rendered in 1896, and the Brown vs. Topeka, Kansas Board of Education decision, rendered in 1954. The same held true for much of the nation. In some southern states, school segregation meant that separate and inferior facilities were the norm for black students, but in other cases it meant schools for whites and no schools for blacks.

It was also true that in those instances in which states made funding available to educate black children, huge disparities existed between the funding provided for blacks compared to whites, particularly southern states. Per capita expenditures for public education were 65 times as great for whites in Alabama during the 1920s and 1930s as for blacks, a gap probably larger than South Carolina's, but part of a consistent pattern of education funding. Funding voids for the education of blacks were partially filled by support from northern philanthropic organizations and foundations like the

Rockefeller Foundation, the Phelps-Stokes Fund, the Sterling Foundation, the New England Conference, the Rosenwald Foundation and others. And budget and curriculum planning for black schools in many states revolved around ensuring children's availability as tenant farmers - farming and harvesting laborers - in which case the school year lasted four months.

Differences of opinion about what constituted an appropriate education for blacks – a classical/liberal arts education versus a vocational or technical education - had raged on early into the 20th century and added complexity to the education issue. Booker T. Washington[ii] was a huge proponent of vocational training for blacks and a national figure of prominence as this debate played out. His approach garnered mixed reviews. He founded Tuskegee Institute upon whose campus the Tuskegee Army Air Field was built, and where Tuskegee Airmen trained. Robinson's assessment of Washington's approach is as follows: "I think that the more educated you were as a black person, the less you could appreciate his point of view, his philosophy. He was a proponent of farming, industrial training, and manual labor; he was high on that. That's the philosophy that Tuskegee Institute was built on. They had an awful lot of land, taught farming, and had a very good veterinarian school; they called it animal care, husbandry, or something similar. What he did, worked, but it wasn't freedom. He was an important and educated 'Uncle Tom.' He did get favors from whites for his college and for blacks in the community and was a very good salesman for his point of view, but I thought he had faulty views. One of his beliefs was that black people should have been willing to forego any desires for political power until they got on their feet. That was Washington's way of solving the problem - bringing us up by our bootstraps. However, I must say the veterinarian school at Tuskegee Institute still remains strong to this day."

But so rooted in the belief that an education was critical for a person's ability to improve his lot was the ex-slave, Christopher Zeigler Robinson that he sent his oldest son, Thomas Robinson, to Claflin College in 1870. In subsequent years Thomas G. Robinson purchased land specifically near Claflin College so that his children might have an opportunity to get an education there, too. He would extend his help and hospitality to several children in his family as well as promising children of members of his church. "My father and his brothers and sisters were all educated at Claflin College between 1890 and 1900," Robinson informs. "There weren't a lot of blacks acquiring normal degrees or going on to college in the 1880s and 1890s, but my parents, aunts and uncles were. Their normal degrees were the equivalent of a junior college degree today, but "normal" also meant it wasn't vocational training." A normal degree qualified Robinson's father to teach. Usually he taught in rural places where the school year lasted four months and where there would be two to four teachers to a school, but sometimes he taught in schools where he was the only teacher and taught all the grades.

The city's system of schooling for blacks was very poor, almost nonexistent in the Orangeburg, S.C., of the 1930s. Public elementary schools in the city were for whites; they had two elementary schools and one really good high school. The elementary school for blacks was run by the Sterling Foundation until 1924 and went as high as the eighth grade, which was added during Robinson's brother George's last year. It was a wood frame building with about eight to ten rooms. Robinson never attended that school, but all his brothers, with the exception of his oldest brother, went to school there. Glenn, the oldest, went to Claflin on a work scholarship beginning in the fourth grade.

The Sterling Foundation was formed right after the Civil

War. Among its other philanthropic work, the organization was responsible for building many schools in South Carolina for blacks prior to the state's inclination to provide such funding. And Sterling schools provided a free education for black students who lived in the city. It had ample teachers, but classes were sometimes crowded, although not as crowded as they were in the county school, a public school that would eventually replace it. In fact Jesse Jackson[iii] went to a Sterling school in Greenville, S.C., that had been a junior college twenty years prior to his attendance there. But by the time he got there, it had become a good high school and it was still run by the Sterling Foundation. The state took over the Sterling schools in Orangeburg around the time that Robinson started school in 1924.

In addition to the Sterling schools, both colleges, South Carolina State and Claflin, had broad pre-college curriculums encompassing kindergarten, elementary school, and high school that afforded educational opportunities to the more fortunate black children. "My sister and my oldest brother went to Claflin Elementary School, which went to the eighth grade" Robinson recounts. "Claflin's elementary school had class sizes of about fifteen students per class. Claflin also had a four-year high school that went from ninth through twelfth grade and a four-year college. The school charged tuition, but I don't think it was very much because we were able to afford it even though we were poor."

Robinson went to the first public school for blacks built with state funds in Orangeburg County; he remembers seeing the school being built. "When I was about four or five," Robinson says, "they began to build this school during the summer on the grounds of Claflin College's athletic field. Claflin had sold some of its land to the city to build a black elementary school there. It was a three-story brick structure with thirteen classrooms, as I recall. It opened in September 1924. I turned five in August so I went directly to the first grade there."

Children came from several miles around to attend the school, and indeed some children came from what Robinson's community called 'over the river' and boarded in town so that they could go to the new elementary school. Consequently, the school was overcrowded from the beginning. There were two classes each from first to fifth grade, one sixth, one seventh, and one eighth grade class. As the students got older, they began to drop out of the higher grades to go to work. This was the only public school in Orangeburg County for blacks besides the Sterling school that went as high as the eighth grade because most schools in the county went to fourth grade and only operated four months out of the year. That meant that students had to go for two years to make one grade. A situation Robinson characterizes as "That's a shame but that's how it was."

The schools run by the city compared unfavorably with those operated by the Sterling Foundation or the Rosenwald School at South Carolina State. In the new elementary school, overcrowding was extremely bad. There was one bathroom for the boys and one for the girls; this was for a student body of almost 1400 kids. It was easy to see that it was overused. The new school would start the year with between 100 and 110 students per class and end with about 80 because of dropouts who did farm work. The Rosenwald School and the Sterling school had smaller classes – about fifteen to thirty students per class. However, education at the public school was free while students had to pay to go to the elementary school at both Claflin and South Carolina State, and the city school was also large, and new.

On very cloudy or rainy days when kids likely couldn't

work in the fields, additional students would come to school. Classrooms would be so overcrowded on those days that some kids would stand along the walls. Often when the older boys came to school they seemed to revel in the pleasure of being away from fieldwork. Some sat in the back of the classroom and would shoot wads of wet paper from rubber bands or throw bits of crayon and small pebbles, and talk loud and laugh all day long. All the poor teacher could do was to hit the desk with a big stick and holler, 'Quiet!' During recess the older boys would pluck the smaller boys heads or twist their arms in a hammerlock fashion and generally make it miserable for their younger and smaller classmates when they chose.

George had just turned six and couldn't cope with the bigger, older rowdy students. When he was in the second grade, he already was an avid reader. If the brothers were out in the field and found a piece of paper that was lying around, he'd pick it up, read it, and he could remember everything he'd read. At one point it appeared that the teachers in his elementary school were not maintaining order in the classroom, so he refused to go to class even when everybody else went. The reason for the disorder was that the classroom was overcrowded with more than fifty children. The big boys were bad and were menacing him. A neighbor of the school saw him alternately either going under the building or hopping in and out of an empty coal bin, hiding. The neighbor informed an instructor, Professor Sharperson, who nabbed him. He called George's brother Ben, who, in turn, called George's first grade teacher who agreed to take him back and prepare him for the third grade.

Students would really fall behind when they only came to class during inclement weather and during the winter months. Parents of such students would let them go to school when it didn't interfere with farm work. The situation was only slightly better for students who diligently attended schools with truncated school years. This situation created another classroom problem, according to Robinson. "We were getting students from out of the county for the second, third and fourth grades who were much older because they had to spend two years making up one grade. It would show in their ages." In the second grade, Robinson was six or seven, but there were children in his class who were ten to twelve years old. When he finished the eighth grade, some of the students graduating with him were nineteen-years-old. And there were more of them than there were of students who had been progressing at the rate of a grade per year.

Curtis Robinson and his brothers and sister were more fortunate. From an early age, the Robinson children were given books at home. The family had a large dining room where everyone would gather around the dining room table with a lot of books, and the children all had a study period even before they started to attend school. Although CC Robinson was the youngest, his brothers and sister didn't teach him much except for George. It was his parents who taught him. His mother would listen to them read and his father would check everyone's arithmetic. "My mother read to me so much that I sometimes memorized the entire book," Robinson says of the effectiveness of their sessions. "I would look at the pictures and listen to my mother as she read. One book was called *Baby Ray*. It was a first grade book for rural people. It started out with numbers. It went, 'Baby Ray had one cow, the cow is red' – using all short, three and four letter words. 'The cow says moo, and Baby Ray loved the cow,' so on and so forth. It went on to say, 'Baby Ray had two ducks, the ducks said quack, quack,' et cetera; then it went on to, 'Baby Ray had three cuddly kitty cats, the cats said, 'meow, meow, meow.' "I still remember that book after all of these years."

It became his favorite book, the one he always took with

him. So when he first went to school and the teacher asked him to read, *Baby Ray* was the book he presented her. She turned to the page that had the picture of the cats and CC began, "Baby Ray had three cuddly kitty cats," and continued as if he were reading. He knew all the words that went with the pictures and he cited them from memory. The teacher said his reading was "marvelous" and "wonderful." She didn't know that he couldn't read; he had already memorized that entire book.

Elementary school curriculum consisted of the basics – reading, writing, arithmetic, and spelling. Luckily the schools he attended, the city school and Claflin, had good teachers who knew their subjects well and could teach. They made sure that all students understood the lessons, at least the children who were coming to school regularly. Most teachers in the county were graduates of South Carolina State and Claflin College and, with one or two exceptions, were very dedicated teachers. They all had big rulers or big sticks and would use them. Students knew this, so discipline was usually very good. "I got struck a few times, myself. But, as a rule, most of us got a good elementary education," Robinson says.

During the summer, South Carolina State College would have teachers attending classes there from all over the state. On some nights, they would have movies that were open to the public in their large chapel which held two or three thousand people. They would let young children attend, too. One of young Robinson's most crushing moments happened when he was in the second or third grade and involved a teacher that he thought was very fond of him. She would bring him up to her desk and hug him, and she gave him a lot of attention. At one of the movies he attended and while sitting in the balcony, he saw the teacher sitting a distance across from him in the balcony, and she was waving and smiling in his direction. He began smiling and waving back enthusiastically, too, almost the entire time. The next time he saw her in class, he told her that he liked the movie. She asked, "Oh, were you there?" His heart dropped; she hadn't even noticed him. He found out that her boyfriend was in the balcony somewhere behind him. She had been smiling and waving at her boyfriend – not him; that almost broke his young, infatuated heart.

In the third grade, students began to take geography, and from the fourth grade up, history – this was in addition to reading, writing and arithmetic. Students stayed in the same classroom all day long until they got to the sixth grade. At that point, most of the boys went over to another building for shop and agriculture, but other than that the kids would stay in the same room all day long. In the sixth grade, boys learned agriculture and girls, home economics. Then in the seventh grade the girls took sewing and the boys took shop. In the seventh grade students were also taught literature and English; in the eighth grade algebra, and another math class above arithmetic. Each teacher taught about four courses.

Teachers also enjoyed having students participate in performances, and Robinson recounts how it affected him in elementary school: "Teachers loved plays; it was all they wanted. One little girl, Charlene, was always matched with me, and I didn't like it. She was plump, had big jaws, nappy hair, and wore homemade dresses. She had a habit of wiping her hands on the sides of her dress and it was always dirty there. Sometimes two or three times a year they'd have plays and would match me up with her. I was getting to the point where I really resented it, but I couldn't say anything because, boy, if I had, I would have gotten it from everybody –my teachers, my parents, everybody! Of course, I wasn't that great looking, either. I was scrawny, had nappy hair, big eyes, and wore homemade clothes, too. I certainly wasn't a prince, but I sure wanted to be matched with one of those little girls with pretty hair and high cheekbones – a "trophy" girl." After the sixth grade, Charlene seemed to have gotten to the point that she didn't like the match-up thing either, and that was the last time we were matched up."

They graduated after the eighth grade, and since there was no public high school for blacks in Orangeburg, Charlene didn't go to high school because her parents couldn't afford to send her. Robinson, however, went on to Claflin High School where he had to work to pay for his tuition. He played sports and coached. It would be years before they saw each other again. One day during his senior year of high school while he was walking on campus, Robinson saw a group of guys and a young lady; it was Charlene, the plump little duckling that he was always paired with as a little boy, sitting there and he remembers, "She had grown up to be a gorgeous young woman; she had become a trophy girl. She had a cute face, pretty eyes; a nice perky chest – ah, she was a bomb. They were having the time of their lives. When I approached them, I said, 'Hi, Charlene.' She said, 'Hi, CC,' but she never looked up. She left town soon after that, and I never saw her again."

Soon, CC Robinson completed high school. It was almost automatic that he would continue along a path of educational achievement that had been established in his family almost fifty years before he was born. And since that time the family tradition had continued. One of his uncles was a teacher, another taught, then went to Philadelphia and eventually became a preacher in his later years. Ednora Robinson's uncle was a doctor who had earned a medical degree from Meharry Medical School around 1928, but unfortunately he was killed in an automobile accident. Robinson's brother Glenn began teaching in one of those one-room schools after he graduated from college in 1930. Then he landed a job at a school that had two teachers and about forty students. "Although we didn't discuss it much, I knew as a young child when I was in elementary school that I was going to college;" says Robinson of how fundamentally his family embraced education. "No one talked about how it would be financed, but it was just understood that I would be going to college like my brothers before me. My four older brothers all went to college and my sister finished high school before she passed away at an early age; it was just one of the things that we all did." After he graduated from high school in May of 1936, the most immediate issue for Robinson was that of continuing his education. Orangeburg was a college town and in the fall of 1936, he was headed to college.

Coming of Age

Claflin College is a United Methodist college and at the time Robinson attended, its funding came from the Methodist churches in the state supplemented by funding from the New England Conference, a regional Methodist conference in the northeastern United States. Claflin was named after Lee Claflin, a Presbyterian minister from New England who raised a lot of money for the school and was one of the founders together with his son, William Claflin, who was the governor of Massachusetts at the time. The college had approximately 300 students in 1936. Including the high school and the elementary students, the institution had a total of about 410 students. A fence separated the Claflin College and South Carolina State campuses with a gate that connected one campus to the other, but it was almost like one campus. South Carolina State was three times the size of Claflin and had many more students there. They had a lot of agricultural, mechanical and industrial majors, but they didn't have many students majoring in liberal arts areas.

Claflin's focus was more in the area of liberal arts. It was a setting where Robinson met lifelong friends, some of whom would figure prominently in his life - especially his wife, Florie. She came to Claflin during his junior year. They met as he was leaving a fraternity meeting, and they dated intermittently. During his senior year, she transferred from Claflin to South Carolina State, and he didn't see her too often after that.

College introduced him to his social and intellectual contemporaries from all over the South, and to a limited degree, the Nation. Aspects of his peer's value systems that were not so obvious in his peer group in Orangeburg could now be observed. He could see that skin tone seemed to be an issue or a consideration with some sororities and, to a lesser extent, fraternities. It was a time when having a lighter complexion appeared to give some students more prestige in their early years. It was also a time when some within the black community - discounting the societal mindset underlying Plessy, who had a single black great-grand parent, v. Ferguson and the 1/8th rule - perhaps equated lightness in hue with superiority within the race. Putting a premium on lightness may have seemed a way to mitigate the penalty of race, maybe it was out of self-loathing, or perhaps being light or so associated seemed a logical way to soften the blows of racism and escape its evil commensurate with ones skin tone. Or it might simply have been mere preferences based on notions of beauty. Whatever the reason, it was a judgment factor and value criteria in the consciousness of some.

Fortunately as young men and women progressed through their college years and beyond, a person's complexion didn't make that much difference in Robinson's view, particularly in the case of males. Robinson recalls that within the college fraternities and when he competed with black guys later in life, performance and merit tended to win out but he suggests, "It might have been different with females." Both fraternities and sororities were in their infancies at South Carolina State and Claflin. It was believed that the Alpha Kappa Alphas (AKAs) at South Carolina State were smarter, but socially, the Deltas appeared to be what most girls aspired to. They were higher on the social ladder, more popular, sought-after, and most were light-skinned. But the bottom line, particularly for a guy, was that you reached a point where you had to bring something more to the effort when competing than a light complexion."

Claflin College held an extremely serious attitude towards education. The instructors there were well-trained. Having a master's degree in 1936 was a big thing, like a Ph.D. is today. Claflin only had three Ph.D.s. on campus then, but everyone else had master degrees and had gotten them from major U.S. universities. Many of the instructors remembered Robinson's brother George, two years his senior, who was a straight A student when he attended. "Why can't you do as well as your brother?" they would often ask as a veiled challenge to equal his record. But Curtis Robinson doesn't believe he was as smart as George Robinson and thus he says, "I received grades accordingly." Nor was he a particularly serious young man like his brother George, whom he described as "dead serious." Nonetheless, Curtis Robinson was a solid student who studied hard and excelled in his major.

Medicine seemed appealing to Robinson. There was one doctor in his family, his uncle on his mother's side, and the accident involving his brother Glenn highlighted the need for more black doctors. So Robinson majored in chemistry and minored in zoology thinking that he would become a physician, but it didn't turn out that way. A course in comparative anatomy changed his mind. First the class used dolphins as he recollects, and then they experimented on cats and rabbits – dissecting and examining their organs. That was too much for him. It turned his stomach, and he couldn't handle the odor. "I decided that medicine wasn't for me after my comparative anatomy class, but I didn't know what I was going to do after that."

Students had to take at least four courses per quarter, earned two or three credit hours per course, and needed to attain approximately 120 credits in order to graduate. Certain courses such as psychology, sociology, religion, calculus and trigonometry were required for all students. Robinson stayed with chemistry though he changed his mind about becoming a doctor. The decision to pursue chemistry would turn out to be a good one in the short term and an underlying factor later in life in his final career choice.

Part of Robinson's success in his major was due to his chemistry lab-mate. She was about five years older, a very pleasant young lady and a lot of fun. She had attended Claflin a few years earlier, gotten married, left college to be with her husband, and then returned to Claflin to complete her education. They worked beautifully together as lab mates and she was very smart. Her husband was from Orangeburg and they lived near Claflin.

As his sophomore or junior year neared its close, it was time to begin to study for finals. Robinson needed to redouble his chemistry study efforts and that meant studying with his lab-mate, particularly the last three weeks before final examinations. She was keen and took excellent notes so he headed to her house to study. In Orangeburg there were very few telephones and in most cases visitors simply dropped in on each other un-announced. If someone were home and could entertain you, they would; otherwise, you tried again later.

Robinson took his work over to his lab mate's house, unannounced, with the hope of catching her at home and doing some home work, but she was out. She had a younger sister,

Sophia, who was a year behind Robinson at Claflin, who was there, and she greeted him at the door after he knocked. She invited Robinson inside. He went inside and stood for a moment recalling her campus image: "She was totally different from her sister. The sisters were from out of town. As this one, the little sister, walked home from class each day, the guys would constantly hit-on her. They called her 'ice-berg' because she seemed so cold. She didn't seem very fun-loving, at all. But she was beautiful, one of the prettiest women on campus, yet she had no personality. She took no part in any activities after school; she joined no clubs and attended no social events. When classes concluded at day's end, she would fold her arms across her books, clutch them to her chest and without looking right or left, walk straight home. She lived about a mile away with her sister, and during her walk home she would barely speak to anyone but just kept walking while maintaining her pace and remaining unsmiling. The guys were all trying to woo her but they never got anywhere with her.

"Please have a seat," she said pleasantly and motioned Robinson towards the large sofa. He went inside and sat down on the sofa near the center. She told him sweetly, "Laura's not home right now, and I'm not expecting her for quite sometime." "Oh, I see," replied Robinson not really knowing what to say. He felt awkward sitting there and didn't know if he should leave. "Laura and Robert won't be home until about 7:30," she continued as she sat down right beside him, very close – which surprised him. It was now 5:30; he raised his arm and put it along the back of the sofa and somewhat around her to see what would happen. He began to tell her what a beautiful home they had when she leaned over into his arm.

Robinson hardly knew what to say. He told her how she was even lovelier sitting there than he had noticed from afar and she smiled. Then he marveled at how beautifully her hair framed her face and accented her eyes whose beauty he had not noticed before, and she thought that was a charming thing for him to say. Then he pulled her closer to him; they smiled a delightful, secretive smile as if knowing that this might be the beginning of something special. He tilted his head towards hers and kissed her. She responded, so he wrapped his other arm around her and held her tight, and things proceeded from there. "I found out that she was very passionate, extremely lustful," Robinson recalls of that moment and his new friend. "Sometimes it's hard to know how much fun a person can be until you really get to know them."

After their first evening together, Robinson felt so lucky, Sophia was a hidden treasurer. Wow! What a passionate woman her façade masked. He had gotten lucky! Robinson remained extremely discreet about what had happened. He never told a soul about the incidence, didn't mention it, ever, until this time. Sophia saw him on campus several days after their first evening together and told him it would be ok if he stopped by to see her right after classes. When classes ended, he spotted her heading home. Robinson began heading there, also. He followed her casually at an inconspicuous distance – fifty yards or so – while greeting his friends, stopping and talking briefly so that no one would suspect them of anything, but refusing to linger. The two walked through Claflin's campus and past South Carolina State's while she coolly eschewed all advances as was her style. When Robinson went over to her house the first time to study with his lab mate, he didn't know that her husband was a tailor with his own business, and she headed over to his shop everyday after class and stayed and worked with him until he closed. This meant Sophia had the house to herself until they got home. She and Robinson had a couple of hours alone there almost everyday for about three weeks, and nobody knew a thing.

It was a passionate relationship, full of energy, an affair so steamy that the fellows would never have believed it anyway. Had the school year not ended so soon after their affair began, it's possible that the two of them might have really fallen in love. After commencement, school closed and students headed home. About a week later and month into the affair, without giving Robinson any advanced notice, she left town. Sophia didn't usually stay with her sister during summer breaks; instead she would return to her home in North Carolina for the summer, but when the upcoming school year started, she did not come back. From that point on, Curtis Robinson and Sophia would not see each other again for almost fifty years.

Summers by now were taking Robinson in a different direction than those of his youth. The Edisto Hotel job now had long been a thing of the past. Music was holding as much of an interest for Robinson now as did athletics during his high school years. He had begun to learn music early in life. When he was six or seven, his grandmother taught him to play the piano – the basics. "I played like she did," he says, "which was very slowly and carefully. But I knew music." Later, he learned to play music under a program sponsored by the NRA, or the National Recovery Act[iv]. Under the authority of the NRA, students who were highly skilled in music were paid to teach music to other students, and this allowed Robinson to upgrade his musical talents. He was in high school when he first went on the campus at Claflin and noticed that six or seven musical groups were being formed. With an eye toward joining one of them, he began to take a course in music for about nine months after he entered college, later he joined one of the groups.

Soon, at least in his mind, he became a professional. He took the college's bass fiddle home and practiced all summer long, and when he returned to school for its upcoming term, he was good enough to play with the college's string ensemble. He was very proficient at reading music and using the board. The next school year he gave a solo performance on his bass fiddle in Claflin College chapel using the bow almost exclusively and according to his late brother, George " President Randolph gave him many accolades - very positive comments for several minutes. It made his family very proud."

One summer just before he graduated from college, he went to Asheville and played in a band. The group consisted of college guys whose trumpet player was from Claflin. It just so happened that the band was missing a bass fiddler. Robinson's classmate contacted him via telegram and said, "We need a bass fiddle player. Can you play with us?" Robinson didn't have any money and neither did his mother. Fare to Asheville cost two dollars and ninety cents. They borrowed it from their neighbor across the street, an older lady who rented to boarders, and Robinson got his ticket and headed to join the group. Most of the band members were from schools like North Carolina A&T or Johnson C. Smith, North Carolina colleges. They played in resort areas like Black Mountain, Spartanburg, and Greenville, S.C., and in places like Kingsport, Tennessee, up in the hills in that area, and also in Asheville, N.C. They played mostly to white audiences and had their own uniforms.

It was a ten-piece band, and with all of them traveling in one fully packed station wagon, traveling was miserable. But it was quite an experience, and he got to meet a lot of pretty girls that would follow the band around like latter day groupies. As band members, some young women saw the musicians as more interesting than the local guys. Plus, the musicians had a lot of time to stand around and talk to them; they enjoyed flirting and talking romantically with the girls. It was a summer that he enjoyed immensely, and much like his older brother after he had gone to New York, Curtis Robinson went home broke, too. He was forced to negotiate a financial arrangement with

President Randolph, the President of Claflin College, in order to return to Claflin and complete his senior year.

It was somewhat ironic, but Robinson and his chemistry instructor would go on to share closely related military experiences. In fact his chemistry instructor would go on to become the first black navy pilot in the United States. His name was Oscar Holmes. Robinson describes him as "a West Virginia boy who got his masters in chemistry and physics from Ohio State University and came to Claflin as an instructor. When the war started, Holmes landed a job in Erie, Pennsylvania, as a chemist in a power plant. He had lots of time on his hand so he took up flying. The Navy was recruiting pilots then and when their recruiting personnel had an opportunity to observe him flying, they recruited him for their flying program. So he went into that program just like Curtis Robinson did for the Army Air Corps. There was a small problem. Holmes looked white, but the Navy never noticed that he had written 'Negro' on his form where it asked for "race" and didn't discover that he was black until his graduation; then they refused to assign him to a squadron."

After he graduated, Holmes noticed that new pilots were getting assignments, but he never saw his name posted on the assignment board. All of his classmates were pulling out, but he was still there. Concerned, he questioned his leader about his assignment status. The Navy pulled out his records, showed them to him, and said, "It says on your record that you're a Negro. Is that true?" He said, "That's right." They asked, "Why didn't you tell us?" He said, "You didn't ask." After that, they absolutely wouldn't assign him to a squadron, but instead sent him to New York as a recruiter. After he stayed there a couple of years and had not gotten any rank, he told the Navy, "Look, either let me fly or let me out." He was sent to Canada where he ferried planes. Robinson remembers that

Holmes was a fine chemistry instructor.

Curtis Robinson graduated from Claflin in 1940 with an impressive group of classmates. His graduating class produced the first black United Methodist bishop in the country; it included ten chemistry majors that yielded two pharmacists, two doctors, two dentists, two builders, a principal and a chemistry teacher - his lab-mate, and several ministers and teachers.

Teach, Preach, or Sell Insurance

After graduating from college, Robinson's chances of continuing his education were very slim. He had taken courses geared towards pre-med but did not want to go into medicine after going through a comparative anatomy course at Claflin. "My senses were too susceptible; I couldn't stand those odors," is his reason for not pursuing medicine. "I decided to become a house painter like my daddy, who taught school during the winter, painted in the summer, and had all of his sons painting, too. When I was sixteen or seventeen, I began taking on painting jobs for myself and had some previous experience. So when my classmates sent out applications all over the state for school teaching jobs, I declined. I decided I was going to just continue my painting business. My mother counseled me that the season for painting was mostly the summer and that winters were very slow, but I initially ignored that advice."

When Robinson graduated from college in 1940, opportunities for professional careers for blacks were extremely limited. The only things a black college graduate could realistically expect to do were to teach school, preach, go into insurance sales, start a small business, or continue his education if he could obtain enough money to do so. There were no other options unless you were a tradesman. Much of the reasoning and thrust behind Booker T. Washington's philosophy concerning vocational education as preferable for blacks sadly was in response to that reality, i.e., the discrimination that black college graduates faced in the job market when seeking professional careers.

"It was interesting how I got into teaching," Robinson says of that time of his life. "After I graduated, the summer was passing and I was painting, but jobs were really getting scarce. I heard of a school near Spartanburg, S.C., that needed teachers, so I prevailed on one of my schoolmates to write a letter for me. Her name was Ruth and she was a very good student and a great typist."

Ruth Williams was the wife of Robinson's good friend, Frank Williams, who later became the pastor of his church, Ashbury United Methodist Church in Washington, D.C. After completing his application letter, she also completed the accompanying application to be submitted with it. Robinson read it quickly, just signed it, and sent it off immediately. It turns out that it was such a great letter that the superintendent of the school system with the vacancy came down to see him. He interviewed Robinson, and on his way out he said, 'That was a fine letter you wrote.' Then he asked him, 'Did you really write that letter?' Robinson said, "No, I didn't write it," and he told him who had. The principal said, "Well, she certainly thought a lot of you." He thought it was such a great letter that after interviewing Robinson, he offered him the job on the spot."

As far back as his childhood, almost all important decisions seem not to have been totally up to Robinson. He believes God has played a tremendous part in his life. Things just seemed to develop out of nowhere, and he just kept going from one thing to another. The teaching position he had just landed turned out to be one of the best paying teaching jobs in the state. The school paid seventy-five dollars per month. His brothers, one of whom had been teaching for ten years and the other for seven years, were making fifty dollars per month, and here was little brother CC walking in at a starting pay of $75 dollars per month.

While his two older brothers were earning $50 a month, George was making $60." The reason George made more, Robinson remembers, "is that around 1936, the state of South Carolina decided to standardize test scores for all teachers, white and black. They tested teachers and their salaries were based on their test scores. The total possible score was 700, but 300 was passing and the state paid each teacher $50 a month who made at least 300 and who was also a college graduate. My brother George took the test and made the lone perfect score; they couldn't believe it! He was paid a little bit more." New teachers who made a score of less than 300 or who didn't have a degree were paid $40 a month. "We had a lot of teachers who had not earned a college degree," Robinson says, "but they had to go to summer school every summer to build up their credits." But when lucky CC Robinson came out of college two years after George, he was hired to teach in Spartanburg County and that made a difference.

Spartanburg County sported textile factories all over the county and surrounding areas. Those factories made different types of fabrics and materials, nothing else, just that, and they made and sold a lot of it. The area was such a factory town that the factories supplemented black teachers' salaries by $25 per month and white teachers' salaries by $35 a month. That made Spartanburg a very good county in which to teach. The state still paid teachers their customary, $50 dollars a month, bringing Robinson's income to $75 per month which was pretty good money to be making in South Carolina in 1940.

After having just turned 21 in August, Robinson began his career as a school teacher in September of 1940. The school was in a small town about twelve or thirteen miles from Spartanburg, the third largest city in the state. "And luck was with me further. I didn't have an automobile. The principal of my school found a nice place for me to stay with an old man and his wife who rented out rooms," Robinson says of his additional good fortune. "Most of our meals consisted of rabbits, squirrels or whatever the old man could catch when he hunted, which was all the time. His wife was a good cook and they had a big garden. We would usually have food for a nice meal consisting of whatever meat he brought in from his hunting outings and the vegetables they grew. The place wasn't far away from the school. In fact, the old gunslinger sometimes walked that distance."

The school was a wooden structure with enough grounds for the kids to play. It had a maintenance man, but no electricity, no running water or cafeteria; however, the school did supply books and materials. There were eight teachers and a small student body. The class sizes were very small compared to the class sizes of most of the schools around there at that time which ran anywhere from 29 to 32 students. There were so few kids that one teacher taught both the first and second grade. The third and fourth grades were taught by another teacher. Single classes didn't begin until the upper grades. The school went to the tenth grade which was taught by the principal. Robinson taught geography, history, general science and mathematics, but not chemistry, which was his major. Some students would go from the tenth grade at the school directly to college and many colleges had a special prep class for them to help their transition. Although Robinson was teaching in a county full of textile companies, blacks couldn't get those types of jobs and were mostly tenant farmers, instead. Many students were poor farm kids who only got to play during recess because they had to go home after school and do their chores.

Spartanburg County and the surrounding counties were comprised mostly of whites because the cotton mills provided jobs that paid more and produced higher standards of living than the agricultural ones. Consequently, blacks weren't allowed jobs in the cotton mills but did a lot of farming around there, or, as in the case of the old guy Robinson lived with, hunted and collected rent. You could tell who had mill jobs among the whites by the way the kids were dressed. Because the core of the city was white, the city school system was white, segregated, and had about thirty school buses, all of which were used to pick up only white children. The city schools were about three times the size of black schools. Robinson's school was the only black school in South Carolina that had a school bus. The PTA sponsored the school bus which transported students over two counties; they paid for it, kept it running, and paid the bus driver as well, even though there weren't a lot of black school age kids in those two counties. "That PTA was impressive," acknowledges Robinson. "We would have a PTA meeting once a month at the school, and all the parents would be there! I've never seen anything like it. That was a great PTA."

After Robinson filled his teaching position, there were two remaining vacancies in his new school, one for a home economics and fifth grade teacher, and the other for a music and fourth grade teacher. On his third day on the job, the principal brought the new home economics teacher out to be housed where Robinson boarded; she would be living there, also. He described the new boarder: "She was not the average type woman. She was tall, about my height, slender, had a lot of brown hair, a sandy complexion, large eyes that would look at you and through you at the same time, and sensual lips. She was unsmiling, but smiled easily. She would look at you in a serious way, but if you said something charming or engaging, she would smile very easily and that was why we got along so well. In fact, eventually we would kid each other back and forth as we rode to school with the principal each morning. He would crack up as we would have our verbal exchanges."

About ten days on the job, his school got a new music and fourth grade teacher. That young lady had just graduated from Spellman with a degree in music. Robinson remembers, "She was from Boston, had married a guy who had gone to Claflin, and they resided in Spartanburg. Her husband's nickname was 'Pig'; she loved him very much and called him "my piggy." She developed a beautiful choir at the school and it often performed at teacher meetings and statewide events. She was a great organizer, a brilliant teacher, and a very pleasant woman. She was black but looked Italian - real light with nice hair."

His new housemate, who taught the fifth grade and home economics, had graduated from South Carolina State in 1935 and was about six years older than Robinson. He found out later that she had lost a very good position in a school in another county because she was caught having an affair with the principal. In those days, there were very few married female teachers, at least in black schools. School systems, for some reason, didn't want any married female teachers on the staff. Perhaps they were afraid the married ones would get pregnant, and they would lose them in middle of the school-year. But the men were often married while the women weren't. After this teacher lost her job, the principal at Robinson's new school hired her and put her in the same house with the old man, his wife, and Robinson.

The house where Robinson and the new teacher lived had a kitchen, a dining room, and a bedroom in what was the old part of the house. The owners had just built a new addition to the house consisting of a bedroom, a living room and a hall downstairs, and two rooms upstairs. They gave the new female teacher the downstairs bedroom and Robinson the upstairs one. "But where I was designated to sleep there was no heat whatsoever, and it was cold in those mountains," says Robinson of his chilly, unheated room, "so when the weather got cooler, I slept downstairs, in the living room which was heated."

Robinson's move to the first floor did not go unnoticed. Soon this friendly teacher resumed with him where she had left off with the principal at her previous school. Robinson says cheerfully of her style, "She was a very attractive young lady, and I was surprised that she was so romantically aggressive. After I started sleeping downstairs, she came in from her room to talk with me because she said she couldn't sleep. We talked for a while about school matters and she went back to bed. But she returned again the next night still talkative but surprisingly very playful and a little suggestive. We became intimate and lived almost like man and wife for the first year. By the second year, she told me that life was passing her by, that she didn't have any children, and was interested in getting married. She was twenty-eight, six years older than my twenty-two years and I told her that I could understand her desire to get married. Twenty-eight seemed old for women then, but I was not looking to get married, and I told her so. Then I told her that I would love for us to continue our special friendship."

Robinson decided to try one possible guy that might be a good mate for her. There was a friend of his brother's, the principal of a school not far from there, who was a nice guy and who Robinson figured was her type. He also had a car. One day right after the Thanksgiving holiday of 1941, Robinson approached him about coming over to meet the teacher which he did. The two of them met and began to date. Robinson had no car. When he visited, Robinson would sit with them for a little while and then ask to borrow his friend's car. Of course he would comply gladly, eager to get him out of there. And Robinson would leave to pursue a former classmate, a cute young lady he'd run into at their daylong teachers meeting. After about two or three months of that, the teacher and his friend got serious. They got married in February, but it was a secret marriage because she might have been fired if the school system had known she was married. "I didn't know her before she became my housemate. But she came from a good family in Greenville, S.C. I met her mother and father, who were very nice, respectable people. She was an only child and, I guess, was used to having her way. She had had her way with me, and that was just fine. It worked out well for everyone."

Among his students, Robinson remembers that there were kids who were quite smart. He said, "If I gave them an assignment, they would do it, but they had no drive. They were smart kids who could do things, but would not take any initiative on their own; you would always have to push them and push them. But there were some smart kids who were motivated to learn on their own and whom I didn't have to push that much." He also coached the girls' and boys' basketball teams, but didn't receive any pay as a coach. Robinson tried to be a disciplinarian but knew the kids could see right through him. "I had one child who was hyperactive – I don't remember the official educational term. I would bring him up and seat him next to my desk. I'd look up, and the next thing I knew, he had gone to the back of the class. I had no trouble keeping order, but he was an exception, and he did whatever he wanted whenever he wanted to."

Robinson learned to enjoy teaching. He was from a

family of teachers so it was a natural profession for him. It was also enjoyable because he had a supportive principal who was a good educator and who thought Robinson had the right attitude towards teaching. "I think my biggest contribution to teaching was that some of the kids tried to act like me," says Robinson. "They thought I was a role model, someone special. I was able to motivate and inspire them, and they pulled up their grades, changed their behavior, and everything else. I really tried to engage the children in class. Otherwise, I don't think they would have tried much of anything. I don't think they were ever challenged away from school. Helping those students to believe in themselves, helping them to see that they truly had potential, and helping them understand that they really were as good as anybody else were my biggest teaching accomplishments." And Curtis Robinson might well have remained a teacher his entire life, but world events would halt his teaching career and beckon him away from the teaching profession.

PART 2

THE WORLD WAR II YEARS

A Few Were Chosen

On December 17, 1903, Orville Wright piloted the first powered aircraft in a flight that lasted 12 seconds and covered 120 feet in Kitty Hawk, North Carolina. New milestones in aviation continued at a brisk pace after that historic moment. In May 1919, the first trans-Atlantic flight occurred during a journey that started on May 8 and ended on May 27, having originated in Long Island, N.Y., and terminating in Lisbon, Portugal. In 1927, Charles Lindbergh became the first person to fly solo across the Atlantic Ocean in a flight from New York to Paris that lasted 33 hours; he flew directly between two trans-Atlantic cities and was the first to do it alone. On June 17 and 18, 1928, Amelia Earhart became the first woman to fly across the Atlantic.

Black Americans, too, were quite involved with aviation and flying early in the 20th century. Eugene Jacques Bullard, born in Columbus, Georgia, was the only black pilot of World War I. Since blacks were not permitted to fly for the United States at that time, he flew for France's Lafayette Flying Corps. During the 1920s and 30s, several black flying clubs were in operation, and black men and women were receiving licenses as pilots. Several aviation milestones were met: Bessie Coleman graduated from the Caudron Flying School in France in June 1921 and received her license there; she was the first black woman to make a public flight in the United States. In October 1932, James H. Banning and Thomas C. Allen became the first black Americans to make a transcontinental flight. Other well known black fliers were C. Alfred Anderson and Dr. Albert E. Forsythe, who made pan-American flights during 1934.

Still, in the mindset of America, questions remained about the suitability of blacks as aircraft pilots in general and fighter pilots particularly. Fundamental questions about their courage, intellect, and resourcefulness remained and were documented in studies commissioned by the War Department and War College. Twice, once in 1925 and again in 1937, the War Department commissioned studies that concluded that "blacks were cowards, and poor technicians and fighters..." The study went on to comment on black brain sizes, reasoning ability, and other factors working against them. But because of war preparation for World War II and common sense, the War Department stated that blacks would be called into service in proportion to their percentage of the population, but would be segregated, and would not be eligible for the Army Air Corps. For a group whose valor and courage had been documented from the time of the Continental Army, the Civil War, frontier battles by the famed Buffalo Soldiers[v] between 1866 and 1892, the Spanish American War, and World War I, it was obvious that blacks were patriotic and courageous and would be quick to rush to defend the country even as it ran tests as a means of discrediting them.

The Army had a very large camp in Spartanburg County, S.C., called Camp Penn, now long since de-commissioned. There were about 50,000 troops there and about 1,500 were black. During his second year of teaching, Curtis Robinson visited the camp one day and saw how blacks were being used by the Army. He observed soldier going about their tasks. "Cap'n, we're going to be finished before the end of the day," Private Brown told the officer in charge as the men worked on a drainage ditch at Camp Penn. "Well, we'll see. If you do, I'll let you call it a day," the lieutenant in charge responded. Robinson looked sadly on the activities that played out in front of him. The black soldiers were doing latrine duty, kitchen duty, sweeping the streets and digging ditches. They had a white second lieutenant who was in charge of this one group of blacks that Robinson observed, and they all called him "Cap'n." Regardless of his rank, they called him captain, like prisoners would call the whites who guarded penitentiary road gangs. And he walked down behind them like a prison guard.

Robinson took mild offense that the group was improperly addressing the officer at a rank higher than his true status, and that the officer, a second lieutenant, hadn't corrected them – not that he should have needed to – but was basking at his elevated status and role. "Why are they doing that? He's not a captain," Robinson thought. "Can't they tell?" He told himself that there was no way that he would allow himself to become a serviceman in a group like that. It seemed that they all had picks and shovels, brooms and dustpans; they weren't doing any soldiering. Robinson was determined not to get into such a situation and not to become one of those type soldiers.

The Presidential election of 1940 provided an opportunity for the issue of segregation and blacks in the armed services to receive more serious thought and debate than the issue had theretofore been given. Wendell L. Willkie, the Republican candidate, promised to integrate the Armed Forces if elected. This caused President Roosevelt to take action on the issue during late 1940. Previously, in 1938, President

Roosevelt had approved $100,000 of National Youth Administration funds to begin a Civilian Pilot Training Program (CPTP) at thirteen colleges and universities in the United States. In 1939 after the Nazis invaded Poland, $7 million of additional funds were appropriated to train pilots until 1944 when the program was scheduled to end. At its height, nationwide, the program would have approximately 1100 educational institutions involved, approximately 1300 flight schools supported, and a significant numbers of black pilots trained.

In December 1940, the War Department submitted a plan for an "experiment" involving black pilots. But the Army Air Corps still refused applications from blacks until Yancey Williams, a Howard University student, filed a suit through the NAACP in 1941. Then in March 1941, the Selective Service Headquarters said in part, "The Negro pilots will be trained at Tuskegee, Alabama, in connection with Tuskegee Institute..." Shortly thereafter a training center was established there.

By February 1941, Tuskegee Institute had received certification to provide advanced flying courses and would soon receive $1.7 million for an air field. When speaking with the Pittsburgh Courier, once the nation's most widely distributed black newspaper, during the spring of 1941 about the Tuskegee Pilot project and what considerations blacks should use for choosing candidates for the program, Major General Waller R. Weaver, the commander of the Army's Southeastern Air Corps Training Command, pleaded: "For God's sake, send us your best men...For their sake and for our sake, give us your best." Against that backdrop and while Curtis Robinson was teaching near Spartanburg, South Carolina, the Germans began to stir things up in Europe, so America decided to institute the draft in the event of its entry into war. Teachers were used by the War Department to administer the draft examination to the populous. Then they had to take it themselves and administer it to other teachers. Everybody knew that the war was coming. Besides that, the military was expanding rapidly. Early in 1941, the Army began to build camps all over the United States with the country entering war after the bombing of Pearl Harbor on December 7th. Three of Robinson's brothers were called to duty, and so had most of his friends. He decided to take matters into his own hands to avoid the fate he'd just witnessed at Camp Penn. So after his visit there, he went home and met with one of the highly respected black men in the community.

"In the South of my youth, whites always had a 'black connection' to inform them of everything going on in the black community because although they were segregated from blacks, they had a desire to know what they were doing at all times," Robinson says of the existing social order. "Everything was run by whites, but if a black person wanted to get something done, you would start with the 'connection.' There was this successful black businessman who had a reputation for wielding power. He was the upper state representative of a group of insurance companies. A big man by the name of Mr. Bolden, he had sent his children to Claflin to be educated, and more importantly, he was a consultant to the draft board."

Robinson paid Bolden a visit. "Mr. Bolden, I've just left Camp Penn and witnessed what they have Negroes doing over there," Robinson began. "Oh yeah, so what do you think?" Bolden asked. "I can't do that, I can't dig latrines and toilets, I'm a teacher; I have a college degree. What can I do about a situation like the one at Camp Penn?" Robinson asked.

"Well," Mr. Bolden told him, "there's nothing you can do about that situation, but recently I saw an article in the paper stating that the Army Air Corps is accepting applications for black cadets who are interested in flying, they have a program starting at Tuskegee Institute in Alabama. I have the information and address right here. Why don't you write them a letter?" Bolden also added, "As a cadet you'll make $200 dollars a month, and when you graduate, you'll make $350." Now that really impressed Robinson. Soldiers were only being paid $21 per month and he had making $75 a month as a teacher and had a hard time living on that because he was a young big spender. Robinson wrote a letter to the Army Air Corps that same day requesting information about the program at Tuskegee. In about a week they responded.

The corps sent him an application and told him where to go to take a physical. The Army required his college transcript and three references. This was a time when black candidates had to have a four year college degree to get into the pilot cadet program at Tuskegee and white candidates were required to have just two years of college for pilot school. Once his paperwork was in order, everything had to be notarized and then sent back. He filled out the papers and went to Columbia, South Carolina, for his medical examination. The Army Air Corp had the beginning of installation there with flight surgeons on staff. Robinson was examined there and passed his preliminary physical. To meet his requirements for his references, the president of Claflin College, the dean of the Agriculture Department of South Carolina State College, and his minister wrote letters of recommendation for him. He had to sign them and have them notarized to ensure that everything was true and proper.

Curtis Robinson compiled his package of information and took it to be notarized by a woman whom he was told was the only notary public in town of Orangeburg, and he tells what happens next. "Her office was in one of the huge antebellum homes over on the west side of town, on Russell Street. She was on the second floor in this large room sitting behind a big desk. I stopped at her door with my information, knocked on the door which was ajar and said, 'I'm looking for a notary public and was told to come here. Can you help me?' 'Yes, come in,' she replied. I entered her office and stood beside a plush fabric chair that faced her. But she didn't offer me a seat or anything, so I stood in front of the desk and gave her my packet of information and told her what I needed. She looked over the papers and talking to herself she said, 'This is the recommendation, this is the application, this is the college transcript,' and then she said to me after affixing the seal, 'And this is where you put your X.'"

In the South it was customary for people to put an "X" on documents as a substitute for their signature. This was the manner in which illiterate individuals represented their signature. Robinson continued, "I stood there looking down at the notary public and she kept looking down at the forms; everything got real quiet. Finally, she looked up at me as I continued looking down at her and she said, 'Oh! You can sign your name,' almost as though it were a question. She had just gone through my college transcripts and said, 'This is where you put your "X"' and 'Oh! You can sign your name.' I was left to surmise that she assumed that most blacks couldn't write their names and without thinking, her comment came automatically. Perhaps she could not believe her eyes. She saw this black guy and even with my college transcript, her mindset was such that she wasn't sure that I could sign my name. Those college transcripts should have given her a clue!"

After his information had been notarized, Robinson sent it to the Army Air Corps, and about two weeks later they sent him an acceptance letter and said he would hear from them. But it was a year before they ever called him.

His friends and relatives, it seemed, were all being drafted. One friend who had been drafted a year prior had been in Burma for six months already before Robinson even signed-up for cadet training in the Air Corps. Robinson's brother, Benjamin, was an Army enlisted man but somehow managed to maneuver himself out of menial work. George and Eldridge entered the Army and became officers, but Glenn, who had been in a bad car accident, could not serve. Only about six of the black college graduates from the county out of about 150 got commissions. Many others fared well within the enlisted ranks and most came out as sergeants.

Robinson's brother, George, was drafted and sent to Fort Bragg in North Carolina where he had to take a test. After he had taken his test, the Army called him to headquarters, placed him alone in a room and retested him. Afterwards, he noticed that people kept coming by to look in on him. He didn't know what was going on. It turned out that he had made the highest grade in the history of Fort Bragg up to that time. So they shipped him right off to Officers Candidate Training School. That was around 1941. George was very bright; he could go through a crossword puzzle like he was writing a note. George was definitely the smartest of the Robinson brothers, according to CC.

While all of this was going on Curtis Robinson hung around South Carolina literally doing nothing and in limbo while he was waiting to go into the service. "Everybody had been drafted. I was the only physically fit guy left in town and virtually the only guy in town in his young twenties. I wasn't teaching after May of my second year, or 1942, because I was waiting to be called to report for service at any time. Two of my brothers had cars they had left at home, so after they went into the service at least I had a choice of two cars to drive. Beginning in the summer of 1941, I started driving around in my brother's cars, visiting school friends and some of the girls I knew who lived throughout the state thinking I'd be leaving any day," Robinson added.

Eventually he was called to Columbia, South Carolina,

for another physical examination; all in all he took three examinations. He was one pound short of the required weight. The flight surgeon told him to take a break, go eat some bananas, drink a lot of water and come back. After having done so, he went back, but the doctor didn't even re-weigh him. He merely said, "You're all right," and Robinson passed the physical. Then he returned home and waited, and waited some more. This all started in the summer of 1941, and it wasn't until July of 1942 that he was called. The regular army contacted him twice during that time, and he had to keep writing them, telling them that he had been accepted by the Air Corps because after having visited Camp Penn, he wasn't about to go into the Army.

Robinson was finally contacted by the Army Air Corps and told to report to Shaw Air Force Base in Sumter County, South Carolina, where there was a large airfield for training with a tremendous amount of land. Actually they had an airfield within an airfield. In fact, they had a grid of runways on the side of a large runway that cadets practiced on. They were flying BT-13s which appeared to be used for basic flight training. Shaw Air Force Base was the first air base Robinson had ever seen that had runways. The few air bases that he had ever seen had grass fields. Actually, he had only ever seen three airplanes on the ground prior to this. Orangeburg is positioned west of both Charleston and Columbia, S.C. This was the primary route for air travel in the state, so flying in a direct route between those cities, planes never flew over his town of Orangeburg, and he seldom saw a plane unless it was inadvertently forced to land there. Shaw Field was the first place where Robinson had ever seen planes on the ground at a close distance. He knew the basics of how they flew, however, because his brother George had instructed him on all of that, but he had never really seen a plane up close.

There were approximately 2,000 personnel at Shaw Field, and when he arrived, Robinson was taken into headquarters, introduced to a major and a captain, duly sworn in, and partially processed. That means they gave him some uniforms and insignia to go on the uniforms, but no instructions as to where the insignia belonged on those uniforms. Then after the induction, they had no place to put him because as a black air force cadet he was in a peculiar position. He was not really in the Air Force, per se. He was not an officer, yet he was not an enlisted man, either, nor had he been assigned to a base. So he was totally on his own, and he answered to no one except the commandant of cadets. The MPs – Military Police - had nothing to do with him, nor did anyone else; he was an entity unto himself. This is what Robinson encountered when he first went into the military and before he was assigned anywhere; the program operated on the honor system. The commandant of cadets told him what to do. In turn, he committed to what he was going to do, and that's what the Army Air Corps expected to be done.

Because of segregation, the situation he initially encountered at Shaw Field cost Robinson almost all of his money. The Army Air Corps had no place for him on the base because it was segregated and he couldn't stay there, and since his class hadn't yet formed at Tuskegee, the authorities at Shaw Field really didn't know what to do with him. He overheard a captain and a major discussing his situation. "We can't send him to regular cadet training – he's a Negro," the captain said (there were about 300 white cadets there). "Well we can't send him to any of the Negro squadrons, either," countered the major, so they gave him a three-day pass. With this pass he was on his own, and the military didn't provide him with any funds or vouchers. Robinson had to arrange for transportation back home. The base was about 49 miles from Orangeburg, but the bus didn't go directly there. It went first to Columbia, S.C., which was about 40 miles from his home, and then on to Orangeburg, another 45 miles. Upon returning home and given his extroverted nature, Robinson did more traveling and visiting to occupy his time.

Three days later he returned to the base and the same thing happened again. His class still hadn't formed at Tuskegee so they still had no place to put him. As a result, they gave him another three-day pass. His salary as a teacher had been $75 per month. It was now late July of 1942 and his teaching job and pay had ended in May. Unfortunately, not knowing what to do with himself, he had spent money on a new suit, shoes and accessories that he would never need and was running low on funds. By the second time he returned to base, he had only about four or five dollars left and the same situation occurred. They sent him back home again, and again he had to pay his fare back home and buy food and such.

When he returned to the base after the expiration of his second three-day pass, he was virtually broke with less than a dollar in his pocket. Before the personnel at Shaw Field could tell him that he was going to get yet another three-day pass, he told the officer handling his situation, "Sir, I cannot afford another three-day pass because I don't have any funds." The officer replied, "Well we are going to have to send you down to Tuskegee and let them decide what to do with you." They cut some requisitions for travel and sent him to the train station.
Getting to Tuskegee was a story within itself. Another Tuskegee cadet, Bill Delaney, was also scheduled to report that same morning. The Army Air Corps sent the two of them down to the rail station to get their tickets to Tuskegee Army Air Field, each with a requisition which they presented to the station master.

Because Bill Delaney, who had been a star football player

at South Carolina State College, looked white, he had no problem getting his ticket. Robinson, however, had a lot of problems getting his. The ticket clerk didn't seem to believe that he should have it. He looked at the requisition and he looked at Robinson; he kept looking at him and walking back and forth, and finally he made a telephone call. Evidently someone must have told him to give Robinson the ticket because he finally came back, wrote it out, and gave it to him.

That's when it dawned on Robinson what the problem was. The ticket called for a Pullman coach reservation. In the South, blacks were not allowed to ride Pullmans in those days. Not even many whites rode Pullmans, which were sleeping cars generally used by affluent whites who traveled from New England to Florida. The train was very slow, and for long trips the railroad needed those types of cars to accommodate the demands of the well-to-do. Noting this, Robinson was surprised that the station master didn't try to force him to ride coach. Today he says, "Honestly, at the time, I hadn't realized it was a Pullman, but I would not have changed tickets or cars."

Between 1:00 and 1:30 in the afternoon, the train pulled into the station and the passengers boarded. The conductor approached Robinson as soon as he took his seat and tried to put him to bed. He said, "Look, we can break your bunk down right now and put you to bed." Robinson figured they were trying to hide him from view of the white patrons, but he said, "No, I'm not sleepy." The conductor went away, but a few minutes later the porter came back with the same message, "Let us put you to bed." Again Robinson said, "No, I'm going to sit here," and he sat there with Bill Delaney.

The train was very slow. It chugged along and finally around five o'clock p.m., they rang the dinner bell to have people come to the dining car for dinner. Robinson didn't move because he only had fifteen cents and couldn't afford dinner, so he remained in his seat. Bill Delaney didn't go back for dinner either, perhaps out of camaraderie, or perhaps he was also broke. Either way, he sat with Robinson through dinner. So Robinson rode hungry. After dinner Robinson finally allowed the train personnel to break down his bunk and put him to bed.

From Sumter County, South Carolina, to Atlanta, the distance is less than 300 miles. The train arrived in Atlanta at 8:00 a.m. the next morning. Robinson had ridden from 1:30 p.m. Tuesday afternoon until 8 a.m. Wednesday morning – seventeen and a half hours – without food. He had gotten on the train with about five cents. There was another South Carolina State guy named Demery that Robinson knew who just happened to be on the train. He worked in the lab at Shaw Field. Robinson borrowed a dime from him and then had fifteen cents. They pulled into the station for an hour and a half layover, un-boarded, and many passengers sat out in the yard surrounding the station.

There was a USO at the station, a huge place. It was segregated, however, with the white USO on the first floor and the black USO on the second floor above it. Delaney, Robinson, and his new friend, the lab technician from South Carolina State, decided to go to the black USO club. Inside, there were several long tables laden with coffee, donuts, milk, bananas, apples, and other pastry items; there was also a hostess present who asked Robinson, "What can I get you?" He was surveying the table trying to figure out what to buy with his meager 15 cents that would last the longest, so he told her, "Nothing now, thank you. I'll just wait." In the meantime, he noticed that a steady stream of soldiers kept coming in and getting coffee and donuts and walking out without paying, and that went on for quite a while. Finally he realized that everything was free and that he could have whatever wanted;

and he helped himself.

A couple of hours passed before the train left for Chehaw, the stopping point for Tuskegee and about 150 miles away. Chehaw is located about four or five miles from the city of Tuskegee and four or five miles from the air base. The train station was located near the widest part of the highway with one or two houses nearby; that was Chehaw, a bend in the road. Robinson and Delaney un-boarded at Chehaw after several more hours of travel, collected their bags, walked to the road and looked up and down. Robinson set down his bags because he had not imagined that they would arrive in a place so remote with no transportation. "Man, we're in the middle of nowhere," Delaney said. "No, I don't think we've even made it that far," Robinson quipped. A few minutes later as they began walking towards the base, Captain Dreyer, the band director of the base, came by in a squad car, asked where they were headed, and gave them a ride to the base. They were glad to see Dreyer because it was both disappointing and desolate where they found themselves. It was literarily in the middle of nowhere. Dreyer dropped them off at the cadet corps where they were properly fitted with clothes, the insignia, and everything they needed. From there they were immediately put on KP (kitchen patrol) because their class had not yet formed. It was now late July of 1942.

Tuskegee Airman Cadet

"It's nice to meet you. You guys must be the re-enforcements," chuckled 'Woody' Crockett, who is now Robinson's good friend, a fellow "Airman" and member of the Arkansas Aviation Hall of Fame. He smiled, extended his hand, and introduced himself to Tuskegee Army Air Field's two newest arrivals as they reported for kitchen patrol assignments on their first day. Crockett had arrived a few days earlier and was doing KP after having just missed his class' start-date. He was to have been in the class ahead of Robinson and Delaney's, which had already formed. Initially the instructors weren't sure about what to do with him. But two or three days later they put Crockett with his class, and that left Robinson and Delaney doing KP. That assignment was short-lived and by the first of the month of August 1942, Robinson's class was formed. Its pilots would graduate as Class 43-D-SE which designated the year and month, respectively; the SE indicated single-engine plane. The first class was 42-C-SE which graduated March 1942, with proficiency in single engine planes, also. Cadets were forced to sign a release from the United States Army.[vi] Upon graduation, Robinson would be a full second lieutenant in the Army Air Corps of the United States.

Being accepted into the Tuskegee Cadet Program allowed Robinson to avoid dreaded military duty like the army assignments that he had seen black soldiers performing at Camp Penn. But he really had no idea what he was getting into when he joined the Tuskegee pilot training program; most of the black cadets probably didn't. In fact, what he wanted to do was simply get away from the low-level, unskilled duties that the military was giving black soldiers in the Army at that time. Later he would say, "I would have done anything, whether it was an assignment with a tank division, the infantry, flying airplanes or anything, just to get out of a situation where I would have been assigned menial duties like I saw the black guys doing at Camp Penn. The Army Air Corps offered me that opportunity."

The routine at Tuskegee began with a 6:00 a.m. call of reveille. Breakfast was 7:00 a.m. followed by physical fitness and calisthenics. After that, the cadets would fly either in the morning or afternoon. The most amazing thing that happened to Robinson early into the program had to do with the morning and evening routine. Every morning at 6:00 a.m. the cadets had to organize in a formation. The band would arrive, and cadets would march to headquarters and raise and salute the American flag. Every afternoon they would form, march back to headquarters, and take down the flag. "Just performing that ceremony somehow made me feel a whole lot of love for my country that I couldn't understand," Robinson says of the patriotism he felt as a new cadet. "It was amazing how just marching up there to salute the flag every morning and returning at night to retrieve it made me feel about the flag and that procession, even after having done it for a long time."

Until a cadet reached advanced training, there was a system of hazing in the cadet program whereby upper classmen, those in advanced training, got to haze or make lower classmen, newer cadets like Robinson, do ridiculous acts. One of the things they did during hazing was called "bracing" during which the cadets "sounded-out." It meant that they stood at attention and gave a read-out of their autobiography in a flow of words that lasted no longer than thirty seconds. They were required to give their name, hometown, address, alma mater, college major, sports, fraternity – all of that had to spoken smoothly and evenly. Whenever they came out of their training segments for breaks, upperclassmen seemed to have nothing else to do but get that information out of new cadets.

Also as underclassman, the new cadets had general orders that they had to learn. An upper classmen would approach Robinson and say, "Dummy, give me your first general order." Robinson would start his recitation, "Sir, my first general order is to walk my post in a…," but before he could finish, they would interrupt him and say, "Give me your second general order,' he would begin the general order and again he would be interrupted by the interrogating upperclassmen. So he became very proficient at rendering his responses. For example, even if Robinson didn't know his third general order, he would begin to recite it before they asked, knowing that they would interrupt him. Cadets were never allowed to completely recite a general order. He realized early-on that he only needed to know about half of each general order to successfully negotiate that hazing drill. As a result, Robinson mastered the beginning of all of the general orders early as a new cadet but didn't know any of them completely except the first two, and when asked today says, "I eventually learned all of most of them."

Cadets came to regard the hazing as fun and accepted it in good spirit. Of course, upper classmen couldn't touch them, but they could give new cadets a lot of punishment like duck walking for an hour or running. One hazing activity was called dial-a-button where cadets in advanced training would make new cadets perform a series of squats in which they successively lowered themselves eventually ending in a sitting position, but unsupported. "It was an awful physical position to be in," says Robinson further describing it as, "very strenuous. But it was great, especially for me since I tended to have weak legs anyway. The process was one of successive bending of the knees, as you lowered yourself downward with arms outstretched in four inch increments: down four inches, then down another four inches until almost in a squat. Then I would be braced on my legs and thighs and would have to maintain that position for a long time. That really built up my leg muscles and it also helped to condition my legs. That proved very valuable later for flying some planes, particularly the P-40."

Practically all of the young men entering the Tuskegee program were high achievers, well educated and some of the most promising and accomplished of the black community. One of the surprises for Robinson, and somewhat intimidating, was that he had classmates from major colleges and universities all over the continent – the University of Chicago; several from UCLA; one had a law degree from McGill University in Canada. His class also included alumni from Hampton Institute, Howard University, from West Virginia State College, from Morris Brown College, from Indiana State College, and a few others. These guys were all college graduates, but his college was quite small compared to those larger schools many of his fellow cadets had attended. Of that experience Robinson says, "During hazing, upper classmen would ask me to sound-off, and I would say that I graduated from Claflin College. Almost no one knew of Claflin unless they were from South Carolina, or at least the South. They'd say, 'Claflin? I've never heard of it. Where is Claflin College?' That was one issue that I had to get over, and I did."

TUSKEGEE AIRMAN CADET

When Robinson arrived at Tuskegee in the summer of 1942, flying was limited there with few pilots and planes. Also a lot of construction activity was going on that caused the airfield to be very muddy because of an abundance of red clay. Some enlisted men lived in tents while barracks were being built. Quite a few of them had to stay in those tents for several months, but cadets had their own barracks and the air field had an orderly room or essentially the office. Work on the barracks was completed in 1943 producing new barracks including one for the cadets in pre-flight training and primary training, and a barrack for cadets in basic training and advanced training. By the time Robinson's class completed primary training, those barracks had been built and that's where he resided.

On the Tuskegee Army Air Field, they had two classes of basic and advanced flying school. There were only about fifteen or sixteen black fellows actually flying at the time, not many. The cadets were to be there for eight weeks of pre-flight training - four weeks of lower pre-flight and four weeks of upper pre-flight. In pre-flight training the cadets were either on the air field or in classes all day long. This was also the time that cadets were challenged with very demanding academic work, too. After the pre-flight training was complete, cadets went over to Moton Field for primary training - upper and lower primary training. Then they returned to the Tuskegee Air Field for basic flying school. So on the Tuskegee Airfield, the first class of basic and advanced flying school was being conducted, and on Moton Field, they held upper and lower primary flying school. The sequence was pre-flight training, then primary, basic, and advanced flying school with each training segment becoming increasingly more difficult.

Some classroom work was quite difficult, and cadets spent a lot of time studying. For example, instructors would give them a pamphlet on carburetors as they left class. When they returned the next day, there would be no classroom instruction, only an examination on those items that had been covered in the pamphlet about carburetors that they were expected to know. Consequently at night after training, the cadets had to learn on their own as much as they could about things not specifically covered in class. Academically, everyone was a college graduate, and many had master degrees. So they all could do the classroom work, and they received training the entire nine months they were there. Areas of study included weather (meteorology) the whole time they were there; navigation, Morse code, aircraft structure, aircraft engines, and mechanics. They took mathematics, too, because navigation depended on mathematics, and they received plenty of physical training. Robinson found navigation to be a tough course. Flight instructors allowed cadets to use a computational device that was similar to a slide ruler but which was a circular instrument, to solve navigation problems. They could perform various mathematical computations with it and match figures up against each other; it could also be used to add, multiply, and get square roots. It was a very versatile tool.

"One of the toughest navigation problems to solve," Robinson says by way of example, "was one involving riser action relative to a moving object such as the following: If a plane on an aircraft carrier took-off towards the enemy while the carrier was going north, the enemy was east, and the aircraft was going at a certain given speed with the wind direction another speed, and the plane had a certain allotted hours of fuel – then the problem was – how far could a pilot go towards the enemy and fight? How long could he stay and yet have sufficient fuel to safely return to the aircraft carrier? Where would the aircraft carrier be when the pilot returned – because it was moving all the time? How much fuel would be remaining? The answers can be figured out using algebra, but it takes forever. But with the computational device, it didn't take cadets too long. The instructors made sure that we fully understood what those type problems were all about and how to solve them, so we had to do a ton of them manually, first."

During primary flying school, half a day was used for flying and half was spent in classes, with an hour of physical training in the morning. Cadets would perform take-offs and landings. They learned the fundamentals of flying, how to operate the controls, how to fly the planes solo, and they went through a proscribed group of maneuvers for the first twenty hours. In this phase, instructors would black out all the instruments with the exception of the altimeter, the turn back indicator, and the tachometer, so cadets literally flew by the seat of their pants. Instructors would have instruments up front, but all of the cadet's instruments were blacked out. "We had to learn how to glide at a certain speed that the altitude of the plane would allow us to attain. If we put the guidelines on the horizon, the plane would travel eighty miles per hour, or if we put them higher that would give us a slower speed, and so on; we had to learn to judge that ourselves," Robinson notes. Wash-outs from the program usually started during primary training.

As Robinson settled into primary training, he became more self confident and his desire to succeed grew stronger as his flying proficiency progressed. "I'll tell you, when you want something so badly," Robinson says, "sometimes you tend to overreact. In situations like that during training, if we weren't careful, we could get washed out."

"I guess almost all of us had that eagerness in us, that confidence that we could do whatever we tried, and you didn't have to tell us more than once," is how Robinson characterized cadets. "Most of us had been what you called BMOCs, 'big men on campus' during our college days, guys who were well known and accustomed to having things our way and that was the attitude we had. But when we went to primary flying school, we met what we called the elephant, the flight instructors. There was a story about the elephant and the lion; the cadets were lions meeting the elephants, the instructors. The lions foolishly thought that they, the cadets, were the kings of the jungle, that being Tuskegee Army Air Field. One day in the jungle, the lion ran into the elephant and roared, 'Do you know who the king of the jungle is?' The elephant looked at him, smirked, wrapped his trunk around the lion, twirled him around his head and slammed him down onto the earth. The lion staggered up and said, 'You didn't have to be so belligerent just because you don't know the answer.' So we were the young lions. We wanted to get through those elephants, and they were slamming us down like mad; they could be brutal, merciless."

"Well, I was one for trying to get a notch in my belt, some place where I could make a name for myself, but I didn't worry too much about flying. I was doing very well at flying, but I was a little bone-headed. Before I took off on one of my solos, the instructor and I were flying on a very large field. It's important to note that when you start to do a take-off, you go down the field, and as the plane accelerates, the tail rises and the torque in the engine (i.e., the turning of the propeller in one direction) causes the aircraft to veer off a little to the right just two or three degrees. As I initially did that, the instructor said, 'Correct that, don't you see that?' I said, 'Yes, I see it, but I've got this whole field. What difference does it make?' So I didn't bother. With that, the instructor finally said, 'Look, unless you make the correction, I'm not going to let you fly this plane.' I made the correction, all right. On the next take-off, I kept the plane perfectly straight, and he said, 'All right, that's good.' Initially, I didn't see the significance of keeping it straight. The significance was that when you're flying on the battle field, you don't have big fields all the time or you may be in crowded space. You may fly from runways and sometimes from carriers."

Next in the training sequence was basic flying school. There were just three planes and three instructors when Robinson's basic training class began, but there were fifty-two cadets. So that was a dilemma immediately. Prior to Robinson's class, the typical class size ranged between fifteen and nineteen at the most; the first two had counts of about ten to thirteen cadets in them. On the first day of basic, Robinson's class didn't fly at all. They sat outside and talked to the instructors. The second day, the head instructor told them that it didn't look like they were going to get any additional planes soon, so they were going to take each of them up. If the cadet demonstrated an aptitude for flying, they were going to keep him, but if he didn't, he would be washed-out. And that's what they did. Some cadets didn't have much of a chance; it was one flight for about half an hour, and they either flew well or were gone. After Robinson's class had completed a week of basic flying school, they received four new instructors and six more planes, and the training situation became manageable.

At this stage of the program cadets trained on planes with lots of speed, retractable landing gear, and adjustable prop pitch for the first time. "The significance of prop pitch," Robinsons says, "is that we could adjust the propeller pitch to any speed we wanted as far as the turning of the engine went. If the prop pitch was very slant, that meant we could generate a lot of RPM, but we wouldn't be pulling in much air; that's how they would be set when we were cruising. If we were taking-off, we would want the prop to go slowly and to pull in a lot of air so it would be set at another angle. That was the way I'd control my speed - by adjusting the angle of the propellers." Cadets were also operating planes with two-way radios for the first time and planes that were much heavier, probably 2,000 pounds heavier with a much larger engine than those used in Primary Training. Another consideration in basic training was that cadets had to master all of the instruments available to them at this point.

"I was lucky and unlucky, too," comments Robinson. "I had one of the new instructors. His home was Birmingham, Alabama. He evaluated me solo in the plane for about three hours. I was the first guy in my class to solo. After that, we covered aerobatics and he was crazy about that; he saved me for last during aerobatics."

"When my chance came, we got in the plane and flew over to Birmingham, Alabama, about 120 miles away towards his parent's house, or whose ever it was. He went through all the aerobatics himself and we headed back, but he hadn't shown me anything or allowed me to do one thing. This went on for a couple of weeks, so I began to ask my buddies what they were doing when they went up. They told me that they were doing this, and they were doing that, and a lot of other things that I wasn't doing. So I tried to do the things my classmates told me they were doing, but I tried to do them like we had done them in primary flight training. In basic flight training, however, since we used bigger planes, maneuvers were executed differently than in this plane. Evidently the instructor had been giving me excellent grades."

Cadets were continually evaluated. One morning soon after aerobatics training, the chief instructor called Robinson in and said, "Come on, hot shot. Let's see what you can do since you're supposed to be such a Hot Shot aerobatics pilot." He took Robinson up and said, "Do a chandelle." So Robinson did a chandelle like he had done them in primary flight training where they had been relatively simpler. His chief instructor asked, "You call that a chandelle? That's no chandelle; let me show you how to do it." He demonstrated it, and Robinson followed doing it just like the chief instructor did it. Then he said, "Do a Lazy Eight." Robinson did a Lazy Eight and the instructor said, "You call that a Lazy Eight?" Then he showed Robinson how to do it, and sure enough, Robinson managed to do it just like he had. Whatever he showed Robinson, he did it just as the instructor had done it.

When they landed, his chief instructor asked him, "What was that you were doing up there?" Robinson honored the "Airmen's code" and replied, "No excuse, sir." Robinson didn't tell on his instructor because in the cadet corps they always individually accepted responsibility for whatever went awry and would say, "No excuse," regardless of what the reason might have been; they didn't tell on anybody. Then the chief instructor asked, "What have they been teaching you?" Robinson said, "No excuse, sir." But it was obvious that his chief instructor could tell that the aerobatics instructor hadn't been teaching Robinson anything. He said, "You know how to fly a plane, but I don't understand what just happened." But he let Robinson through.

After an initial introduction, the cadets went through a group of more advanced aerobatics for the last twenty hours. "That's when I really fell in love with flying - when I went through aerobatics. I loved that!" recalls Robinson of that part of his training regimen.

At this stage cadets would have been in the program for more than four months. The training program was intense and men had very little time for socializing, but over a period of time cadets naturally picked certain guys in their class that they clicked with, guys who became their pals and with whom they bonded. When he got to Tuskegee, Robinson didn't know anyone. Every month the Air Field would have big dances, and people from all over the United States would attend them.

Each cadet had to have a guest. Robinson had a couple of buddies who knew plenty of young women, and the local ladies must have sensed that the Tuskegee Airmen Cadets were special young men. So a friend of Robinson was able to arrange a date for him with his girl friend's sister as Robinson's guest at his first Tuskegee dance.

He's never forgotten his date or the occasion. "She was from a large family of 23 children, nine boys and the rest girls. When I arrived for our date, I noticed that she was attractive, which was encouraging since I was meeting her for the first time. She was dressed nicely, and I felt good about taking her to the dance. On this particular Saturday night, Colonel Davis and Dr. Fred Patterson, the president of Tuskegee Institute, attended the dance. When the dancing began, she started dancing in such a suggestive and even raunchy manner that it embarrassed me. She was leading me around, too. As soon as the music would start, she would grab my hand and pull me onto the dance floor. She was something else. On the way home, she took me by the house where she worked – a large stately home with a huge yard surrounded by hedges. She knew where an opening in the hedges was and tried to pull me inside her employer's yard! I had never seen anyone like her. I didn't see her anymore because she would have certainly gotten me put out of the Air Corps."

From that point on, whenever he had time to date, Robinson decided to leave the local town women alone. The cadets were living on the campus of Tuskegee Institute, so he decided he would go to the campus library, dormitory lobby, or some place with his peers and try to meet some of the female students. But Robinson remembers, "One of my instructors in particular, if he saw me out socializing, would come up and soon start talking about flying during my free hours, even in the library. I didn't appreciate that at all. I had taken to flying very easily and my instructor was proud of me, but I wasn't always happy about him, we had only about two hours off at night where we could go out, and he was cutting into that. To make the situation worst, co-eds were not even allowed to go out."

Robinson managed to meet other eligible women who weren't locals or school girls. He began to spend his free time with another young woman, a nurse that he met. The United States Veterans Administration had a hospital in Tuskegee for blacks. In fact, it was the only one in the country for blacks, recalls Robinson. "It was a large institution. It had residences for nurses and most of the nurses lived there. A friend of mine, one of my classmates from Chicago, knew one of the nurses. She got one of her friends, a fellow nurse, as my next dance guest. It turned out that the two of them were the two youngest nurses out there. They were in their early twenties. The rest we thought were old; they were mostly in their thirties. But we were young men; I was twenty-three and my perspective about youth was different then."

Usually on weekends, especially Saturday night, they would go out to visit these young ladies. Robinson and his buddy had to catch a bus to get out to the veterans hospital to see them. It was a special bus, and their timing was important because the bus ran every hour. The last bus headed back to the base at midnight. As for the dates, he says, "We would meet in a large recreation room. The room would be full of nurses, and we were the only two guys there," he chuckles. "We would usually leave there around 11:00 p.m. to head back to base, and the room would still be full of nurses. One Saturday night, we decided to wait the 'old' nurses out."

"The nurses would start leaving about 11:00 and would all be gone by 11:30 or 11:45. It didn't give us much time with these girls. But after they were all gone, my buddy would get in one corner and I'd get in another and we smooched and had our time with these girls. Then we would have to run to catch the bus. This went on for a little while; those nurses were nice and wonderful women. They used to complain that we never took them any place. And we didn't; we would just sit in the recreation room with them. There weren't really any places to take them. There were no cafes or clubs to frequent. We could have taken them to the USO, but who wants to take a girl to the USO? So we dated in the recreation room. Once the old nurses left, we would just do a lot of petting. I guess we could have taken them to the base officer's club, but for the most part, time for dating was scarce."

As cadet training progressed to advanced flying school, cadets would get a check-flight after twenty hours of flight time to be conducted by one of the chief instructors. There were two groups of instructors, one for morning students and one for afternoon students. Each of these groups had a chief of instructors, and each of the chief instructors was overseen by the commandant, who would sometimes take the cadets for a flight to see how well they were progressing. Everyone received what was called a "twenty-hour" ride. Robinson remembers his: "Well, I drew the commandant. I believe his name was Captain White. We took off, and I gave him such a beautiful flight that when we landed, he asked, 'Where did you learn to fly?' I said, 'Right here.' He asked, 'You mean you've had no previous flying?' I said, 'No.' 'That's amazing', he said, 'You fly very well. Come on, I want to show you something.'"

"So we got back in the plane and went through all the aerobatics he could show me. We had a ball. One of the maneuvers was called a 'snap-roll,' which is a maneuver that calls for very exquisite timing. To execute this maneuver, you have to cut the fuel to the engine, bring the engine up, elevate it, and just before it stalls out and falls out the sky, you pull back on the stick, kick the rudder, and the plane snaps and rolls. To come out of it, you do just the opposite thing. If you could do a perfect snap-roll, it meant that you had mastered that plane. Well, I did it very well. This was about Wednesday."

All the rest of the week, Robinson snap-rolled and snap-rolled every day, every chance he got. He thought he was the king of the snap-roll! He had an aunt and uncle down at Tuskegee. His uncle worked in the agriculture department at Tuskegee Institute, and he often visited them on Sundays. On this one particular Sunday right after he had mastered his new maneuver, he said to his aunt, "Watch out for me tomorrow. I'm going to come by and show you something," and she said, "O.K."

The first thing the next morning, Robinson got in the plane and took off. He describes it, "I went directly over their house and buzzed my aunt. She came out in the back yard, and one of her neighbors did, too, as I pulled up. Now this maneuver, the snap-roll, should be done at three or four thousand feet because it's so delicate that you can literally fall out the sky. But I pulled up to only about eight hundred feet. I was so anxious to get into it that I didn't wait for the motor to stall. I went ahead and kicked the rudder and pulled back the stick, but instead of snapping, my plane turned over and came straight down. I know my mouth and eyes must have been wide open, and I didn't see myself ever getting out of it, I really didn't. I thought I was a goner for sure. I had given it full throttle, but I kept coming down and down, and there was nothing else I could do. But just before I hit the ground, it leveled off right over the clothesline – I could see it - and my aunt and her neighbor were ducking and running for cover. The plane pulled up just as I was about to hit the side of a house nearby. I was so scared that I went directly back to the base and landed. I was terribly shaken by this near tragedy. I had almost killed myself, my aunt, and her neighbor. I had never had anything to scare me so badly during my entire life. Even in combat, I have never been that frightened."

Chief Anderson, the chief instructor at Tuskegee Army Airfield, came out after seeing Robinson land so soon after having just shortly taken off and asked him, "What's wrong? Why'd you land? Is there anything wrong with the plane?" Robinson replied, "No." So Anderson asked, "Why did you land? What's wrong with the plane?" Again Robinson said, "There's nothing wrong with the plane, and I don't know why I landed." He said, "Get that plane back up in the air!" and Chief Anderson made Robinson go back up. Robinson says, " I fooled around on the ground until I got myself back together, but I really scared myself that day. I had been afraid that I was going to kill my aunt, her neighbor and anybody else around there that day; worst still, I could have ruined the program. On a perfect snap-roll, the plane turns over. It's a quick roll, and the technique is to keep it from going over again, to stop it smoothly on that one roll. My aunt and her neighbor got the impression that I was really good because they thought I had planned to dive that close to the ground. They didn't know what a close call we all had and I never told them."

Robinson was now flying a fancier aircraft. The planes were much faster, a lot more maneuverable and flying was more enjoyable. At this stage, the instructors were trying to get them oriented to flying a fighter plane. Cadets also made a lot of cross-country trips during advanced flying - some at night and longer cross-countries during the day. At the end of their training, they went down to Eglin Field for four days of gunnery training. Cadets received some basic gunnery training at Tuskegee on a range that was used for practice, but just before graduation, they had to go to Eglin Air Force Base, Florida. It was equipped with tracks laid out for ground gunnery and air gunnery training. Cadets had to pass their test on that gunnery course. "I'm happy to say that I got an 'expert' gunnery rating in ground and air," a proud Robinson reports. "I was one of five guys in my class who made expert gunner."

After that, it was graduation upon which, when he reflects, Robinson says, "I think I succeeded at Tuskegee because I was able to learn things quickly and was absolutely determined to succeed. My understanding of what the airplane would do and how it functioned helped me tremendously. I think some of the guys who washed out never really understood that. They thought that the plane was flying them instead of fully understanding that they were flying the plane. From day one, I knew that I was flying the plane. I could make it do what I wanted it to do and was very comfortable with it."

"All of the guys who came through Tuskegee were not going to pass regardless of their flying proficiency. Despite having sterling credentials, some very smart young men washed out. Brilliant guys who would have made such good pilots, or who would have been good at anything in life, washed out. Racial quotas, not enough planes – you name it - but some capable pilots washed out. Robinson's view, "The Army Air Corps was only going to accept a certain number; there were quotas. They took the very best pilots and washed out the rest. Sometimes it was half that made it; sometimes it was less. That was the way it worked."

Army Air Corps Pilot

Every month a class of new pilots would graduate from the flight school at Tuskegee Army Airfield, but there would only be a small number of pilots. The first class had five graduates. Then shortly thereafter, one had three graduates followed by the next class which probably had eight or ten pilots. "The class with the highest number of graduates finished about three classes before my class and had about twelve graduates out of a class that started with twenty cadets, so they had a good production rate," Robinson says of Tuskegee's graduating efficiency. "The class before mine had about twelve who graduated also; they started with eighteen. My class started with fifty-two; we graduated seventeen. That wasn't very good. I believe the overall success rate for the entire program was about sixty percent."

"I graduated in class 43-D-SE in April of 1943. Graduation was a big ceremony with a lot of guests from out of town. Parents who could afford it came in from all over the country. My Aunt Anna and Uncle Nick attended my graduation. They were very nice to me while I was in Tuskegee. I would go over to their house to have dinner with them practically every weekend, sometimes bringing my friends with me. In fact, later in life I would eventually get married in their house."

By the time he graduated, Curtis Robinson had flown several different planes: The PT-17 Kaydet which he flew in primary flying school, BT-13 Valiant in basic flying school, and North American AT-6 while in advanced flying school. The PT-17 was an old, small, bi-wing plane that was the first plane the cadets were trained on. It had between 90 to 110 horsepower and a cruising speed of about 80 miles per hour. Next, during basic, cadets trained on the BT-13 which was larger than the PT-17. Cadets finished their advanced training with the AT-6, which had a lot of gunnery. The new graduates had not yet done any formal pursuits, attacks, evasive tactics or similar maneuver at this point in the training program. It was only after they became pilots, and were very proficient in flying that they began to do those more complicated maneuvers that required really good skills.

The types of planes flown changed again after they became pilots. "We transitioned to the fighter, the P-40, after graduation," Robinson explains. "This was the last portion of our training at Tuskegee. They had about four or five P40s there. In the book *Black Knights*, Lynn M. Homan and Thomas Reilly describe the P-40: "Following graduation, the final aircraft was the sleek P-40. It had a bad reputation for being a man-killer. The P-40 was a good but unforgiving airplane; pilots had to give it their undivided attention. A heavy airplane with sluggish controls, it was not an aircraft conducive to easy and clean maneuvers."

Taking it from there, Robinson says, "That is the plane that killed two of my classmates – James Brothers (from Chicago) and Sidney Mosley. There were various maneuvers that we had to do everyday while training. In one of them, we climbed to 10,000 feet and then dived to see how fast the plane would go. I got it up to 470 miles per hour. Both of those guys were killed while performing that maneuver. I think they kept their eyes on the speed when they should have pulled up; perhaps they were looking to see how fast they were going, tried to pull up too late, and flew into the ground. I'm not sure if they were trying to reach a certain speed or what."

Completion of the advanced maneuvers and fighter training marked the end of their training at Tuskegee Army Air Field. They had a ten-day leave. Then it was on to Selfridge Field in Michigan. The new pilots spent a couple of days at Selfridge Field getting assignments, and then they continued onward to Oscoda, a resort town in Michigan right on the beach of Lake Huron where the army had a gunnery installation and the pilots received gunnery training. "The place was really like a recreational 'escape', having all types of cabins and a beautiful beach, but it was a segregated town and the citizenry protested our presence," Robinson says of the Airmen's time spent there.

There were no other people there except the pilots and crews, very few people who did anything else. Lots of cabins were available to the new airmen as residences, and they lived two per cabin. Guys who were married were allowed to bring their wives there, and they had a very nice time. Because of segregationist policies in place, there were no whites in this setup; there were only black pilots and crews. Robinson believes that facilitated better bonding among them, "That's when we really got to know each other and the guys in classes other than our own. We established strong ties and had a great time flying. I really enjoyed it there."

Usually there would be four or five classes at Oscoda at a time. This current group consisted of the three classes ahead of Robinson's class, his class, plus the class behind his. There were plenty of planes to go around - new planes - and the pilots flew everyday and had as much freedom to fly as they wanted. Oscoda had both an aerial and ground gunnery air field. "We took gunnery courses and went through a lot of simulated dog-fights with each other," Robinson says. "This was the good part of flying – dog-fighting without really having to worry about getting shot, and of course we flew over lakes such as Lake Erie for our gunnery training."

Though this part of training was less stressful, with the new graduates having already made the grade, they were still being evaluated. One example involved the firing of their machine guns. "After our planes, which had 50 caliber machine guns in each wing, were loaded with color coded ammunition, we would start our practice. We had a plane piloted by a fellow pilot which was equipped to pull a long target behind it. The rest of us pursued the plane in our aircrafts and shot at the target. When pilots fired, we shot all six of our machine guns and aimed through a sight that was made of glass. Every fourth bullet from our guns was a tracer bullet that would light up and show us whether or not we were hitting the target because they were so easy to follow. After the plane dropped the target following our runs, ground crews would retrieve it to see what color the bullet holes were. The instructors would check to see if we were hitting the target by checking the color of the bullet holes in it. They would know who was firing accurately and who wasn't. We also practiced dive bombing, strafing, and other maneuvers. Additionally, we target practiced for ground gunnery on large targets located on the ground."

After four weeks at Oscoda, the young pilots went back to Selfridge Field and began practicing formation flying and aerial and tactical gunnery training. "Just before I left to go overseas, we found out about the types of formations that the 99th Fighter Squadron was flying;" Robinson says of the famous squadron that he would soon join. "They were different from the formations we were practicing. We flew with wingtips about a foot apart during training. A pilot has to have very quick reactions to any movement of the leader in tight formations like that. We would fly about a foot behind our leader and about a foot off of him. If he turned in a certain direction – say, to his right and we were on his right, we immediately had to pull back on our throttle and drop down; otherwise, we would get ahead of him. If he made a turn to his left and we were on the right, we would have to increase our speed and pull up. A pilot had to be very alert. They taught us a little bit of formation flying early in flying school, but it wasn't the type of formation flying that we flew in those fighters."

Until he went overseas, Robinson had always had a great time flying, but of this stage of his training he says, "This period of time was the best time I had flying while in the service. It was a great experience for anybody who loved to fly. When I flew overseas, there was no extra time for just leisurely flying, or really, the fun flying that training allowed. Overseas, I was always flying missions, but this phase was fun."

After the formation flying training that the new pilots received, they had the skills, decision-making ability, and a sound knowledge of flying techniques for "air warfare" formation flying. Overseas there were several formations being used, but in some cases pilot who were engaged in warfare were more on their own than they found themselves in training. With some formations, pilots flew quite far from the leader, at least fifty to seventy yards away so they could cover each others' tails and would be able to maneuver and keep abreast of what was going on about them. When flying in spread-out formations like that, the pilot usually didn't need anyone to point anything out for him – unless someone saw something he couldn't or didn't see, such as a distant plane far off on the opposite side of the formation. For the most part, he could see for himself what was going on.

"I got to the point where the airplane felt like it was a part of my body after so many hours of flying," Robinson says about having become a pilot and having spent almost a full year just flying. "Knowing and keeping in mind the limitations of the plane, I could make it do practically anything I wanted it to do, whenever I wanted to. It's not like driving a car, where there are limitations of the road and lots of traffic. In the air you could do whatever you wanted to after you had a certain amount of experience and skills. You did not have space, terrain, and congestion constraints that encumber your movement in a plane as with automobiles. For about six weeks we did nothing but flying, shooting, and whatever we wanted."

And unlike Oscoda or Tuskegee, Selfridge Field was located near a major metropolitan area. It lies between Lake St. Clair and Mount Clemens within twenty miles of Detroit. After our last flight of the day, on many days guys headed into Detroit right away, not even staying around for dinner. I was one of those guys running into town. There, we could meet young ladies, go to clubs, and have a good time."

Probably ninety percent of the guys were single with a few having gotten married after graduation. A friend of Robinson's, Albert Manning, who was a class behind him, was one such pilot. Right after he became a pilot, he married his college sweetheart who had been the queen of South Carolina State College. "She was, indeed, a queen - a beautiful person," Robinson says of the wife of his friend who was working behind the scene trying to be a matchmaker. "He kept telling me, 'I want you to meet our landlady.' Now Robinson had come from a college town that sported numerous boarding residences primarily for college students and he had seen tons of landladies. The landladies who ran those sites in his hometown were old women, and not necessarily attractive.

They formed his frame of reference as to what landladies looked like. Robinson was young and handsome. So meeting Manning's landlady didn't sound very appealing to him. "I told Manning I didn't want to meet his landlady," Robinson says of the matchmaking, "but he persisted and a date was arranged."

Manning and his wife invited Robinson over for Friday dinner at their place before they were all to head off into Detroit to a club. He accepted their invitation and showed up at their house at the designated time. "Another friend of ours, Pearlee Saunders and his wife, were there, too," Robinson says of this date. "And there was someone else in the dining area with Manning's wife. We all chatted for a while in the front room and then gathered in the dining room where the six of us were seated at their dining room table. I looked up as if drawn to do so involuntarily; and then I viewed the most beautiful woman I had ever seen, and was she ever beautiful! It was the landlady! Her name was Loraine. She was about 23 or 24 years old and was sitting directly across from me. She couldn't keep her eyes off me, and I couldn't keep my eyes off her. I couldn't wait to get close to her."

After dinner they all headed into the city for an evening of fun at one of the clubs. Everyone got into Manning's car. Robinson's date got in the front with Manning and his wife, and he got in the backseat with his friend, Pearlee and his wife. Once they got to the club, it was the same thing as at the dinner table. She just kept her eyes on Robinson, and he told himself, "Gee whiz, she is mine." The two of them had a very enjoyable conversation, laughing most of the evening and having a wonderful time. The evening seemed to pass quickly.

"When we got ready to return home, Loraine got in the backseat and sat in my lap," Robinson says of the trip from the club. "It was a playful ride. I could smell the fragrance of her perfume as she tossed her hair aside and leaned close while I whispered to her; she would kid and tease, so I blew lightly on her ear and neck. We smooched all the way back and were still smooching when suddenly the car stopped. They all lived in Detroit, but I lived on the base, and Manning had stopped to drop me off at the bus stop so I could catch a bus back to the base. I was surprised at how quickly it seemed that Manning had arrived at the bus stop. I looked up and saw where we were and said, "Manning, drive around the block." He asked, "For what?" I struggled to find a sensible answer but couldn't, so I got out. She asked, 'Are you coming to see me tomorrow?' I kissed her and said, 'Yes.' Then she said, 'Please come to see me tomorrow.' I said, 'I'll call you as soon as I'm done flying in the morning and whatever time it may be, no doubt, I'll come by.'"

As he headed back to the base, Robinson was excited about the way the evening had gone. He was smitten by his new friend, the scent of her perfume still lingering about him, and he thought - what a bombshell. She had a keen sense of humor and had been teasing him. He would show her how to tease when next they met. Walking briskly on this memorable autumn night, he returned to his barracks.

Robinson was scheduled for gunnery training the next morning. He arrived for his morning training routine, fired up his plane, and went through his series of training maneuvers. In no time at all he was done and glad that he had quickly dispatched those items that stood between him and his most divine new friend. He had been thinking about her the whole time he was in the air, "There was nothing on my mind except that girl after our first date," he says. "Just before I completed my flying session I received a call from the office informing me that Colonel Davis wanted to see me, so I came down."

"I landed, went immediately to his office, knocked, entered and saluted him." This was just the second time that

Robinson had met Colonel Benjamin O. Davis, Jr. face-to-face. Colonel Davis was tall – about 6' 2, stood erect, as straight as an arrow, looked Robinson directly in the eyes, and said, "Robinson, as of right now, you are grounded; we are sending you overseas. You are not to speak of this to any of your friends. You are not to use the telephone or write letters to anyone; this is between you and me. Do you understand?"

Robinson's replied, "Yes, Sir! His heart dropped. Of course the first thing he thought about was his date with the most beautiful woman he had ever met. It surely never crossed his mind to call her, for Colonel Davis's men held him in high respect and admiration bordering on fear. They would absolutely not go against his orders; besides, Robinson was a professional. "As I headed out of the office, my friend Manning was coming in to meet with Colonel Davis and Davis told him the same thing," Robinson says. "He couldn't even tell his wife; he sent someone to his house to get his gear and things, but his wife didn't know what was going on. I never saw Loraine again - never again. I've always told myself, it must not have been meant to be."

The first class of cadets had entered Tuskegee Army Air Field in November 1941. Its graduates became the first members of the 99th Pursuit Squadron, later to become the 99th Fighter Squadron, and they first arrived on the combat scene in April 1943, seventeen months later. The squadron's involvement in the war was continually delayed because the military brass didn't really know what to do with the 99th Fighter Squadron. The armed services were all segregated, so the 99th Squadron couldn't be assimilated into any existing groups. Most Army Air Corp fighter and pursuit groups were comprised of at least three squadrons – usually four, but there were no other black squadrons to produce sufficient numbers of squadrons to form an all black group. Consequently, the men of the 99th had continued to train endlessly - it seemed to some - for months. Later, ironically, some in the military leadership rank would claim that this showed that the pilots of the 99th required more training than white pilots.

To make matters even less certain for the Tuskegee Airmen, at the time Robinson was receiving his orders from Davis, the War Department brass in Washington, D.C., were becoming a much greater threat than the enemy abroad. They were trying to shut the Tuskegee Airmen down. Army Chief of Staff, Gen. Henry Arnold, visited Capt. George "Spanky" Roberts, who had taken over command of the 99th from Colonel Davis. General Arnold dropped in almost immediately after Davis' departure to return to the States. Roberts characterized Arnold's statements during their meeting as "discrediting" and "maligning." Arnold had visited him because of criticisms brought by Colonel William Momyer. The 99th Squadron had been attached briefly to his group, the 33rd Fighter Group during the spring of 1943, and Colonel Momyer detested it immensely. Davis had returned to the States to become Commander of the 332nd Fighter Group, a newly formed all black group initially comprised of the 100th, 301st, and 302nd Fighter Squadrons in September of 1943. And as importantly, he would have to defend the record and performance of the 99th Fighter Squadron before he returned abroad.

These developments would later become a matter of record. But in the meantime as they played out, Curtis Christopher Robinson was now a freshly minted Army Air Corps pilot, a hot shot fighter pilot, a first lieutenant who was oblivious to the political drama attendant to his squadron. He had received his orders to head to the Mediterranean Theatre of Operation to join the 99th Fighter Squadron on the battle field. And he knew that he was ready!

Quest for the 99th

Toward the latter part of 1943, battles between allied forces and German and Italian forces raged on in Italy as part of the World War II Mediterranean Theatre of Operation where combatants fought to control territory. The Army Air Corps played a huge role in securing victories in Pantelleria and Salerno. Bombardment of Pantelleria, considered important for protection of the allied flank for their planned invasion of Sicily, began in May of '43, and the island passed to allied hands later in June. This paved the way for the assault on the European mainland. Victories at Salerno followed in September, as Army Air forces disrupted enemy supply lines, reinforcements, and sought to isolate enemy divisions.

On April 2, 1943, the first war-bound members of the 99th Fighter Squadron had departed Tuskegee Army Air Field by train to New York. There they boarded the USS Mariposa on April 15th en-route to the war and arrived in Casablanca, French Morocco, on April 24th. But prior to their departure, and as the first of their ranks prepared to embark for Europe, their commander, Colonel Noel Parish, told them, "You are fighting men now. You have made the team. Your future is now being handed into your own hands. Your future, good or bad, will depend largely on how determined you are not to give satisfaction to those who would like to see you fail."

After they arrived overseas, the lead-off men of the 99th received a month of intensive training in Tunisia and were attached to the 33rd Fighter Group to gain combat experience. The 33rd was an all-white group lead by Colonel William Momyer, and he did not consider them part of that group. On June 2, 1943, William Campbell and Charles Hall became the first members of the 99th to fly in a combat mission for the United States as wingmen with the 33rd. But the Tuskegee Airmen reported a series of problems with this group: a reluctance of its members to fly with the black pilots; continually receiving separate, segregated briefings, and on-going hostility and racial slurs, among other things. Spann Watson, who was one of the first four black pilots to fly with the 33rd, recalls this experience in *Black Knights, The Story of the Tuskegee Airmen*: "After my fiftieth mission with the 99th, I came back to the States; then I went back to Europe and went over to the 332nd. On the day before Christmas, the bombers were forced to land at the fighter base. They were snowed out down in southern Italy. Up around where we were, the field was open. At that time we had a stand-down. All the enlisted men on those bomber crews found shelter somehow or other with our men, and at that time I was the censor officer, the mail censoring officer for enlisted men's mail."

"I picked up this letter; it was from one of the bomber crews, a gunner. And it said, 'This is the time, just before Christmas, when we all should be together. I'm not even at my own airfield. I'm at a nigger airfield, sleeping in nigger beds, and eating nigger food.' He signs it 'Sergeant Schwartz.' I picked up the thing, gave it to the adjutant, and he gave it a cursory look. I looked at that thing and I said, "If I were to take this outside and show it to somebody, there would be a riot here tomorrow." This was Christmas Eve of 1943.

Call it "a matter of following the shadow of the leader" because Colonel Momyer himself had tried to have the 99th Fighter Squadron eliminated and the program at Tuskegee terminated in September of 1943. After they finally integrated the unit, things got so bad that Robinsons recalled a story about pilots from the 33rd having gone on a mission with a couple of black pilots from the 99th. Seemingly, all of the pilots went through one of those big clouds, and when they came out, two white pilots had disappeared and the two black pilots were still flying. Nobody knows what happened to those pilots; they have no idea and no pilots from the 99th were ever accused of foul-play, but the point is that things were so bad that you could expect almost anything to happen. For emphasis Robinson adds, "That's a true story, and they never found those pilots. While my squadron was attached to the 33rd, the 99th lived on one side of the field; the 33rd lived on the other. The men of the 99th never saw them, didn't have briefings with them, did not eat together, nor did they socialize with each other."

Their association with the 33rd didn't last very long. On June 29, 1943, the 99th Fighter Squadron became part of the 324th Fighter Group based in Cercola, Italy. And in July, while flying as wingmen with the 324th Fighter Group, Lt. Charles Hall scored the first aerial victory for a Tuskegee Airman. This was a happy and significant moment since Tuskegee Airmen weren't usually given assignments where they encountered the enemy and had opportunities to engage him. Their job was usually to dive bomb enemy ground targets and not get caught.

This was a period during which any accusation that could be levied against the pilots of the 99th was levied. They were criticized for having a low number of enemy engagements and kills, though they were given missions bound to yield such results, missions where they went as many as nine months without encountering enemy planes. Many believed that Colonel Momyer, who precipitated the visit by General Arnold to Captain Roberts after Colonel Davis had returned to the states, and the subsequent investigation of the 99th Fighter Squadron, seized on Davis' departure and absence as an opportunity to terminate them. Momyer strenuously criticized the 99th and was backed by his bosses, Major General Edwin House, who was the commanding officer of the 12th Air Support Command, the command under which these men did their fighting, and Major General John Cannon. The concurrence between these two led to a formal investigation of the 99th.

In October of 1943, Colonel Parrish and Colonel Davis testified before the McCloy Committee, a War Department committee headed by Assistant Secretary of War John J. McCloy, that had been formed to investigate the matter of the charges that Momyer had levied against the 99th. His charges stated that they lacked discipline, motivation, and he practically called them cowards. These charges were captured in a report termed the Momyer Report. In their testimony, both Parrish and Davis thoroughly supported the 99th and defended its record. The Committee, nonetheless, forwarded a recommendation to President Roosevelt to kill the Tuskegee program. Wiser heads prevailed. Fortunately, Cannon's boss, Lt. Gen. Carl Spaatz, ordered more studies be done on the suitability of blacks to serve in the Army Air Corps. Colonel Emmett O'Donnell of the Air Staff suggested that the recommendation be reconsidered and never forwarded it to the president. As a result the program survived.

While the political drama surrounding the survival of his

squadron played out unbeknownst to most Tuskegee Airmen, Curtis Robinson was heading out to join the 99th Fighter Squadron in battle. "There were four of us headed overseas together, and we were en-route from Michigan to Camp Patrick Henry in Hampton Roads, Virginia, by commercial air," Robinson says of the new pilot's upcoming journey. "We hopped a plane in Detroit, landed in Pittsburgh, and then flew on to Washington, D.C. When we got to Washington, the weather was terrible and all planes were grounded; they wouldn't hesitate to fly in that kind of weather today. Florie, my wife-to-be, was living in the city with one of her sisters. We had lost contact with each other after dating during our college days. I don't recall how I managed to get her address or telephone number, but somehow I found her. I spent three days in Washington, D.C., and we started our romance again."

"After three days, the weather still hadn't cleared, and the four of us guys caught a train out of town at our own expense and continued on to Hampton Roads. This was the first part of September of 1943. We probably should have waited until the weather cleared and caught a military plane, but we thought that we really needed to get there expeditiously. Upon arriving in Hampton Roads, the four of us were put in an entire barracks by ourselves; we ate alone and were left alone. The military didn't want to mix us in with the rest of the troops because Camp Patrick Henry was segregated. Art Carter, a black correspondent from the Afro-American newspaper, was being sent over to cover the war in Italy at the same time. He arrived in Hampton Roads during the second week we were there and lived in the barracks with us. We continued to be segregated for the entire two weeks we were there."

Camp Patrick Henry was a huge installation built on what appeared to be virtually swampland. It had a large stockade and from all over the United States, the military had sent unruly guys there to the stockades. One group of black guys was so unruly that they had taken away their clothes after they went AWOL (absent without leave) and had given them only raincoats. That's all the clothes they had – raincoats - so that they couldn't go anyplace. "I saw them playing basketball in those rain coats, lining up and eating in those raincoats – all day long, those raincoats." Robinson thought it strange. "They had arrived with a major. After he reached the point where he couldn't put up with them any longer, he turned them over to a captain. The captain tired of them and tried to turn them over to us four, but we weren't going to have any of that. We were pilots, not military police. As the time arrived for de-embarkation to Italy, those guys balked. They said they weren't going, that they had been in the service for six months without having being paid, so they refused to go. The captain promised them that they would each be paid $10 if they got on board, and he set up a table at the end of the boarding ramp. There were about sixty-five of them who boarded, and they were each given $10 each."

Even on the ship they continued to be unmanageable. Two of the guys had a roulette wheel, and they gambled all day and all night for about two days. After that, there was no more gambling. "The two guys that had gotten on with the roulette wheel ended up with all the money; they really were quite funny," Robinson laughed. "I don't know what they had done, but Art Carter tried to interview them. They were so vulgar that he told them he couldn't put what they were saying in the paper, so they cursed him out and wouldn't talk to him. No one was able to get any information out of them. I don't know what happened to them, where they were headed, or why the U.S. was sending over guys from the stockades to the Mediterranean."

The four newest members of the 99th traveled abroad in

a large convoy, about fifteen ships wide and twenty ships deep and totaling almost 300 ships. They were traveling on a liberty ship.[vii] These were ships which had been built quickly specifically for the war effort. "During the trip Germans would attack on the southern side of the convoy," says Robinson of the journey over. "We were heading east towards North Africa and the Mediterranean area, and after about a week into our trip, we would see fire and a ship going down every night; the enemy really attacked steadily. For protection we had aircraft carriers, many destroyers, and destroyer escorts; even so, we lost a lot of ships during the voyage. Our planes would patrol during the day so we were not usually attacked during daylight hours."

About three days before they were to have arrived in Gibraltar, at about 8:00 in the morning, Robinson's ship was rammed by one of the ships in the convoy. The four new pilots had been sleeping but were awakened, grabbed their life jackets, and rushed out on deck. The captain of the errant vessel said that he lost his steering control, and instead of going straight, he accidentally ran into the side of their ship. That knocked a hole in their ship's hull, and water started rushing in. It was a big hole about fifteen by thirty feet. The ship that rammed theirs pulled out, made its correction, and went on.

To help the ship stay afloat, the crew transferred some of the airplane fuel and the ship's fuel from the side that had the hole to one of the other ships. They then dumped enough additional fuel so that they got rid of the list and got the hole in the ship above the water line. But the convoy kept going. It didn't stop and it didn't linger. A destroyer stayed with them for a while, but it left, too, once it looked as if they weren't going to sink. The crew used canvas and boards to patch up the hole and keep the water out. "We limped along for three days and three nights that way at about four knots with a bright moon;" Robinson says of the ordeal. "It was a little scary given the way Germans had been knocking off ships, and we figured we'd had it. Everyone was busy from that point on scanning the ocean to see if there were signs of any German subs."

"We got into the harbor at Gibraltar and stayed there overnight. The military brass was considering the possibility of transferring us to another ship, but they could find no other available ship. It was a frightening experience because someone, probably the Germans, had divers swimming over from Spain's side of the harbor during the darkness of night and placing explosives - depth charges - near the ships, and rocking our ship most of the night. In order to stop it, we began dropping depth charges every fifteen minutes, all night long. Those charges formed a protective barrier out a safe distance from the ships since they made it dangerous for any divers to swim near them. We didn't get any sleep at all. The next morning, we pulled out."

The 99th was a segregated unit that for all intents and purposes stood alone, isolated, nomad-like, living in tents, flying from barren dirt strips and significantly on its own. It was a squadron that was also almost continually on the move. The four new pilots had no idea of where the squadron was. The last Robinson and his group had heard, the 99th was in North Africa, but they knew the war had moved on. They figured the squadron was no longer there, but they had to start somewhere.

"So after we left Gibraltar, we headed to Oran in North Africa," says Robinson as the search for the 99th began. "When we landed, it was raining like mad, and we were put on an army truck. The driver took us out to a big field, threw us a canvas sack, and told us to pitch a tent. There I was, wearing my dress uniform, and they're telling me to pitch a tent in a barren muddy field. So I asked the driver, 'Where is this truck going?' He said, 'I'm going back to the post.' So I said, 'Well, I'm going back to the post, too.' So the four of us got on board and went back to the post. We spent the night on board the truck, and the next day we went to the officer's club. We got boarding there. They put us up in the French cadet barracks; this was in Oran. Then we had to make a decision about how to catch up with our outfit from there."

The new pilots were given their orders in Oran. The orders said, "Proceed to outfit; air, by first priority, to unit." "That was it," adds Robinson. "No mention was made of what unit, where the unit was, or anything. My squadron didn't have a physical home, and they didn't have an organizational home at this point. It was up to us pilots to determine which way to go from there. The Army Air Corps had planes going up and down the coast, everyplace all the time. And as pilots, we could hop a plane any time, any day. So we went out to field operations and asked them, "Where is the 99th Fighter Squadron?" "No one knew anything about them," says Robinson. "The first sergeant, one of the fellows that we had met and talked with briefly the night before, knew that they had been in Casablanca and Fez, so he suggested that we go there and inquire."

"Accordingly, we hopped a plane headed to Casablanca - then called French Morocco - for a trip to Fez," Robinson says as their search continued. "There we were told our squadron had left weeks previously. We hopped a plane and went to Tunisia and then back to Oran. We stayed there for a couple of days and went on to Algiers. Since we had seen the movie 'Algiers' starring Charles Boyer and all those beautiful French girls, we wanted to check out the place. Algiers was very interesting; we spent three or four days there just sightseeing. We found out that no one there knew where the 99th was. One of the guys was becoming chicken and said we were wasting too much time. So we resumed our search. We went out to field operations to catch a plane. They had a plane going to Constantine. I'd never heard of Constantine but learned that it was a little town on the coast of the Mediterranean in Algeria. When we landed there, they were having a big USO show. We took in the show and spent the night there."

The next day the young pilots flew over to Tunis, made inquiries, and were told that the 99th had been there but had gone on to Sicily; then, the story changed, their source really didn't know where they were. Robinson and his comrades ended up spending a couple of days in Tunis, a sea town in Tunisia, a country east of Algeria, and after a couple of days, flew over to Sicily. "No one in Sicily that we spoke with knew anything about the whereabouts of 99th. But over at field operations, a base officer told us that he had four P-40s coming in that needed to be transferred and didn't have anyone to fly them;" Robinson says of situation, "He asked us to hang around until they came in. We hung around there for four or five days waiting. Finally the operations guy said it didn't look like the planes were coming, and for us to go on."

From there, they caught a plane going to Foggia, another Italian city. They landed in Foggia and were just getting set up when they encountered Ollie Stewart who was a black correspondent for the Pittsburgh Courier, another black newspaper. He had been there reporting about six or seven months and was getting ready to go home. Ollie told them that the 99th Fighter Squadron was down about forty or fifty miles from there. After he left, one of the guys suggested, "Let's make a quick trip to Naples," which was on the other coast.
So the men hopped a plane for Naples and got there about six o'clock in the evening. Robinson described what happened next: "It was just getting dusk. As we were going into town, the Germans started an air raid. In town they had smudge pots containing oil that the townspeople burned when they came

under attack. They began burning them and it created huge clouds of smoke all over the place, so you could hardly see your hands in front of your face. They did it to obscure the German's ground visibility and limit their ability to locate strategic targets. We couldn't see anybody on the street and couldn't hear anyone. Everything was quiet except for the shrapnel which was falling, hitting the pavement, and ricocheting all around us. We took cover under a truck until the air raid ended."

After the bombing stopped and things settled down, the pilots began walking around checking out the town. As they walked down the street, people began following them; the town's people, seemingly, had never seen any black people up close before. A soldier they met while walking about took them over to the officers club. The officers club was part of a larger complex; it was huge. It was eight or nine o' clock in the evening and people were having dinner. The greeter at the officer's club, he wasn't really a maitre d,' sat them at a table. There was a beautiful ballroom and an officer's mess. There were young twenty-year-old girls waiting tables.

A group of girls started crowding around the handsome young pilots and began playing with their hair. "They hadn't seen hair like ours before," and Robinson laughs as he recalls the incident. "Their hair was straight, and they thought our kinky and curly hair was great. It was the most amazing thing. Finally this major came in and jumped on them saying, 'You're all fired unless you get back to your tables.' They thought we were cute and that hair like mine was great. They acted like I had the greatest hair in the world. We spent about five days in Naples, which was fine, but we couldn't go anyplace because wherever we went, we would draw a crowd."

But despite being thousand of miles from home in the Mediterranean, the world could still seem relatively small in some respects. Who could have imagined that Robinson's search for his squadron would also lead to an encounter with his brother. He tells it, "I had an opportunity to meet up with my brother, George, while in the port city of Naples. He was an artillery officer in the 598th Field Artillery Unit, which was a part of the 370th Combat Team. They were part of the 92nd Infantry Division. The 92nd Division was over 15,000 strong and was the only black unit of its size in the Mediterranean Theatre of Operation. It was comprised of three all-black infantry regiments, four all-black field artillery battalions, and an all-black engineering battalion; however all senior commanders and staff for the 92nd were white. George was broke, as usual, and had asked his friend, Warrant Officer Fox, that if he saw an Army Air Corps officer who had a strong family resemblance, advise him that his brother George wanted to see him. Sure enough, Warrant Officer Fox got the message to me, and that's how we rendezvoused during the war - so that I could lend George some money!"

"We spent another three days trying to catch up with the 99th and late in October of 1943, we flew back to Foggia. After six weeks we finally caught up with our unit," says Robinson of the conclusion of the search for his squadron.

The four pilots' search had actually been very enjoyable and most exciting for them. During their journey, they could catch a plane at will and go from city to city to city, or country-to-country. They got up when they wanted – maybe nine or ten o'clock - had breakfast, and wore their dress uniforms all the time. They would go out to an airfield, and the installations always had transportation for them. "Once we got there, in almost all of these airfields, there would be a big drum with nice, hot coffee brewing. That was something! We were living the life then," Robinson says. "For over a month, we traveled. First to Casablanca for about two days, then on to Fez where we spent a day, back to Oran for two or three days, and then on to Algiers where we spent a week. Then we went to Constantine and Tunis, with four days in Sicily, and a few in Naples."

When the four new pilots finally found their unit, no one in the 99th Fighter Squadron asked them, "Where have you been? What took you so long?" or, "What happened?" Not a word was spoken about their long search.

Paternal grandparents: the Reverend Thomas Glenn Robinson and Mrs. Anna Robinson, circa 1890.

Post Office Department.

Walter Q. Gresham.

POSTMASTER GENERAL OF THE UNITED STATES OF AMERICA.

To all to whom these Presents shall come, Greeting:

Whereas, On the 27 day of December 188[illegible] Thos. G. Robinson was appointed Postmaster at [illegible] in the County of [illegible] State of South Carolina and whereas he did, on the [illegible] day of January 188[illegible] execute a Bond and has taken the Oath of Office, as required by law:

Now know ye, That confiding in the integrity, ability, and punctuality of the said Thos. G. Robinson I do commission him a Postmaster, authorized to execute the duties of that Office at [illegible] according to the Laws of the United States and the Regulations of the Post Office Department: To hold the said Office of Postmaster, with all the powers, privileges, and emoluments to the same belonging, during the pleasure of the Postmaster General of the United States.

In testimony whereof I have hereunto set my hand and caused the seal of the Post Office Department to be affixed, at Washington City, the [illegible] day of [illegible] in the year of our Lord one thousand eight hundred and eighty [illegible], and of the Independence of the United States the one hundred and [illegible].

W. Q. Gresham

Postmaster General

This is a copy of the Reverend Thomas G. Robinson's commission as Postmaster of Bamberg County, South Carolina.

Parents: Mr. Christopher Capers Robinson and Mrs. Ednora Robinson circa 1943.

Robinson's oldest brother, Capers Glenn Robinson, and sister, Anna Ella Robinson; pictured circa 1932.

Curtis Robinson and three brothers in their armed services uniforms circa 1943.

Historically significant

Trinity United Methodist Church, located at 185 Boulevard NE, is now listed in the National Register of Historic Places, the nation's official list of documented historic properties. This older photograph (left photo) is a view of the present sanctuary shortly after construction was completed in 1944. Members of Trinity United Methodist Church, originally named Trinity Methodist Episcopal Church, first met in a school operated by the Freedmen's Bureau. The first separate sanctuary was constructed in 1870 at the corner of Amelia Street and Pittman Alley – where the Orangeburg County Courthouse now stands. A second larger sanctuary (above) – a Romanesque Revival building – was constructed in 1891 and served the congregation until 1926, when trustees of the church traded with trustees of South Carolina State College for the property where the church is now located. (Photo special to The T&D)

"Trinity United Methodist Church, where virtually my entire family were members; condemned by the "city fathers" and moved to make room for a Courthouse, circa 1926."

Claflin College, Claflin High School, and Claflin Elementary School combined classes; circa 1940.

Curtis C. Robinson, Tuskegee Airman; circa 1943.

Clockwise from top left: Ulysses S. Taylor, Harold E. Sawyer, Luke J. Weathers, Lewis C. Smith, Leonard M. Jackson, Curtis C. Robinson, Vernon V. Haywood, James Y. Carter, Walter T. Foreman, Charles P. Bailey, Charles I. Williams, Sidney J. Mosley, Wilson V. Eagleson, Freddie E. Hutchins, William J. Faulkner, Paul Adams, Arnold W. Cisco, James E. Brothers, and Heber C. Houston. Tuskegee Army Air Field: Graduating Class 43-D-SE, April 29, 1943. (Prints and Images, The Library of Congress.)

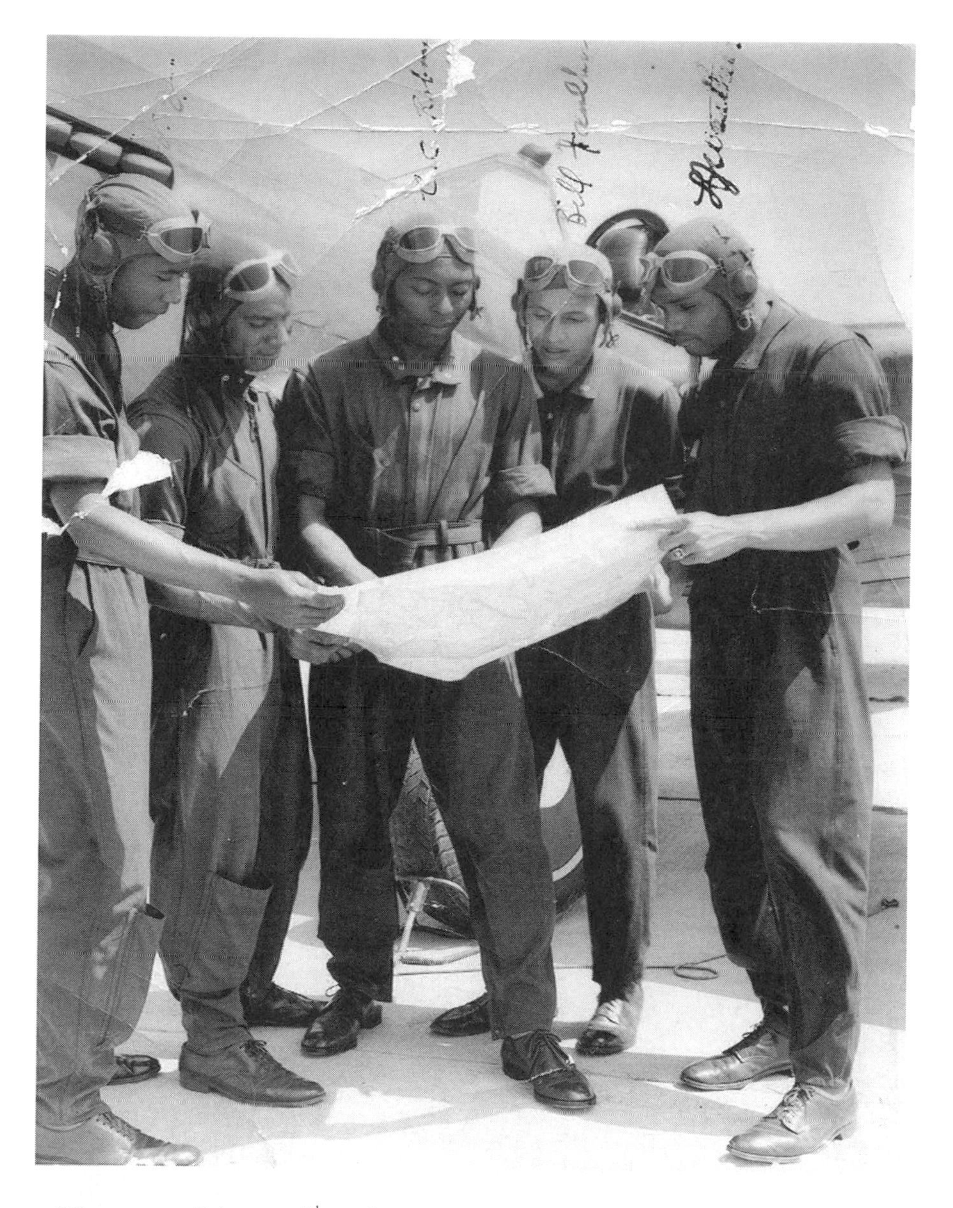

Veterans of the 332nd Fighter Group: Vernon V. Haywood, Sidney J. Mosley, Curtis C. Robinson, William. J. Faulkner, and Luke J. Weathers review flight plans prior to mission.

Instructors conduct formation flying at Tuskegee Army Air Field, circa 1943, photo by USA Army Signal Corps – with permission.

P40 Warkhawk Pursuit/Fighter aircraft similar to plane flown by Curtis Robinson, circa 1943, photo by USA Army Signal Corps – with permission.

Members of the 99th Fighter Squadron have a meal in their tent, at Foggia II, in Italy, circa 1945; from left Curtis Robinson, George McCrumby, Erwin Lawrence, Pearlee E. Saunders, and Henry Perry, private collection.

Good friends: Leonard Jackson, Curtis Robinson, and Albert Manning circa 1945.

Curtis C. Robinson and wife, Florie Frederick Robinson, circa 1945 shortly after marriage; photo from private collection.

Top photo: From left, father-in-law, Henry Frederick; mother-in-law, Mary Frederick; brother-in-law, Henry Frederick, Jr.; his bride Hattie McCullum-Frederick, and her mother, Mrs. Mildred McCullum.
Bottom photo: Florie's sisters, Ernestine Frederick-Fields, May Frederick-Bacon, and Allie Frederick-James.

Curtis Robinson and wife, Florie, spend an evening out at one of Washington, D.C.'s new club, in 1950.

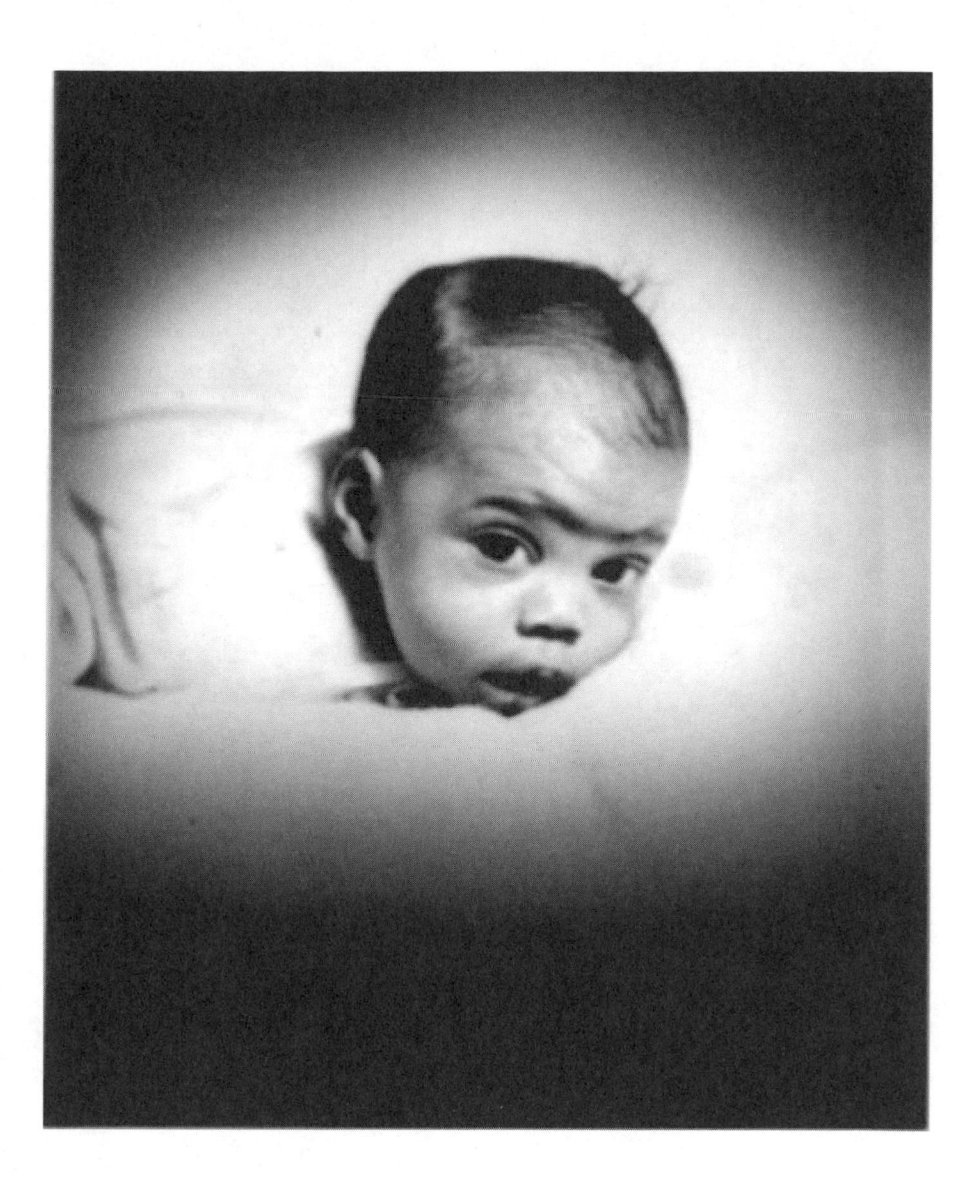

Daughter: Linda Robinson, circa 1947.

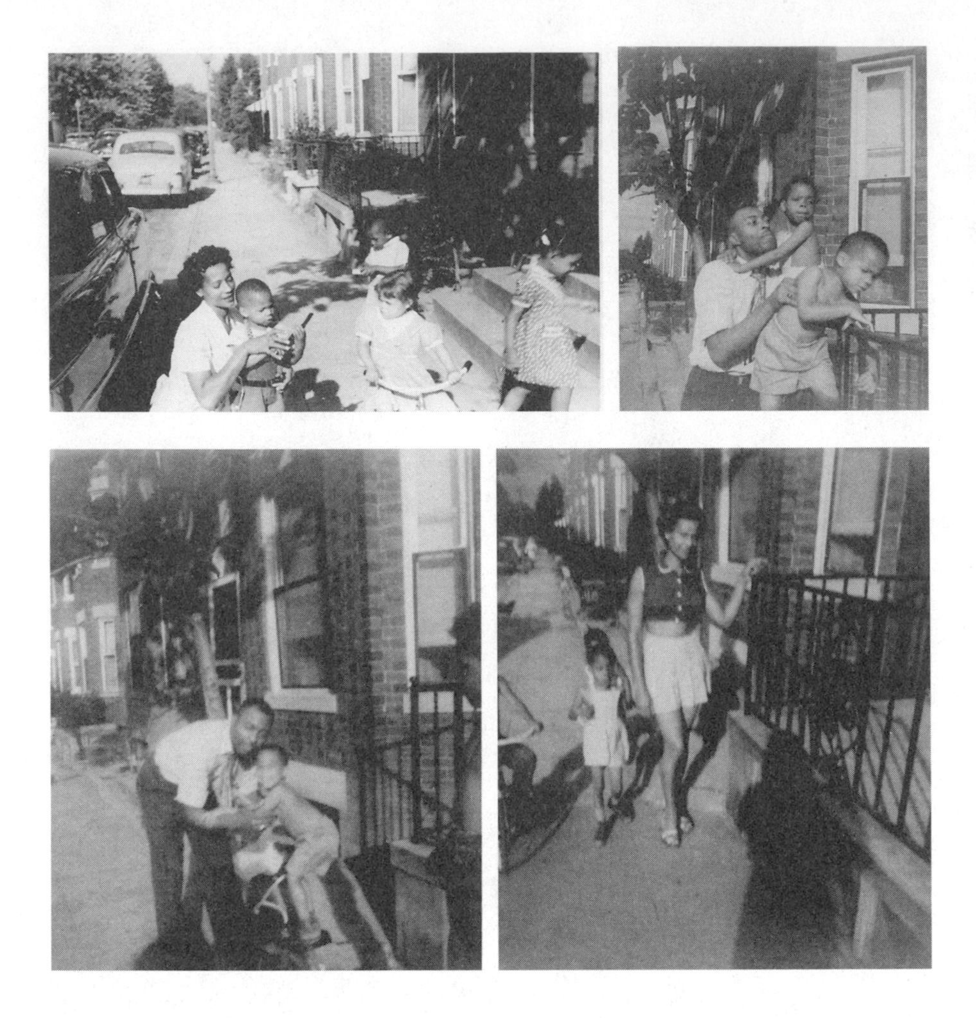

Top, Clockwise from left: Florie with son, Chris, and other neighborhood children when the family lived on Lamont Street; next, Curtis Robinson with daughter, Linda, and son, Chris, at play in the neighborhood. Bottom from left: Curtis Robinson playing with son Chris, and Florie Robinson with daughter, Linda.

Left: Curtis Robinson, third from left, as a new graduate of Howard University's School of Pharmacy in May 1952. Right: From left, friend, Robert Freeman, Florie Robinson and Curtis Robinson in the Alabama Avenue Pharmacy circa 1956.

Daughter: Linda Robinson at age 10 in 1956. Son: Christopher Robinson at age 7 in 1956.

Curtis Robinson and Florie Robinson are shown here on vacation in Tangiers in 1973.

Curtis Robinson and Florie Robinson pose during a trip to Bermuda in the early 1970s.

Curtis Robinson, Percy Sutton (former Manhattan Borough President) and Tuskegee Intelligence Officer, and two un-identified gentlemen photographed at the registration for Annual Awards Banquet in 1984.

Curtis Robinson, fellow Airmen General Daniel "Chappie" James Jr., and Willie Fuller pose for a photograph taken during Tuskegee Airman Reunion in Tuskegee, Alabama, circa 1983.

Curtis Robinson and brothers in Orangeburg, S.C., circa 1987.

Claflin College: 50th anniversary class reunion for the class of 1940. Bottom row from left: Hubert Manning, former Georgia Blassengam, Barbara Meyers-Freeman, and Ruth Carr-Williams. Top row from left:, Curtis Robinson, Elliot Lewis, James Milton, Manny Roseman, and Roscoe Deveaux.

Presentation of "Red Tails" planes at Army War College Exhibit Hall. Curtis Robinson is 2nd from right in upper photo and 3rd from right in the lower photo. Top photo from left: Woody Crockett, Charles McGee, John Suggs, un-identified female, Wiley Selden, Curtis Robinson, and Luke Weathers. Bottom photo from left: Un-identified gentleman, Luke Weathers, un-identified gentleman, John Suggs, Woody Crockett, Luke Weathers, Curtis Robinson, Charles McGee, and an un-identified gentleman.

PARADE

Fifty years ago, nearly 2 million veterans, home from World War II, entered the nation's colleges at government expense to begin reclaiming normal lives:

It Was Called
The GI Bill
And It Transformed
A Nation

A REPORT
By James Brady

Parade Magazine cover August 4, 1996, devoted to the G.I. Bill; Curtis Robinson is lower left: ©1996 Parade Magazine; reprinted with permission.

Former Tuskegee Airmen pilots from left Louis Purnell, Curtis Robinson, Charles M. Bussey, Harry A. Sheppard, and John Suggs pose in 1998 photo shop in Fredericksburg, Virginia, during signing of Tuskegee Airmen commemorative art.

Curtis Robinson, Bill Cosby, and unidentified friend at funeral of General Benjamin O. Davis Jr. in July of 2002.

Above: Curtis Robinson shown beside the entry way to his remaining pharmacy – Robinson's Apothecary - on East Capitol Street in Washington, D.C. during 2003.

Left: Award from Howard University Alumni Association in April of 2003 for fifty-one years of service as a pharmacist in Washington, D.C. He is the only remaining practicing pharmacist from his 1952 graduating class.

Curtis Robinson relaxing in front of Robinson's Apothecary for a photo shot.

Curtis Robinson and the author, George Norfleet, shake hands in this photograph taken on December 18, 2004.

2005 photo by Paul Morse of President Bush and Laura Bush in celebration of Black History Month with: Ms. Mary Louise Mohr (widow of Tuskegee Communications officer Dean Mohr); Tuskegee Airmen: Wiley W. Selden, Walter L. McCreary, Howard L. Baugh, Edgar L. Jones, Ira O'Neal, the President and Mrs. Bush, Curtis Robinson, Claude Rowe, James Pryde, Charles McGee, and George Watson. Courtesy White House Photography Office.

It's Time to Fight

"When I finally caught up with the 99th Fighter Squadron in Italy," says Robinson recapturing that moment, "they were serving as wingmen attached to a group which, as I recall, had been part of the 79th Fighter Group. In the Air Force, groups generally have four squadrons of similar types of planes. That's why the 99th had been having problems flying over there and were being moved around a lot. Nobody wanted them to be attached to their group; they were an all-black squadron and nobody wanted to fly with them." They had previously encountered problems with a different fighter group, the 33rd, the group to whom they were first attached after having arrived abroad. Colonel Momyer, a strict segregationist, commanded that group. In contrast, their stint with the 79th Fighter Group, which lasted six months, was beneficial and much better. They gained a lot of experience, learned better tactics and takeoffs, and felt included

Still the 99th Squadron had almost been taken totally out of the action in late 1943 when Robinson caught up with them. What they were doing was dive bombing, and they were very good at it. It was called "close-support," but that wasn't much of a war for them then. There were a total of three squadrons performing patrols. The 99th's slots were 8:00 a.m. until noon, and from 3:00 p.m. until 6:00 p.m. "We would send a group of eight planes, or sometimes four, to fly over the front;" Robinson says of their missions. "The group had a spotter up front, and they'd have a grid mat. The spotter would tell us that there was a gunnery nest at a certain spot on the grid and he'd say, "Let's take it out," and we would take it out. Afterwards he might say, "We have some oil tankers," at a certain spot on the grid and we would take those out, too. That's what the 99th was doing everyday. There were very few anti-aircraft guns to worry about, and it was very easy work. We used five-hundred-pound bombs. We'd drop those bombs on enemy targets, and that would knock them out."

When the 99th was sent to hit a target, you didn't have to send them twice. After they visited, it was demolished. They were highly skilled bombers. "On occasion we'd get a strafing mission where we would fly in somewhere and see what we could find and strafe it," Robinson says. "We were experts at strafing and dive bombing." But strafing didn't produce aerial victories, of which the unit had only one for the last six months. The morale of the 99th Fighter Squadron was suffering. Even the enlisted men had almost lost faith in the courage of their pilots, questioning their willingness to engage the enemy considering the low number of kills they had tallied.

The war was at a stalemate. Robinson observed that there was a line all the way across Italy from about forty miles above Naples all the way to about sixty miles above Foggia, which is on the east coast of Italy, almost straight across the peninsula. In most wartime literature it was formally called the Gustav Line, and it extended from Netunno on the western side of Italy and Ortona on the east. There was a little fighting on the western side, but not much. The fighting was being done on the eastern side of Italy and that was the area where the 99th had been bombing machine gun nests, gunnery installations, and other targets that posed problems for the allies; they'd take them out, and the enemy didn't advance. It was just a line.

Mediterranean Allied Forces decided to advance and land at Anzio in the early winter months of 1944. Anzio is located about forty miles south of Rome and had a nice beach for landing. The allied forces deployed troops in there in an effort to force the Germans to back out, which is what they did. It turned into a terrible loss for allied forces, however, because when they landed, they could have gone on to Rome, but they chose to dig in. The Germans saw that they weren't going any place, that they were entrenched, so they regrouped, reorganized re-enforcements, came back to meet them, and began bombing ships in the harbor and attacking troops. As the battle at Anzio bogged down and its ferocity picked up, the 99th was called over to the western coast because allied forces needed patrols there. Allied troop movement, coming in and going out, was continuous. There was just a lot of activity going on, and the 99th protected the troops on the ground, too. They were then flying out of Naples, and Anzio allowed them to become more actively involved in the war.

When Anzio was invaded, hundreds of ships filled the harbor and the 99th was brought into the action to protect the ships. "The 99th began to fly missions over Anzio, which is where I did most of my fighting and where I really saw the enemy," says Robinson of the increased involvement of his squadron in the war. "On my very first flight, I went up with a group that included Charlie Hall, who was somewhat of a legend and the first guy in the 99th squadron to shoot down a German aircraft in a dogfight; it happened in July of 1943 while flying with the 324th Fighter Group." It was now January, 1944. Robinson had a plane assigned to him that he said, "I wish I hadn't. They assigned old Number Ten to me, which had come over from the China Burma Theatre of Operation, the Flying Tigers. It was one of those old raggedy planes that even had Chinese writing still on it. The senior fellows in the squadron assigned that thing to me. Nobody wanted it. The guys said, 'You're the rookie, it's yours.' Those planes had two engines. They were paired from three types: an Allison engine, a Rolls Royce, or a Chrysler engine – they were interchangeable. It didn't fly very fast and only cruised about 275 miles per hour."

During Robinson's first few days with the squadron, they patrolled up and down the coast between Ponziane Island and the assault beach. Charlie Hall, who was a captain, was his flight leader, the person responsible for ensuring that pilots involved in a mission arrived at the right rendezvous point, at the right time. While Robinson and a group of pilots, a total of eight of them, were preparing to go up on the second flight to Anzio, Charlie Hall came to see him. He said, "Look, Robinson, I know you're not an experienced combat pilot, but you're going to be on my wing; you're my wingman. As soon as you take off and you see the mountains over there," and he pointed, "I want you fly in a protective mode." Robinson says, "Now I have to explain a 'protective mode.' When the 99th flew in formations, they did so with few planes; the Germans always had more planes than we did. The British taught the 99th to fly what they called line-abreast. In that formation, there were about four planes in a line with fifty to one hundred yards of separation between them, so that a pilot could turn inside another plane and see what was happening behind him and other pilots. Visibility in a plane was very limited and pilots couldn't see behind themselves very well. Their wingman could turn in behind them and see if there was anything coming behind. And that's how we flew, line abreast about fifty yards apart. Charlie had said, 'Now as soon as you see those mountains up there, go into protective mode because the Germans have radar. If you fly in any direction straight, they can track you in eight seconds, and they'll shoot you down. So when you fly, you have to fly this way, then that way, then over here,' he motioned and described. 'I want you to fly that way, all the way as soon as you see the mountains.' It was a very erratic pattern the way he described it."

To start his P-40 Warhawk aircraft, Robinson set its twenty-one switches prior to turning the engine on. The chief mechanic then connected an external battery to his engine, and Robinson started the plane, set the flaps and the trim tabs – a small tab that sets the horizontal tails and end-runs so as to off-set the torque of the engine. He taxied to the take-off point, checked his magnesium power sources which powered the engine, sped down the field to about ninety miles per hour, pulled back on the control, and took off. Five minutes after Robinson took off, he could see the Apennine Mountains, so he went into a protective mode. He was flying up and down and side-to-side, bobbing round and round. Pilots were really only supposed to fly like that when they were under attack. But Charlie told him to go into protective mode as soon as he could see the mountains. That's what Robinson did, and he started almost twenty minutes before the squadron even got close to any German territory.

While all of that was going on about him Robinson says, "I saw out on the horizon about forty or fifty miles a group of planes, maybe thirty of them. They looked like specks, and I could hardly make them out. Being a rookie, I thought that these guys were experienced fighter pilots and must see them, too, so I didn't say anything. The planes kept going as if they were going out to sea. I thought maybe they were our guys heading to bomb southern France. I was still flying in a protective mode - up and down and round and round - and it began to dawn on me that nobody was doing it except me. The guys were cracking up. I was the rookie, so Charlie Hall had set me up to look silly."

Pretty soon those planes that Robinson spotted had gone out to sea. They went far out, but then some of them turned and came up right behind Robinson's formation, causing a commotion. "I could hear all of this static on my radio," says Robinson of the moment. "Sometimes my radio would work and sometimes it wouldn't, but I could hear this scratching and noise. I started looking around and I pulled up. I saw these planes, German planes. Now each of our planes was equipped with an auxiliary tank under its fuselage. You'd fly until it was empty and drop it once it was no good to you. I was still flying on that tank when I pulled up and saw this plane and got ready to shoot. I'd dropped my auxiliary tank, but hadn't immediately switched over to my primary tank. The engine cut out. I said, 'Oh God. This is my first fight and someone is about to shoot me down.' My hands were busy and I hit the tank switch and it caught back up. By that time the Germans were fleeing."

When Robinson turned around, he looked down and most of the remainder of his squadron was headed downward. He noticed that there were about twenty Germans down on what was called the "deck", or right at the tree tops. They had been up about eight thousand feet and the guys were chasing them; they had all dived and left Robinson. "But I spotted one," he said continuing the story. "I looked over to my left, and there was Charlie Hall shooting at a German. He hit him and his plane caught fire, and I yelled 'He got one!' So I picked one out. I was too high up, but I started shooting at him, anyway. Charlie Hall swung around, and it looked as if I shot right through his wing; he didn't say any thing. I thought I had accidentally hit him, but I hadn't. He went down and got that plane. Charlie had two kills on that mission. I saw another plane and I started chasing him. Another fellow by the name of Curtis Smith, whom the guys called 'Smirky' because he always had a smirk on his face, was chasing a plane, too, over at about 11 O' clock, and I was chasing a plane located at about 1 O' clock."

"When you were shooting machine guns in those planes, they would knock ten miles per hour off our speed because they'd recoil significantly since all six fired at the same time. I tried to get close enough to the plane I was chasing to shoot it down. When I finally got close enough and pulled the trigger," says Robinson of his hunt for the kill, "my plane dropped back. I was a little higher than he was, so I had the elevation to dive. I began diving and started gaining on him, and I began to shoot volleys of firc at him again. I saw a large puff of black smoke coming out of his plane and I shouted, 'I got him!' Unfortunately, some of the German planes had water injection which gave them an extra ten to fifteen miles per hour boost. What had happened evidently was that the pilot hit his water injection boosters, the smoke came out, and he took off. By then we were over Rome, and he flew further out over Rome. I don't blame him. If I had been he, I would have flown farther out over Rome, too. I wasn't supposed to go over Rome so I cut back. I wasn't afraid, but I was a little mad. It was my first fight, and I had had an opportunity to get a kill, but it got away."

The enemy plane Robinson usually encountered in battle was the German Messerschmitt ME-109. The ME-109 was the German's best fighter plane at the time, too. It cruised at about 300 miles per hour while a lot of the 99th squadron's planes cruised in the two hundred to 275 miles per hour range. So the

Germans could run away from the 99th whenever they wanted to. The Germans also had the Focke-Wulf, the most common model being the Fw-190 D-9 which had a top speed of over 400 miles per hour; the 99th sometimes encountered it also. It wasn't really a fighter plane, but a light bomber. It had a series of holes in the wings and when it dived, it made terrible noises to frighten everybody on the ground, but it wasn't a fighter. Shortly after, Robinson left Italy around July of 1944 and returned to the States; however, the 99th squadron got faster planes like the P-51 Mustang that were as fast as the German planes. The P-51s were the planes whose 'tails' were eventually painted red because of shortages of paint supplies which resulted in the Tuskegee Airmen being known as "Red Tails." But early on, and while Robinson was flying sorties, the 99th's planes were slower than the Germans'.

On that particular day, which Robinsons believes was January 28, 1944, Charlie Hall shot down two planes, Curtis Smith, Charles Bailey, and Robert Deiz each shot down one. The 99th had good kills that day; they downed four enemy planes for sure - possibly five - without losing any of the eight in their formation. And Robinson adds, "When a pilot is engaged in air battle, he doesn't have a chance to see the whole field. For the most part, he just gets a chance to see what's going on in front of him. The most dramatic thing I saw during all of my air battles was witnessing Charlie Hall shooting down those two planes." The 99th Fighter Squadron and the Tuskegee Airmen were beginning to make quite a name for themselves.

Before pilots headed out on a mission, they would go through a briefing. There would be intelligence briefings and the G-2, who was the intelligence officer, usually told them where they were going, what they were going to see, discuss the weather – and other related matters. Then the pilots would be transported to their planes. "That's when we would begin to feel all alone," Robinson says of the moments just before he took off in his plane for battle.

"The ground crew would transport pilots out to the planes. I'd get off the truck, start walking out to my plane on wobbly knees, and think that I could hardly make it. Then I'd get there and climb in the cockpit. Most times, I would be so nervous I'd have to get out, regroup and get back in. There were twenty-one switches that I had to hit before I could turn the engine on. It was a complicated engine. But I was so accustomed to it that my hands automatically did it; that's why I didn't panic when I failed to first hit my switch to change over to my main fuel tank during my first dogfight. My hand automatically found the switch. It wasn't something I was consciously doing - my hand was checking the switches to see if they were set correctly. The minute I turned the engine on, all the tension went away as if it was a game. I flew more than thirty sorties, but every time I flew, just before I got in the plane, I had the jitters. And every time, just after I turned on the engine, it got my adrenalin going and I had no fear. There was no more tension until the next time I got ready to take off."

And Robinson knows he wasn't the only pilot who felt "butterflies," or anxiety before take-off. He says, "I've asked fellows after we got back to the States about how they felt just prior to a mission. We all had concerns, and before every flight of mine, I had terrible tension before I got into the plane and got it started just like other pilots. I was never afraid during engagements. But on a couple of bombing and strafing missions and several dogfights, I just couldn't see how I was being missed by enemy fire. The bullets would be shot at us in a fire storm of machine gun attacks. They would be coming right past me and not hit me. I never really understood that."

Soon after Robinson's joined his squadron and after his first few engagements and around April of 1944, the 99th became part of the 324th Fighter Group based in Cercola, Italy, under the command of Captain Erwin B. Lawrence. They continued to dive bomb, strafe, and conduct sustained offensive attacks to interrupt enemy supply lines. With three other squadrons of the 324thh Fighter Group, they continued to patrol Anzio.

On July 2, 1944, the 99th Fighter Squadron became a part of the 332nd Fighter Group, an all-black fighter group that was activated at Tuskegee in October of 1942. The 332nd was led by Lieutenant Colonel Benjamin O. Davis, Jr. This group was comprised of four all-black fighter squadrons: the 99th Fighter Squadron, the 100th Fighter Squadron, the 301st Fighter Squadron, and the 302nd Fighter Squadron. They proved to be extraordinarily effective. It was nothing for the Air Corps to send three hundred planes on a mission. Robinson describes: "If one of our units was hooking up with sixty or seventy planes, our other squadrons would be hooking up with other groups of planes of that size, too. So basically there were about three hundred planes involved on missions. Groups of planes would rendezvous at twenty to thirty thousand feet."

Prior to the 332nd beginning the escort of bomber groups, it was common for the Air Corps to lose ten percent of the planes on each mission to enemy fire. That's thirty bombers, and each one of those bombers had a ten or eleven-man crew. "We were losing three hundred or more people on every bomber engagement, and the Air Corps couldn't afford that," Robinson says, revealing why the Tuskegee Airmen became so invaluable.

Pilots from the 332nd Bomber Group put an end to the business of losing bombers during escorts and established a record unparalleled during the war. That bomber escort group never lost a bomber they escorted to enemy fire! Never! "That's because Davis was adamant that we stay with the planes and not let them get attacked. He'd say, 'Don't let the enemy planes make you chase them. Stay with the bombers!' That's why our record was so good," states Robinson proudly.

The need for an operational base for the Tuskegee Airmen increased after the 99th became a part of the 332nd Fighter Group since a lot more men and planes were then involved. The 99th squadron had been flying out of Pisa initially, but the entire bomber group had just established a base in Ramitelli near the site of a huge wheat farm. On the day that he arrived at their new base, Robinson and several other pilots got a long ride on a transport plane to join up with the 332nd at their newly established base. Robinson arrived in Ramitelli after a long day that had started out very early in the morning, and the same thing that had happened back in Gibraltar, happened there.

He and some other pilots were put on a truck, driven out to a huge field, thrown a canvas pack, a hoe and a shovel and told to build a tent. Robinson was with his best friend Leonard Jackson. They had been good friends since their cadet days in primary training together. During cadet training, there would be an hour break each day during which all of the cadets would be together. Leonard Jackson was a graduate of Tuskegee Institute, a jokester who was right at home in Tuskegee; Curtis Robinson was outgoing and loved to tell jokes, also. The two of them would have the cadets cracking-up during breaks as they told jokes. They became best friends and were quite a pair.

The two were tired, and when they received their tools and tents, and Robinson's friend Jackson said, "I'm not cutting down wheat with this hoe. I'm going to burn a clear spot. We use aviation fuel for everything over here - to heat, to cook, for a lot of purposes," to which Robinson replied, "I'm with you." Everything was done with one hundred percent aviation fuel. For heat, the men would dig a hole and pour fuel in it and light a match. It would last for a couple of hours. And they always kept aviation fuel with them, too. Robinson says, "We sprinkled some aviation fuel around in two square areas large enough for two tents and lit a match. As soon as we lit the fuel, the wind came up and the wheat field began burning like mad. The fire was approaching our packs and bags which were lying in the field. We grabbed them, threw them farther away and began to fight the fire. It would approach them again; we'd move them out further and continue fighting the fire. Eventually, I passed out from all the smoke."

When Robinson came to, he was being cared for in what had once been a private hospital about three miles outside of town. It wasn't very large; consequently, he and several other patients ended up living in the basement. There was about half an inch of water on the floor, and planks had been placed on the floor for them to walk on. But it was very damp in those quarters and Robinson stayed down there almost two months and developed a bad chest cold. He reported his condition to his flight surgeon whose specialty, incidentally, was psychiatry. He told the surgeon, "I have a cold." The surgeon replied, "I have a cold, too." Robinson told him, "I want to get rid of mine," to which the surgeon responded, "I want to get rid of mine, too." He offered Robinson some castor oil, an offer that he declined. Robinson headed to see the flight surgeon that had medical oversight for the overall bomber group. The flight surgeon had a staff of doctors and nurses. They examined him and told Robinson that he had pneumonia and needed to go to the hospital right away. They put Robinson in a jeep and sent him to the hospital. After about a week Robinson felt as if he had recovered. The doctors examined him and agreed, but they requested that he return for follow-up.

Robinson revisited his doctors in a couple of days and was cleared. He went back to his living quarters and right back down to the damp basement. And as one might expect, his problems began to recur causing him to go back to the flight surgeon who examined Robinson and sent him to a larger, better equipped hospital this time. While he was at the hospital, he was required to go through a battery of tests as a part of his re-evaluation. During his testing and examinations, the doctors discovered he had elevated hypertension. Faced with his newly discovered medical problems, the Army Air Corps decided to send him home.

The Flight Instructor

From May of 1943 through May of 1944, the 99th Fighter Squadron had been on the move. First they were stationed in Tunisia attached to the 33rd Fighter Group. While flying with the 33rd in June of 1943, several pilots from the 99th made history when they became the first black American pilots to fly in air battles for the United States. Next they were based in El Haouria on Cape Bon in June 1943, as a part of the 324th Fighter Group, and near Salerno in September as part of the 79th Fighter Group. Then they were on to Pisa and in May to Ramitelli where they were added as the fourth squadron of the 332nd Fighter Group. Robinson had joined the squadron just as it was waging air battles and scoring kills and just as it joined the 332nd. He had flown thirty-three sorties. In addition to Anzio, he participated in the bombing of Monte Cassino. He was temporarily taken off of flying duty and put on light duty until his hypertension subsided. Now he was headed home. The Army Air Corps took him to Naples and put him on a ship headed back to the States.

The return trip home for Robinson was taken aboard a

hospital ship. It was full of troops and had hundreds of officers aboard. There were very few black officers in the military at that time, and he was the only black officer on the ship. Primarily for that reason, Robinson sensed that it was going to be a very interesting voyage, and he suspected it might even be a lot of fun, some of which he dared not laugh aloud about.

To help pass the time, Robinson started playing poker regularly with a group of Army officers. One of the players was a big guy from Texas, who had gone to Texas A&M and had played on the Longhorn football team. He was about 6' 2 and weighed about 270 pounds. "We'd be playing draw poker, and when it got to him," Robinson says, "he would say, 'This white man bets so and so and so,' or 'This white man passes,' as if he were the only white guy there, but everyone else was also white except me. At every opportunity where he could work it in he would say. This white man this," or 'This white man that' emphasizing this fact in my presence every time we played. He wasn't joking. He clearly had an attitude, but it didn't bother me, and I didn't bother to look up when he said it. He was an officer, too! I must say, though, that for the most part, the whites that I encountered on board followed protocol and were respectful."

In some respects Robinson's medical attention during the trip offset any negative situations he encountered aboard ship. One of the nurses always treated him special. "Hey Robinson, do you want me to rub your back," his evening shift nurse would ask as she made her rounds. "Of course I'd say, yes, and turn over on my stomach," he says chuckling about it. "She would position herself on my back appropriately for giving a back rub, and rub my back. The other guys would say, 'Hey! I need a back rub, can't you give me a back rub?' and she'd say, 'Ah, go on, go on,' and she'd move on and not give backrubs to anybody else. She was a pretty white nurse from Boston.

She'd come in every afternoon with her line, 'Hey Robinson, do you want me to rub your back?' and I just went along She did it for a while, and that used to burn the white guys up. I didn't particularly have to have a back rub, but I enjoyed it. I also cooperated because I liked the reaction of the other officers and managed to have some playful fun like that."

The trip home took about three weeks, longer than usual because the ship was caught in bad weather. Everyone had to eat dry rations since the ship's staff couldn't cook. Most of the sick had to be strapped into their beds or the thrashing of the ship would have thrown them out. The ship weathered that storm for three or four days. It was supposed to have come to port in Tidewater, Virginia, but instead, ended up docking in Charleston, S.C. The nurse was really serious, Robinson discovered. "After we docked," he shares, "she came up to me and said, 'Robinson, I want you to take me out to lunch.' I said, 'No, we can't go out together down here.'" She thought Robinson was kidding since nobody on the ship had made a big deal of their friendliness. He explained to her, "We're not in Boston. This is Charleston, S.C. That wouldn't be a wise thing to do here; we can't go to lunch together." She was a beautiful woman, but in those days, no black man would dare to be seen in public with a white woman in Charleston, South Carolina, unless he wanted to put his life in danger. It was very regrettable that. I had to turn down her invitation; she was very nice, quite appealing, and desirable, but off-limits considering the circumstances. I took a train from Charleston to a military hospital in Oteen, N.C., near Asheville and stayed there until I recuperated. This was the latter part of June 1944, and I stayed until July."

After recuperating, Robinson was assigned back to Tuskegee Army Air Field. When he arrived, there were also nine other pilots who had returned from overseas there, too.

The Army Air Corps wanted to make flight instructors out of them. The only instructor school that the Air Corps had in the United States was in San Antonio, Texas, at Randolph Field, so the group of pilots was sent there for training to become flight instructors. The Air Corps allowed them ten days to get out there, and says Robinson when comparing this trip to his trip to Chehaw as a new cadet, "I traveled to Randolph Field by train, a Pullman, like I had when I went to Tuskegee as a new cadet. I rode in the Pullman, I ate in the Pullman, and I took advantage of every amenity, so I had a really pleasant trip. We stopped in Mobile, Alabama, with one of my friends. His father was a dentist who had acquired a lot of property there and had a nice summer home. We stayed there in Mobile for three days and then went on to New Orleans and spent another five days there before heading on to Randolph Field."

When Robinson and his companions arrived at Randolph Field, they were housed in the same building with all the other student instructors who had arrived, but the Tuskegee Airmen were the only black instructor students. They ate with the white instructor students and everything was fine. All the pilots went through orientation their very first day, and there the general in command of the base addressed them. He said that the only thing that the student instructors couldn't do was to use the officers' club on base. That club was for the officers who were stationed at the field permanently, and pilots there for instructor training were considered instructor trainees, not permanently stationed officers. This rule pertained to the white officers in the group, also. The Air Corps had an officers' club located in one of the hotels in downtown San Antonio for people who were transients, those just passing through. The base commander said that they were all free to use it whenever they wanted.

"It was a Friday evening, and we had been in San

Antonio all week and had seen just about all the clubs except the officer's club," says Robinson, meaning they had visited practically all of the black clubs. "Now Texas is as southern as any southern state can be," he continues, "and San Antonio is as southern as any town can be. I wasn't about to go into downtown San Antonio to that officers' club, which was located in a white, racially segregated establishment. It was a five-week training course, so I felt like we didn't really need to go to the officers' club. But the following Wednesday, one of the fellows from California decided he would try the officers' club downtown, the one in a segregated hotel. He went there, and when he came back, he reported that there was nothing going on and no one was there except a bartender, one or two guys, and a slot machine. He said that was the only activity there, so he left."

The following morning, however, the base commander called only the Tuskegee Airmen together for a meeting, and asked them, "How are you boys getting along?" They said they were fine. He asked, "Would you like to have separate quarters?" They told him that they didn't, that their living quarters were fine. "What about mess hall? Do you want to eat in a separate mess hall, a separate table, or at a different time? Do you want a place of your own to eat?" he asked. The black pilots told him they were fine, and he dismissed them. But by the time they got back to their room and changed clothes, they received orders by telegram from Washington to move that day and go back to Tuskegee. The telegram stated, "You will leave San Antonio this day and return to Tuskegee." Needless to say, Curtis Robinson didn't complete his instructor training at Randolph Field.

Most likely the move was a punitive act on the part of the military, or it could have been protective. Tuskegee Airmen had encountered situations in the past in which their lives were in jeopardy for having angered local whites. In April of 1942, Colonel Noel Parrish, commander of Tuskegee Army Air Field, was forced to gather a group of white soldiers and go into town to retrieve black airmen - military police and their prisoner - from a local sheriff, the state police, and armed local white men holding them as prisoners. The reason was that black military policemen had taken a prisoner from a local policeman forcefully, and the collective forces of the state and local law enforcement community, and local vigilantes confronted and cornered them, and they had to be rescued. There were enough other instances of threats and assaults against the men for them and the military to seriously fear the repercussions of a black officer having gone into town to the hotel and possible backlash. Whatever the reason might been, the Tuskegee Airmen left town.

Of the incident Robinson stated, "I think we were ordered back to Tuskegee so abruptly because our guy had gone into that officers' club in the hotel in town. We really weren't welcome there. We had also expressed a preference for not being segregated on a base that, up until then, had been segregated, and that didn't help either. If we had stated a desire for separate quarters and stayed out of town, I'm sure everything would have been all right. And until then, I didn't know that the Air Force issued orders by telegram, but we all got the same order, and they told us to leave San Antonio for Tuskegee almost immediately. So the military decided to form a school there at Tuskegee for the purpose of training black flight instructors. I attended the first black instructor training at Tuskegee as a result of that, and upon graduation I became a flight instructor."

After graduating he was assigned to teach basic flying courses. They had gotten better planes at Tuskegee Army Air Field since Robinson had been a cadet. Tuskegee Army Air field was now using the same plane that Robinson had trained on in advanced training, the AT-6, for basic flight training. As the instructor, he sat up front and had use of all the instruments and had to be proficient in their use. Cadets used just three instruments because instructors blacked-out all the others, cadets had to learn to fly without them; they had use of a tachometer so they could see how fast the engine was going, an altimeter to see how high they were, and a turning bar to see if they were coordinating. If students weren't flying correctly, the instructor would let them know.

During basic flying his students received about 70 hours of training over a nine week period. It expanded the skills of cadets who had completed primary training, in basic they would be taught how to fly at night using instruments, how to navigate in bad weather, cross country flying, etc. Therefore, instructors had to be experienced in flying under those circumstances, and students were soon taking instruments courses related to those areas. Primary among them were instruments used as navigational tools.

The navigation solution for flying in bad weather at that time was a system that utilized signals sent from a station that were transmitted in four directions, three directions, or whatever, towards another station, another city, or a certain air field. If a pilot's aircraft were to the left of the signal, he heard a "da dit," and if he were to the right he heard "dit da." But when the aircraft was directly aligned on the signal the two sounds would come together and the pilot would hear one constant sound like "duhhhh." Then he would know that he was on the navigational beam. Even if he was on the beam and got off, he could determine what side he was drifting towards because of the sound and then correct his course. "It was not a very good system," is Robinson's present assessment, "but it was the best system we had then." That's the way they flew with instruments when Robinson was teaching basic flying; that system has long since been replaced.

In the next system used for night flight, the Air Corps positioned rotating lights along the ground every fifteen or twenty miles to assist pilots. The lights, though they rotated, would appear to be flashing and would be located in fields along the flight path. There were signals embedded in these lights; they might be alphabets or what-have-you and pilots could refer to a map, cross-reference the embedded signal against the map, and determine where they were. The air force has long ago gotten rid of that system, too, but those were the aviation developments on the scene during Robinson's flight instructor stint.

Robinson is still proud to say, "I never washed anybody out. In fact, I saved some guys. On a couple of occasions an instructor would tell me that they had a student at risk of washing-out and would ask me if I would fly with them and help them improve their flying. As I recall, I pulled them all through."

Best of all, as flying instructors, Robinson and his peers could borrow military planes on the weekend and fly to anywhere in the country they wanted to go. "That was sweet duty, really sweet duty!" says Robinson of that particular fringe benefit. "I was 25 years old, and I would take out a training plane for use as my personal transportation on the weekend. I would try to schedule all of my cadet's Friday flights in the morning, and when they were all done, I could get a plane, take off and would not be due back until Monday morning. Wherever that plane could take me, I could go, and I could stop and get fuel at any Army installation. I could cover a lot of territory and I did. My destinations mostly were Detroit or Nashville where some classmates of mine resided. I also went to Washington, D.C., several times since Florie was there.

Some of the instructors would fly out to Kansas City and other places in the Midwest. They'd have to spend most of their time off flying, but they would go, anyway."

On one of his junkets, the dean of South Carolina State almost got him killed. He let Robinson borrow his car, which didn't have any brakes. Robinson was driving near a railroad crossing, and a train was coming. He put on the brakes, but nothing happened. Robinson thought he was going to tear up the car for sure and possibly himself, but fate was on his side and he made it through.

Occasionally he would take a fellow pilot with him. "I was allowed to fly military personnel, my airmen buddies, but not civilians, and we would have a ball," is how Robinson spoke of those trips. "I took one fellow home with me which I came to regret later. I had no knowledge of it, but he was going with a girl at South Carolina State, and they were supposed to get married and had even planned a wedding. Her father was an instructor there, and she lived with him on campus, but she had already graduated from there. I had taken this fellow home several times. But on their wedding day, he left her standing at the altar because he was already married. I regretted that, but I really had no idea that he was married and would trick her like that."

Curtis Robinson married Florie Frederick while he was a flight instructor. They moved into a community that was a brand new development called Carter Village. The homes in that community were affordable homes that cost around three or four thousand dollars in 1944, which was very cheap, cheaper than paying rent. There were about fifty homes in that community, and everyone knew everyone else. Robinson said of those times: "Those of us who were married and living in Tuskegee began living very charmed lives. We'd go in to work together, have parties on the weekend, and would go to the officers club together in between. We had a wonderful time. I worked as a flight instructor and we lived there until the military closed Tuskegee Army Air Field. I still have friends there from those days. Many others have died, and every once in a while someone will tell me about the passing of someone else who lived there. After Tuskegee was closed in 1946, I was sent to Lockbourne Air Force Base in Ohio. By then, the war was over."

Of the 932 pilots trained at Tuskegee Army Air Field, 450 served overseas. Other Tuskegee Airmen had been returning from overseas details and were receiving various assignments. Some of the returning airmen were made instructors – between fifteen and twenty of them - some went to other bomber groups, and some went to fighter squadrons. This soon resulted in numerous problems for those men. An all-black bombardment group, the 477th which was comprised of pilots and ground support, was formed in mid 1943 and de-activated two months after it was formed only to be re-activated in January 1944. Prior to its formation, the Army Air Corps issued a report in response to the proposal for its establishment that stated in part: "It is common knowledge that the colored race does not have the technical nor the flying background for the creation of a bombardment-type unit."

Bomber group operations required more men and equipment and were expensive, much more expensive than fighter squadrons or bomber escorts, and that doomed them. The group never made it into battle during the war because the War Department didn't want black pilots commanding bombers because of the associated expense and the traditional mindset of some of its leadership; they didn't want to trust that level of investments to blacks. The 477th was meant to be a failure like the War Department had hoped the 99th Fighter Squadron and "Tuskegee Experience" would be.

Although the War Department denied it, the 477th was moved about in a manner that seemed punitive and continuously disruptive; they moved around more than the 99th. In fact, between May 1944 and June 1945, the 477th Bombardment Group was forced to make thirty-eight unit moves. The War Department kept moving them in an effort to undermine their morale. After being re-activated in 1944, the 477th was based in Selfridge, Michigan. Several other sites were also used: Eglin Field in Florida for gunnery, Hondo Field in Texas for navigation, and other bases in Texas and New Mexico for bombardment. The original commander of the 477th, Colonel Robert Selway, Jr., was a segregationist and deemed by the men to be a racist of the worst kind. He wanted Selfridge Field segregated and issued orders to bring that about. All black and white officers did not cooperate, resulting in the occurrence of some integration. Consequently, the black officers there were sent to Godman Field in Kentucky where segregation was the norm and the facility as decrepit as any on the planet.

On March 15, 1945, the 477 Bomber Group was moved to Seymour, Indiana. Some grocery stores in the area refused to sell food to the new black military men and their families; the local laundry refused to launder their clothes - this was particularly infuriating since the community had willingly accommodated German prisoners-of-war and cheerfully laundered their clothes when they were held there. Robinson's recollection of the events follows: "The Air Corps was training two squadrons of bomber pilots initially for duty in the Pacific at that time. That's what precipitated a situation which ended up with a group of Tuskegee pilots being accused of "mutiny" by the Air Force. The Air Corps had this problem with a group assigned to a squadron, the 477th Combat Training Squadron. The Training Squadron kept trying to segregate the black pilots and keep them out of the officers' club; only white officers could use the officers' club. Many guys insisted on being allowed to go to the base club, and base officials responded by getting the MPs (Military Police) to put them out and ordered the chief of the MPs, who was a major, to stand at the door. But the guys came back insisted on getting in, and they were arrested one at a time until a total of 101 black pilots were arrested and charged with mutiny.

The black officers first had problems over this issue – segregation and discrimination - at Goodman Field in Kentucky where officers were classified and buildings were given designations in a manner so as to racially discriminate against black pilots. Then they moved the pilots to Freeman Field in Indiana where they also faced discrimination and other bad treatment. The men stood up for their rights, and the Army Air Corps accused many of them of mutiny. One of the Tuskegee Airmen, William Coleman, Jr., who was a lawyer and who later became the secretary of transportation under Gerald Ford, was advising the guys and got the NAACP involved. The situation created a big uproar and got the attention of the War Department officials in Washington, D.C. No one knew what to do about it. Congressman Adam Clayton Powell, Senator Scott W. Lucas, and others also got involved.

Around June of 1945, Colonel Davis returned from overseas and was soon assigned as the commander of the 477th Composite Group, replacing Colonel Selway, who was removed for having violated military policy. A court martial was held, and two of the guys were found guilty for resisting efforts to put them out of the officers' club by the MP Commander, who, since he was a major and had a higher rank than they did, allowed the Army Air Corps to accuse the black pilots of disobeying orders. A third guy was found guilty of assault on a superior after he attempted to maneuver around the major stationed at the door. Years later, President Clinton pardoned those guys in 2000 during his last year in office. But they went many years with that on their records."

The 477th Composite Group was moved to Lockbourne Air Base in Ohio in March of 1946, and later the 332nd was moved there, too. They were all under the command of Colonel Davis. Robinson was transferred there with the 332nd and became a technical base inspector. His official title was Acting Base Technical Inspector. And he says, "That's what I was doing at the time of my discharge in 1947."

The 99th Fighter Squadron, the 100th Squadron, the 301st fighter Squadron, the 302nd Fighter Squadron - collectively the 332nd Bomber Group - flew 200 bomber escort missions and never lost to enemy fire, a bomber they escorted, never! They flew 1,578 missions, 15,553 sorties, damaged or destroyed over 400 enemy aircraft, 40 barges and boats, 619 box cars and other rolling stock, 23 buildings and factories, one destroyer – a feat almost unheard of - 87 motor transports, 5 power transformers, 126 locomotives and miscellaneous dumps and transformers. Quite a feat for a group of men deemed "unfit" to serve in the United States of America's Air Force!

PART 3

POST WORLD WAR II

Welcome to Washington, D.C.

"Florie didn't want to go back to South Carolina after I got out of the service," is how Robinson described the key consideration for their decision to relocate, "so we stayed in Washington, D.C. I had thought about going back to Orangeburg and resuming teaching but soon dismissed that idea. I had an aunt who had lived in Washington for as long as I had known her, who retired from the Bureau of Engraving in the 1930s. I also had a cousin who was a high school principal here. Florie's sisters were living here, too. With us both having family members here, and her having spent some time here already, staying in Washington, D.C. was an easy decision to make."

Post World War II Washington, D.C., was a vibrant and expanding city. Fueled by the federal government and the war effort, its population ballooned from 487,000 in the early 1930s to 663,000 in 1940 and 802,000 by the end of the 1940s - the largest population Washington has ever had. Diverse neighborhoods provided a large variety of choices of location, ethnicity and housing costs. And there was much construction going on. New construction was occurring in the Anacostia area, and right after the war, beautiful colonial homes were being built in new suburban-like areas of the city, including areas east of the Anacostia River on some of the city's highest peaks. Post-World War II modernist architecture also started to appear downtown beginning the transformation of the city's character from a southern town to a major metropolitan area.

Much of the growth in the city's population during the late 1930s and the 1940s was fueled by the migration of blacks from the deep-South to Washington, D.C. More than half of the blacks migrating to Washington during this period were from Virginia, North Carolina, and South Carolina where harsh conditions created by the black codes and Jim Crow had become even harsher after the Great Depression. By 1940, in Washington, D.C., blacks numbered approximately 187,000, by 1950 approximately 281,000 and approximately 412,000 by 1960 – then 71 percent of the population. Between 1930 and the end of the 1950s, Washington, D.C. lost 300,000 whites and gained 300,000 blacks. Many neighborhoods and schools were segregated during that time. Virtually all-black Anacostia of today was almost all-white in 1947 except for small sections, but there were some neighborhoods in the Capitol Hill area of the city in the 1950s where communities were somewhat integrated – white and black children played together and black and white adults conversed. But mixing of races did not occur in public places or as a matter of public access, nor were blacks allowed to try on clothing in many of the major department stores downtown. And of course all of the movie theatres and all of the eating places in town were segregated.

The social conventions of post World War II Washington, D.C., and surrounding areas meant that it was routine for Robinson to encounter discrimination in the area upon settling in his new city. He recounted an instance of segregation in the outlying areas of the city that he was not aware of before he got out of service. "The streetcars in Washington, D.C., were not segregated," he began. "Blacks could also ride buses any place in D.C. and Maryland without being segregated. However, the buses going into Alexandria and Arlington, Virginia, were segregated. Blacks would get on the bus in Washington and sit up front, but as soon as the bus crossed the 14th Street Bridge into Virginia, they were required to get up and move to the rear of the bus. I didn't know that the first time I got on a bus in D.C. and sat up front for a trip into Virginia. When we crossed the bridge, I was surprised when one of the white passengers approached me and told me that I had to move to the back. I still had on my military uniform so the bus driver said, "No, he's O.K." I got a break because of my uniform. All of the area's street car operators and bus drivers were white, too."

But still, for a young couple like the Robinsons, practically newlyweds, a move to Washington, D.C., in 1947 marked a promising new beginning. The city had a progressive black middle class and black high schools like Dunbar and Armstrong were then among the best in the country. The Shaw Street area was brisk with black entertainment, businesses, and vibrancy reminiscent of the Harlem Renaissance. Compared to South Carolina, Washington provided more career opportunities and a better social climate. For a young, black, attractive, college-educated couple like Curtis and Florie Robinson, post-WW II Washington, D.C., appeared to be an appealing place to raise a family and a promising place to live.

Fresh out of the Air Corps after the end of the war, the first order of business for Robinson was trying to find a job. With all the training and experience he had in flying and his great love for it, a career in aviation seemed like the natural place to begin his search. He and a friend, another former

Tuskegee pilot, Clinton Mills, whom the guys called "Bo," went over to National Airport to Eastern Airlines to see if they could get jobs as airline pilots. "Eastern wouldn't even give us an employment application," Robinson says of their effort. "After talking with a receptionist, we were taken to another person who informed us that Eastern Airlines didn't give out applications to blacks - even highly skilled fighter pilots, former flight instructors, or former Army Air Corp pilots - and that was the case with other airlines, as well, regardless of their qualifications."

"So that was the end of flying as a career for me. I returned home after the disappointing visit to Eastern and just lay around on the sofa for about two weeks feeling very down. Soon Florie got mad and said, 'No, you can't do this! When are you going to get up and start doing some work?' Florie could be difficult, and she would get mad in a minute. So I resumed my search and soon found a job. It was with the NSA, the National Security Agency."

Robinson began his career as a government employee in 1947 as a GS-1 grade. The way it worked was that lower grades were the lower paying and non-supervisory positions, still the case today. In the federal government of that time, Robinson knew of virtually no blacks above GS-8 or GS-9. He knew of one who was a GS-11, but most blacks were in grades GS-2, 3, or 4. Even with college graduates it didn't make a difference; GS-3 or GS-4 was as high as black federal government employees could generally expect to advance.

His new job was an interesting enough position, Robinson thought, but he didn't like the setup. Within the agency, an all-black unit had just been formed with fifty or sixty people in it working two shifts. Almost all of them were college graduates. The U.S. had radio taps all over Russia intercepting signals from Russian agents. Employees in Robinson's unit reviewed the tapes which held information received via the taps; they came in on little spools like ticker tape. The employees in his group would pull out the tape in order to read the data printed on them and were responsible for transferring the characters from theses spools to paper pages. The NSA had trained them to identify information and patterns they should keep, as well as what to discard.

The Agency had a machine that helped Robinson's unit process those tapes. The operator would sit with the spool in his hand and slip it on to the machine and let it roll until he saw something he thought he should transfer. Robinson came up with a faster method that he describes: "I took a small can and cut out a side so the tape would come through without the operator having to slip it through, and it got to the point where I could process two tapes at the same time. The supervisor found out what I was doing because of my speed and said, 'Oh, no, you can't do it that way. It goes against our procedures.' They got on me for improving efficiency."

That kind of bureaucratic mentality was one reason Robinson soon left the government. The other reason was that he realized he wasn't going to go anywhere stuck in an all-black unit like that. The NSA was then a new agency, the Cold War was getting hot, and the government needed educated people to do that work. "What got my crow," according to Robinson, "was that they put in these high school graduates as our supervisors and assistant supervisors which meant none of the black guys could get a raise until the supervisor and assistant supervisors got raises; so we were locked in. A lot of us were college graduates and former military officers. Our supervisors were young white high school graduates, unaccomplished fellows. I tried to get a raise but my request was denied, so I decided I had to get out of that place. It was run like an old plantation and was fouled up with racism."

These were also painful years for both Curtis and Florie Robinson. They had a sick baby daughter, Linda, who had been born with a heart condition caused by inadequate oxygenation of her blood; the condition was called "Blue Baby.[viii]" She'd be up at night trying to breathe, Florie would be up at night with her, and Robinson would be up at night trying to comfort them both. Linda was in and out of the hospital continuously, and often the Robinsons would have to rush her back and forth to the hospital at anytime – day or night. On most visits they would take her in and the doctors couldn't do anything for her except give her oxygen, so eventually the Robinsons purchased an oxygen tank for their home. The hospital and doctor bills kept piling up, and Robinson had to really work! There were no health care and medical support services like today. Linda's situation was very grave and until she was two and a half years old, she couldn't sit up. They would prop her up, but she couldn't sit up by herself, and she couldn't stand up.

Robinson used to buy medicine for her condition. The medicine didn't cost much, but the pharmacist was very inconsistent as to what he would charge. Sometimes the cost of the same medication would vary by fifteen or twenty percent from one purchase to the next, which was a significant amount of fluctuation. It seemed to Robinson that there must have been a big profit margin in there. He thought about that for a while, and then a classmate of his from college, Roscoe Deveaux, came by to visit Robinson and to see his daughter. Deveaux was an independent pharmacist. He let his friend review his books, and after seeing them, Robinson decided that it looked like something he could do, especially with his chemistry undergraduate degree and background.

His assessment of this potential opportunity was just part of the reason that Robinson left the government and went into pharmacy. "I knew that I had to get out of the NSA," Robinson recounts. "Actually, several of us left NSA and pursued better professional careers. Shirley Clinton, one of the Tuskegee Airmen charged in the mutiny, and Glen Guy went to medical school and became doctors. My squadron mate, who was a linguist and spoke Italian and did our translations while we were in Sicily, went back to school, studied Russian, and went back to NSA at a higher grade, but many of the guys stayed there for years. The work was interesting enough and I liked it, but the work environment was what got me out of the government and into pharmacy. I applied to and was accepted into Howard University's School of Pharmacy in 1948. I gave up my job at the NSA and went to school under the G.I. Bill of Rights. [ix] Since I had five years of military service, I was allowed five full years of educational financial assistance."

Although Robinson was going to Howard University on the G.I. Bill of Rights, the payment that it provided wasn't sufficient to cover his living expenses as a family man. The G.I. Bill paid his tuition, which was about $125 per month and covered the cost of his books. He was also buying a house and the mortgage was about $75 per month. He was able to buy an apartment with the G.I. Bill, too. Some veterans bought houses with it, other veterans started businesses with it. It was a great help to all soldiers. Of the G.I. Bill Robinson says, "Everybody talks about affirmative action these days. I think the G.I. Bill was the greatest affirmative action ever."

In order to make ends meet financially while he was at Howard University, Robinson decided to get a summer job at the GAO (Government Accounting Office) to earn extra money. He went down to their office, filled out an application, and took an examination on which he scored 100. It was a simple test for a messenger job. They hired him and put him in a room with eight or ten other guys, all white. There was a guy who was in charge. He came to Robinson during his first week of employment and told him to go up to the fourth floor to see a particular secretary. "I went up there and told the secretary that my supervisor had sent me there to see her," Robinson says. "I gave her his message. She handed me an out-basket, some money, a list and said, "We're going to send you to go get some coffee." I told her, "You don't understand. My supervisor sent me up here to get a message to take someplace. I don't deliver coffee." She said, "That's fine," and sent me back down stairs. I didn't think anymore of it; I thought they had made a mistake. What I didn't know was that fetching coffee for white employees at that time was part of what black messengers were expected to do. The next day the GAO created a new job for me."

In his next federal government job, Robinson provided support to about fifty or sixty accountants; they were also all white. He was located in a big office with them, and in his new job, he would receive a stack of papers from the chief in the morning and pass them out to all of the accountants – that's what they worked on everyday. Then, for the rest of the day, Robinson would sit and do nothing. Late in the afternoon, he would recollect all those papers, put them in a stack, and deliver them to the chief so that he could lock them up. That's what he did all that summer in 1949 or 1950; he handed out papers in the morning and collected them in the afternoon on his second federal government job.

"My government job at the GAO wasn't appealing at all," assesses Robinson. "Besides teaching, my trade was painting, so that's what I decided to do. I didn't say anything to anybody about my plans. I just got a couple of my friends and landed some painting jobs; I was able to generate enough work to keep them busy and I kept myself busy. Since I was in school and taking a full load, and because I knew I had to work also, I would study very hard in the first part of the semester and learn everything that I could. Then, later in the semester, I would take time off and do more work, stay out on painting jobs later, and study less. If you looked at my record, you would see that I made A's on almost all of my tests and exams in the beginning of each semester. I figured I wouldn't fail, but near the end of the semester I got a lot of Cs."

By the time he started pharmacy school at Howard University, Robinson already had a chemistry degree from Claflin College which was a help in getting through pharmacy school – recognizing drugs and recognizing how drugs could be combined to change products. In addition he had been a school teacher, he had successfully completed Tuskegee's rigorous pilot training program, had been a flight instructor, an Army Air Corps technical base inspector, and was confident that mentally he was capable of handling most anything you could throw at him. He was well organized, took good notes, and also knew exactly where specific information could be located within them. Robinson never flunked any tests or courses, but his grades suffered. "It got so bad that from time to time the dean would call me into his office," he states "and say, 'Robinson, look at these grades; you can do better than this,' and I would tell him that I had to spend quite a bit of time working. He'd say, 'You can't afford to go to school and work at the same time. You've got to do one or the other.' And I'd tell him I couldn't do that. I had to do both. I was motivated; I didn't want to go back to the government and be a Grade 1. Honestly, I was barely making it, but I had no other choice."

For a while when he was working for the government in the Government Accounting Office, there was a merchant on Georgia Avenue who had a chain of street vendor outlets and a little store where he made lotions, creams, cosmetics and the like. Robinson went to see him and asked for a supply of products for himself, some of which he could sell on his job or through contacts made via co-workers. The merchant gave Robinson a supply on consignment (a dozen of this and dozen of that) for which he didn't have to advance any up-front funds. "They sold like hot cakes," says Robinson of the new products. "People liked them and kept buying them; that was a help with our household expenses. But painting made more money than those things so eventually I stuck with that. I really worked hard at Howard, not like I did in college at Claflin. I knew I had to make it. I knew I had to keep my daughter going. My wife couldn't work because she had to be home to take care of Linda. It was all on me, so I really worked very long hours."

Robinson took painting jobs for several residential customers in an upscale neighborhood right off of upper Georgia Avenue in Washington, D.C. When he headed to work in the morning, he would put his drop cloth in a big paint pail with his brush, take his small step ladder, get on the bus with passengers eyeing him curiously, and head to work. He would walk the remaining three or four blocks from his bus stop to his customers.

One such customer happened to be the manager of Roesler's Furniture Store – a very popular store in the area at that time. He went to his house and painted it for him. The gentleman liked Robinson's work so much that he hired him to work in the furniture store where Roesler's had two interior decorators working. When the store sold a piece of furniture, they suggested what the rooms and walls should look like to accent it, and they would have Robinson do the painting. Needless to say, he was a steady painter as a result of business generated through the store; he had constant work that way. In fact he had to hire more help.

For one of his most memorable jobs he says, "I was referred to a Jewish couple on upper Fourteenth Street in

Northwest Washington through the furniture company; I believe they were French, too. They wanted me to paint the whole first floor of their house. They had wall paper in the vestibule, the dining room, and the living room that they wanted taken off and the walls painted. Well, when I went over and evaluated the job, I tested the wallpaper with plain water applied directly to the paper, and it came off easily. I tested another area, and the paper came right off quickly there, too. So I got my friend, who had also been a Tuskegee fighter pilot and was enrolled at Catholic University pursuing a master's degree in microbiology, to help me. I had the business, he had the car, and we took the job. The two of us went up to the couple's home one Friday afternoon. We got started, took out our bucket of water and our brushes so that we could soak the paper and peel it off. But lo and behold, the paper would not come off. Regardless of how hard we tried, it would not come off. So we went out and got some commercial paper remover and put that on it. That didn't remove the paper, either."

"We had arranged scaffolding all over this couple's house. The two of us worked on this project all Friday and Saturday and were struggling so much with the paper that I finally rented a steamer to steam off the wallpaper. I had to plug it in, put water in it, and place the 12" square surface of the steamer against the wallpaper. The machine would emit steam which soaked into the wallpaper, and my partner would immediately follow behind me and remove it. Then we would move to another area, do another square, and repeat the process. We were so late getting started with the steamer that we worked until midnight on Sunday. We got almost all of it off, but we were tired and just did not have the energy to finish the job. The next week was finals week for both of us. So we put everything down and left."

"When we went back that next Friday to finish the job,

the lady of the house met us at the door and was furious! She verbally jumped on us; she was fussing and really laying us out. We started backing away from the door, but after her few initial outbursts, she cooled off and allowed us to finish the job. But she sure gave us a piece of her mind before she did. She didn't appreciate the way we had left her house messed up all week, but we certainly hadn't thought it would take that long to strip the old wallpaper. We lost money on the job, too, not just because the job had taken longer than we'd expected, but because I had to pay for the steamer which I had not anticipated. We lost almost the entire week. The job paid about $150, and the steam machine alone cost $40 to rent."

Curtis Robinson graduated from Howard University's School of Pharmacy in 1952 and within the next few months became part-owner of his first pharmacy on Alabama Avenue in Southeast Washington. Before buying the pharmacy, he had been working part-time at Professional Pharmacy on Georgia Avenue while he was still in school during his last year. He heard about the Alabama Avenue pharmacy through his friend, Billy Sumler, who had just graduated with him from Howard and had also gotten a job at Professional as a pharmacist shortly after he did. The two of them went over to the pharmacy to check it out.

It was a fairly large store, well stocked, complete with a soda fountain, and owned and run by a non-pharmacist. The fellow who owned it didn't have a degree or license in pharmacy but had been working around pharmacies all his life. He had a blind pharmacist there, who held a valid license which he had gotten before he became blind. He was just there sitting in the back of the store, and it appeared that the owner did all the work. "I don't know how they actually operated since I was there only a few times, and they weren't filling prescriptions during those visits," says Robinson of his knowledge of the odd setup. "The owner wanted $4,000 for the store. I had $2,000, Sumler scraped together his money, and we bought it."

Their plan to buy the store brought about the only time that Robinson has ever been fired from a job. While at Professional, his boss came to him and said that he had heard a rumor that Robinson was going around town looking for a pharmacy, and Robinson told him that it was true, he was. To which his boss said, "Well you're fired; I can't support my competition." That made Robinson's decision to buy his first pharmacy one he felt even better about. "I was excited about opening a pharmacy business," is how Robinson describes it. "Given the way things were in those days, pharmacy jobs were hard to come by, and I had just gotten fired. People's Drug Store, now known as CVS, didn't hire black pharmacists then, and they were one of the major chains and very prominent in this area. They hired their first black pharmacist soon after I graduated, but it would be two years before they hired another one. So opening my own pharmacy turned out to be the best career alternative for me."

Almost all of the other pharmacies in town were independents, and there was a pharmacy on virtually every corner in the city. The one Robinson and Sumler opened on Alabama Avenue happened to be a pretty big pharmacy compared to most. Their rent was high, but they thought they could make it. As they operated the first few months, however, they were tittering right on the edge. They didn't have any operating funds when they first started out having used all the money that they had to buy the place. They had no back-up source of money, no "rainy-day" funds, no reserves, nothing, and really struggled for a while

The two partners came up with clever ideas for generating more revenue using what they had learned in pharmacy school plus practices in use in the industry at that time. When Robinson started to learn pharmacy in the late 1940s in Howard University's School of Pharmacy, there was a pharmacology course he studied which was in part the study of roots, twigs, leaves and of herbs used in the field of pharmacy. Pharmacists had to be able to recognize and sometimes use some of them. They would sometimes use them to make whatever medication was called for in a prescription in whatever manner required, and in the amounts the doctors requested sometimes via a process the industry called "compounding."

That was also a time when pharmacists made their own pills and capsules, suppositories and powders, such as Stanback and BC; the state of the art truly was that of apothecary. Those medicines were extremely important and in high demand, but they were very time-consuming to produce. Insights gained practicing the art of compounding and the production of medications meant that pharmacist would also sometimes offer customers their own custom remedies for minor things like colds. Of this practice, Robinson comments: "I laugh about one particular incident involving my former partner and me to increase our revenue. He and I made two gallons of a cough syrup, but we didn't label it nor keep a record of what we had put into it by content. People came in asking for a good cough medicine, and we would prepare four ounces of it and sell it for a dollar. Everybody liked it. Customers responded as if it was the best cold medicine around. Eventually we ran out, and customers asked for more, but we couldn't remember exactly how we had made it, and since we had no record, our secret formula on such a good seller was lost, as well as our product."

A few months after they had been operating, Robinson's partner Sumler got married. They still were struggling as new businessmen. A few months after Sumler's marriage, his partner's new wife told him he wasn't making enough money and that he needed to get another job. By then Sumler was able to get a job with People's Drugs, and he sold out to Robinson.

The partners had been doing about $9,000 per month in business at that store, which was good money in 1953, but after buying out Billy, Robinson's financial situation was even tighter. Another chain, Parkland, opened a store on Alabama Avenue in Southeast Washington, and they were doing about $15,000 of business per month. There was also a People's up the street on Alabama Avenue, but not a large one. Altogether there were three pharmacies in the Anacostia area of Washington, D.C., including Robinson's and he felt the pinch of competition.

Financially, Robinson was nearly in a crisis. "I felt like I was continually 'robbing Peter to pay Paul,'" is how he described it. "Every time a supplier would come through who needed to be paid, I'd have to rush to get some money to pay him. I was paying all my bills, but I was struggling to do so. On two occasions I actually had to go next door and borrow fifty or sixty dollars from the laundry owner because while I knew I had money coming in, I didn't have any on hand to pay a specific bill at the time. Finally, I gathered my ledgers and took them to my bank to get a loan. When we sat down and talked, the banker told me I had very good figures, but then he said, 'I'd like to help you but I can't.' 'What's the problem?' I asked. He said, 'The problem is that your competition has beaten you to it. Your figures will work, but we have already loaned him a substantial amount of money. We can't afford to lend you money, too, because it may hurt his ability to pay us. We have invested heavily in him and we can't afford to invest in you, too.' So I had to change banks."

Borrowing money was a difficult process for established black businesses of the day, and for a small, new businessman like Robinson, nearly impossible. There were a few black banks in Washington, D.C., at that time, and they were good banks, too, but they were ultra-conservative and wouldn't lend any money at all unless they could see that it would absolutely be repaid; they were extremely risk averse. "I tried to borrow money from another bank, the black-owned Industrial Bank," says Robinson. "They kept me coming back and coming back until finally one of their employees called me off to the side and told me, 'They're not going to lend you any money. I know how they are; you might as well try someone else because I believe you're wasting your time here.' She helped me to find another bank, Prosperity, I believe, but they were also too conservative and wouldn't lend to me, either. So borrowing wise, I was out of luck for the time being."

The Robinson's first child, Linda, was born with a serious medical problem. The cost of medical care needed to address their daughter's condition was a huge financial challenge for the Robinson family. The matter of Linda's health and suffering was an emotional one. Every time Robinson would get a little money together while trying to get ahead financially, he would have to take it over to Children's Hospital to catch up on his daughter's bill that seemed to always be increasing. That was really a burden because they made frequent visits. "I remember after we got the oxygen tank home," Robinson shares, "I owed them about three hundred dollars. I scuffled and scuffled for about six months before I was able to pay it off. It took them a long time to find the records when I showed up to pay it off; I waited and waited. Finally, a lady handling billing gave me the receipt and said, 'We're retiring those records now,' and I was happy about that"

Robinson's workday ran from 8:30 in the morning until 10:00 at night, seven days a week in his first store, until he began to make a nice profit. But he describes how it was luck that got him started being profitable: "Launching my pharmacy business really was a struggle, but I'm faithful. I was usually closed on Christmas Day. However on one particular Christmas, I was at home and received a call from an elderly customer whose husband was very sick. She asked me if I would go to the store and fill a prescription for him. I agreed and went to my pharmacy, not meaning to open it, but as I was preparing medication for my customer, people started crowding around out front. I opened the store for business and customers came in and bought all of my Christmas merchandise, everything. That made it a great Christmas for me financially."

"The following Christmas I didn't have money to buy Christmas gifts, and mindful of business on the previous Christmas, I decided I would just work that day like I had been working. By chance, an upstart businessman had opened a new wholesale place in the area called Link. He came into my place early one morning about a week before Christmas, looked around and said, 'You could use some merchandise for Christmas.' I said 'Yeah,' and he said, 'I'll stock it up for you.' He brought in lamps, Christmas trees, watches, clocks, razors, toys and other items – everything on consignment. The store was stocked as full as it could be. I sold everything that day and made a big profit on it." Up to that point, Robinson's inventory had consisted of only patented medicines and drugs. Of course, he also had a soda fountain and fountain foods. But after the guy from Link came in and brought all those other items – cases of watches that had a fast turnover, lamps, TV antennas, shaving items, small kitchen appliances – people bought all of that merchandise. With the money he began making on the other items, he got on his feet again. It was a fortuitous partnering arrangement that Robinson acknowledges when he says, "I never again found myself down financially after that."

Robinson was serving a primarily black community and was located across the street from a housing project, but it wasn't always clear whether that part of his customer base was more a help or hindrance to his business. The kids would run in and out of his pharmacy whenever they weren't in school and would often steal; they'd take up space at the fountain, loved to idle on his fountain seats, and do other things that began to get on his nerves. Robinson had a solution and says, "I got rid of the fountain and I got rid of that problem."

Just as Robinson's first pharmacy was becoming successful, more fortune shined upon him as he was the beneficiary of an opportunity to open another pharmacy. He had met Dr. Ross Clarke during Clarke's last year in medical school at Howard University. Dr. Clarke and a friend of his, Dr. Gerald Shelton, opened a practice in Pomonkey, Maryland. They would come by and purchase medicine from Robinson, and they all became friends. Eventually the three formed a buying club that allowed them to pool their funds, buy in bulk, and receive discounts on their purchases. Later, Dr. Clarke went into practice with another doctor, Dr. Willie Statom, who also had a big practice on Independence Avenue in Southeast Washington, D.C., in the Capitol Hill area. There was already a pharmacy on the corner near their practice that the doctors felt was ripping people off, giving customers poor quality of products and overcharging. The doctors were receiving complaints from their patients and didn't like what the owner was doing. They asked Robinson to start a pharmacy nearby.

"The doctors bought a house next to their practice and asked me to put a pharmacy in it, which I did," says Robinson as he prepared to open his next pharmacy. "I had the house remodeled, too. This was my second pharmacy, purchased in 1962. Because the pharmacy was in such close proximity to the doctors' practices, it did well immediately. I was doing big business in there. And within a few months, I had taken most of the business away from the other guy's pharmacy business on the corner, and he sued us. He lost in court. It was simply a matter of competition. After he lost, we bought him out."

Robinson's fortunes continued to improve. Soon he was approached by a wholesale distributor who was dealing with several pharmacies in town that were all losing money and they each owed the wholesaler quite a bit of money. The wholesale distributor, Gilpen Wholesalers, asked Robinson to come in and take over those pharmacies for them, which is how he got his four other stores. One store was at 9th and U Street in Northwest Washington, D.C. Another was at 16th and U St., Northwest, and there was one at Shipley Terrace and 28th Street in Southeast Washington. Finally, there was one on East Capitol Street in Southeast, also in the Capitol Hill area. The Shipley Terrace store was as large as his pharmacy on Alabama Avenue, but the other stores were smaller.

The owner of Link had stocked Robinson's pharmacy during the Christmas Season of 1959. A year later, Robinson's pharmacy business became profitable and remained so. As he acquired more pharmacies, he stocked them well and efficiently. He used the same business model or approach that had made him profitable in his original store wherever he could and made more profits in some of his new pharmacies. He hired employees, delegated work, and decreased his thirteen hours a day work schedule. Robinson bought his last pharmacy in 1965 and ended up owning six pharmacies at his height. As to the acquisition of the four through Gilpen, "I was asked to take them over because of the performance of my other pharmacies," Robinson says proudly. "Gilpen was impressed with my inventory management and my stores' turnover rates. The average pharmacist was turning over his inventory about 3.5 times per year. This meant that if you had an average of $1,000 worth of annual inventory, you were supposed to be able to turn it over 3.5 times. I was carrying $17,000 worth of inventory in my first store, but I was turning it over more than 6 times per year. That impressed Gilpen, and that's why they asked me to take over those four stores. They literally gave them to me to see if I could bring them out of the hole. I didn't have to advance any money up front."

Robinson managed his inventory efficiently by stocking a set amount of items based on his knowledge of how items were selling; his approach was to order on a tight schedule and only what he needed. Most stores would wait until their inventory got low and order a lot of everything. Robinson didn't do that. He knew what to order, how to order and kept his inventory very current; "If I bought it, I sold it," is how he describes his inventory management approach. But in working with those four pharmacies that Gilpen had turned over to him, his inventory management didn't help; he didn't make any money on a couple of those pharmacies, either.

The corner pharmacy business in the Washington, D.C. area was changing. Technical advances were allowing for the mass production of huge quantities of drugs at lower prices. Mechanized approaches for the process of compounding medicines were beginning to be used as the commercial pharmaceutical companies took this on, and pharmacists didn't have to mix and make prescription medicines or potions anymore, thus also reducing the possibility of human error and fundamentally changing the industry. America took the lead in the growth in research in pharmacy in the 1940s, and other structural changes were also occurring within the industry in following decades. First there were a number of large pharmaceutical companies, maybe 35 or 40, when Robinson started out in 1952 – much fewer now. The business is dominated by big chains now with companies having found it more economical to merge. He observed over and over that one big company would take over four or five smaller companies and keep their products but sell them under the name of the major company.

Back then, it took sixteen years before a product could become a generic. As a product got older, if its price went down, it reached a point where it wasn't financially advantageous for another company to make it as a generic. But in many cases the price didn't go down. It seemed the large companies could have cared less and kept the prices of their products up anyway. "The effect," Robinson says, "is that in the 1950s there were very, very few generic medicines. Eventually it got to the point that by buying generic medicines, customers now save quite a bit over brand names and now they're more popular."

"Later, insurance companies further changed the character of the business," states Robinson as he discusses other industry changes. "They determine how much we can charge and, to a large degree, the relationship between patient and pharmacist. The amount of paper work and insurance company oversight are a huge burden which has become the most stressful part of the business." But pharmacies were just one of Robinson business ventures.

Dr. Clarke, Dr. Shelton, and Robinson expanded their business interests over the years so that Robinson's business activities were diverse. First he and his partners ventured into real estate and bought property in Pomonkey, Maryland, holding on to twenty-nine acres still today, and they sold property, too. Other business opportunities surfaced, and Robinson became the owner of a surgical supply company. It is still doing very well and has about $200,000 worth of inventory.

To describe how he and his partners acquired their supply company, Robinson says, "'The Lord works in mysterious ways.' One of my partners and I opened a pharmacy in the Southwest section of Washington, D.C.; in a new development in the late 1960s. We had to litigate for the right to lease space there. The developer and some of the other tenants didn't want us in the development. The area was segregated at that time. They were white, we were black, but we got in there. There was a clause in our lease which stated that if we were fifteen days late in our monthly payment, the lease was considered broken and we would have to leave. We were doing about $8,000 to $10,000 worth of Medicaid business alone in there every two weeks, big Medicaid business."

After Robinson and his partners had been doing business at their Southwest site for over a year and a half, Medicaid contacted pharmacies in the area and told them that Medicaid had erred in paying them average wholesale prices for prescriptions when they should have been paying average wholesale prices less ten percent. They did that to every pharmacy in the District of Columbia. They went back almost two years and said that Robinson and his partners owed them a refund of about ten percent of their Medicaid business for that time frame. When they did that, it took one of the partnership's monthly checks to make an initial payment plus they also had to work out a payment plan with Medicaid for the balance. Robinson's partner went to the property management office and explained to them that they would be late with that month's rent, and the management office said it wouldn't be a problem. So they paid their rent late.

"Then, boom! Just like that, we received papers from the property management office stating that we were late with the month's rent, that we had violated our lease, and that we had to get out," says Robinson of the management company's betrayal. "We had leased almost the entire first floor of the building, which was almost new at the time, and we had never been late with the rent. We had invested a lot of money in there, and we owed everybody. Medicaid allowed us to pay them in three payments. But for us that was a lot of money to pay in three payments – almost $50,000 and this was 1968. We retained two lawyers and had a meeting with the property management company's lawyers. They brought nineteen lawyers into the meeting. They played hard-nose hard-ball and finally said, 'If you get out in two weeks, you will get $10,000. Otherwise you get nothing; take it or leave it.' One of our lawyers told us, 'You better take it;' the other said, 'Let's fight it.' We had a conference, thought about it, and decided to take the offer and move on. That put us out of business, and I lost $300,000 in there."

Around this time, there was a building owner who had been trying to get Robinson and his partners to locate to another site in another part of town on Brentwood Road in Northeast Washington where he was renting commercial space. He told Robinson and his partners that if they located over there, he would give them six months' free rent. So they took him up on that offer and moved everything over there. After they located there, they weren't able to get a pharmacy license because of zoning problems, but they needed somewhere to move their stock quickly, nonetheless, so the move made sense. In the meantime, the District of Columbia government was forced to close a lot of homes for the handicapped it operated in Laurel, Maryland, and in response to that a former city councilman and his sidekick built about eight or nine homes in the city to replace the ones in Laurel. All of the homes needed supplies. Fortunately, the owners came to Robinson and his partners to supply them. Robinson and his partners were able to meet all the needs of all those homes, and they started making money from their new location very quickly. It was almost as if divine intervention had interceded on their behalf.

After a while the homes for the handicapped they were supplying began having troubles. "Something questionable was happening with the money," Robinson recounted, "and eventually as a result of that, the owners of those homes lost their contract after a few years. A company from Canada was brought in to manage the homes, and they changed suppliers. These houses were generating about $30,000 of business per month for us. This was during the late 1960s to early 1970s. Our business was building up. We started out with $15,000 or $20,000 worth of merchandise, and we built it up to the point where we have about $200,000 worth of merchandise today.

Robinson pursued other business opportunities; some ventures did very well, others didn't. He and his business partners bought and managed property in Washington, D.C., for a while. They kept one building for about ten years and got a much higher offer for it than what they had paid, so they sold it. There were several pieces of property that they invested in with others. Robinson bought one piece of property that was managed by a friend of his who evicted the tenants because they weren't paying the rent regularly. Drug dealers got in there while it was unoccupied and burned the property down. Then he discovered that there was an insurance mix-up and was told that he didn't have any insurance on it. The building was a complete loss.

But there were other instances where Robinson was luckier. During April of 1968 after Dr. Martin Luther King was assassinated, Robinson had a store on the corner of the block in one of the hard-hit areas of Southeast Washington. There was a store next to his and a group of stores across the street: a liquor store, grocery stores, a café and several other retail stores on side streets, too. Every one of those stores was broken into, or bombed with Molotov cocktails except Robinson's; the mobs didn't touch his. He was the only proprietor there whose property was unscathed; he was also the only black owner in the group. The other owners where whites or foreigners; all of their stores were damaged. He was told that one of the neighbors came out and protected his business.

"The riots really hurt the area," Robinson says of that sad moment, "and my luck was minor considering the destructive effect it had on that neighborhood. It was an ugly act. Businesses were burned indiscriminately, and it was a disservice to the community and the people who lived there. Most of the property that was destroyed was located where black people lived and conducted business. We were all angry about the assassination of Dr. Martin Luther King, but the way that anger was vented in parts of this town wasn't right."

At the height of his pharmacy business, he employed fourteen people and says, "I was lucky enough to have somc very good employees. Two of these employees were with me during most of the time I've been in the pharmacy business. One, Ms. Thelma Booker, formerly Ms. Thelma Cunningham from Charleston, S.C., got her pharmacy degree from Xavier University in New Orleans, in 1939;" says Robinson describing his friend and former employee. "Her husband is Simeon Booker, *Jet Magazine's* Washington Bureau Chief. Ms. Booker worked for me for thirty-seven years. The other employee and friend of note is Ms. Alfreda Reavis, formerly Alfreda Miles. One of Ms. Reavis' brothers, Leo Miles, was the first black referee in the National Football League. In 1996, when I had a heart attack, Ms. Reavis, who was retired, kept the pharmacy open for two weeks; I didn't even know this was going on. She has been thoughtful and helpful that way for the almost forty years that I've known her. That event stands out most in my mind. Friends like that made the pharmacy business special."

Robinson is still a third partner in the supply company on Brentwood Road but doesn't get very involved in its day-to-day operation. The business buys merchandise from wholesaler distributors using his business contacts and discounts he established over the years. The bulk purchases help increase his discounts from the wholesaler on stock and inventory he purchases for the pharmacy he still runs. "This supply business, my remaining pharmacy, and a little real estate is enough for me nowadays," stated Robinson at age 85.

Had he not relocated to Washington, D.C., Curtis Robinson might have taught school for the rest of his life like three of his brothers and many other family members did. Or, he really would have loved to have been a pilot and probably would have been a great one. Ideally, a test pilot because he preferred flying alone, but he would have settled for being an airline pilot; but it was not to be. In fact, he may even have remained a house painter were the winters not as inclement as his mother had counseled. In reality, Curtis Robinson had the ability to do or be anything he wanted, and he became a pharmacist and remained one for the rest of his life. Why? Because he loved it.

And of his adopted city, Robinson says, "I love Washington, D.C. It is a changeable city, but it's a fine city. It could be much better than it is now. I think that it still hasn't seen its finest days, but it has seen days finer than it's seeing now. The most disgraceful aspect of living here is the lack of full voting rights for its citizens. As long as Congress has a negative attitude towards the people of Washington, D.C., the city will never achieve what it can. Congress must let us either sink or swim. They're not willing to do that. They like to use our tax funds and send us back only part of it, and send our young people to fight wars for voting rights for foreigners, while not having full voting rights themselves. I think we can handle the business of governing ourselves and electing our own congressional representatives, which we aren't allowed to do today. We are the only federal district that pays both state and federal income taxes but has no representatives in either the House of Representatives or the Senate. It's a shame; it's a short discussion point for us to be free when we have no representation. Taxation without representation is what we have. That's something the British put on us more than 250 years ago, and now Congress and the United States government are putting the same condition on the residents of the District of Columbia still today."

My Family

Tuskegee Airmen had earned the right to be proud of themselves after World War II. They had made an excellent accounting of themselves during the war, had been successful beyond theirs and others' wildest imaginations and had proven to be men of courage and the highest caliber. Those returning to civilian life anticipated returning to an environment in which their race would no longer be a major life's issue and their character and competence would no longer be questioned. Things would be different on the home front.

Generally, men with five years of service returned to civilian life at twenty-seven or twenty-eight years old in the prime of their lives as some of the country's finest men. They expected to resume or start anew lives that would be enhanced by their war time successes. For some, it would be a time to start families. After all, the vast majority of these men were educated, successful, and accomplished before they ever became pilots. Almost all had come from strong and loving families, and they valued their families dearly. Curtis Robinson would marry over a year and a half before leaving service. He and Florie, who had been college sweethearts for a while, would start a family about eighteen months later.

It seemed that times could never be more promising than in the years immediately after World War II as Curtis Robinson left the military and returned to civilian life. They were boom times for the country. Victory was good for the country's morale. The demand for products and services generated by returning veterans and by new families and the resultant "baby-boomers" was good for American industry and the economy. Add the Marshall Plan and the nation's capitol and the country shook off the last vestiges of the Great Depression. Washington, D.C., once a quaint southern town, was growing, and full of opportunities. It seemed like an ideal place for an ideal couple to embrace each other and their future. A young, attractive, smart and outgoing couple like Curtis and Florie Robinson had every reason to expect to happily raise a family, pursue the American dream, and thrive in the Nation's Capitol.

"I first met my wife Florie in 1937 at Claflin College just as I was leaving a fraternity meeting," Robinson said. "The hometown girls didn't take to me romantically during my youth; they saw me more as a friend and a 'play brother.' I had to find someone from out of town, and Florie seemed to like the qualities in me that the hometown girls ignored or may even have thought were square. I had good manners, goals. I am a fun-loving person, I tried to do good things, and I was a gentleman. Some girls liked that and some didn't. And also later when I was in service, my officer's uniform certainly helped make me look pretty good, too."

"Florie and I met one Sunday afternoon when she came up to me and asked, "What were you guys doing in there?" upon seeing me leave a meeting with a group of friends. I explained to her that we were having a fraternity meeting. She wanted to know what the meeting was about so I talked to her a little bit about fraternities, and then we stood around and talked a little more. Over the next few weeks we would meet occasionally and talk a while."

This was a time when coeds were almost guarded by the school. The young ladies couldn't leave the campus and were closely supervised. "At Claflin once a month on Wednesday night, the administration would feature a movie that the school had rented and would show in the auditorium," explained Robinson. "If the young ladies wanted to go to a movie, they had to go in groups, escorted by a chaperon. Dating was strictly a situation where young men would see young ladies in class and flirt, or they could go to the dormitory and call on them. There was a visiting room in the dormitory where male students could sit with female co-eds and talk, but the ladies couldn't leave the campus to go places on dates and often on campus they were chaperoned. That was also the policy at South Carolina State. The school did have plenty of dances, though. There was a dance about once a week. But the dating environment was strict and controlled."

The following quarter Robinson and Florie got to see each other more often when they took a botany class together as Robinson explains, "Most of my classes were science classes. I had taken biology, but because of an interest in pre-med, I also had to take botany. Florie and I worked at the same table; we sat together and flirted, and became closer friends. Then we started dating but it was an off and on relationship. When Florie felt like she was getting too close, or I was getting to close, she would step back, and I wouldn't see her for a week or two; she was very cautious. And if I said something that made her mad, I wouldn't see her for a couple of weeks then, either."

Florie was from Timmonsville, South Carolina, nine miles southwest of Florence. Florence, the largest city near her home area, was a railroad center. Several railroads converged within the town and, to a large degree, made the town. It was one of the largest cities in South Carolina. Florie's family lived close enough to the city for her father to drive her and her older sisters to high school in Florence every day from their home. And according to Robinson, "The majority of black parents in her hometown seemed to have been sending their children to college. Florie, her brother, and her three sisters all attended college; her mother had gone to college at Claflin. When Florie came to Claflin, there were several other hometown students with her, plus many of her high school classmates went to several other colleges. Her hometown only had about six-hundred black families and they were very progressive."

"Coming to Claflin was the first time Florie had been away from home, and she lived on campus," adds Robinson. "She was curious about everything but was fairly protected because she had three older sisters who looked out for her. The two older girls acted almost like mothers towards her. They did most of the chores around the house, so she didn't have a lot of domestic duties either as the baby girl in her family. She had one younger brother, and she, her brother, and next youngest sister were very close."

Florie changed schools during Robinson's junior year because she wanted to major in home economics and Claflin didn't offer that. So she transferred from Claflin to South Carolina State where she could pursue her desired major. She learned home economics well. But after transferring to State, she and Robinson began to lose contact. Of that point in their relationship Robinson shares, "By my senior year, I wasn't seeing her very often. And after my senior year, I went off to a job teaching so we didn't see each other very much at all. In fact, I only saw her once or twice while I was teaching. We did write occasionally. I'd go see her sometime, but not too much."

By the time Robinson graduated from Claflin College,

Florie was dating a guy that went to South Carolina State where she was then a student. He also went into the Army Air Corp's Tuskegee training program while Robinson was there, but he washed out. "I've forgotten his name," Robinson says of his competitor. "I used to tease Florie about him; of course, I didn't know anything about him. I just know that he couldn't make the grade in the Tuskegee program. Then, after the war started, I went off to the service. While I was gone, between the time that I graduated from Claflin and graduated from pilot training at Tuskegee, Florie married a guy from Detroit. However she was married to him for less than three months. They had been living in a one-room apartment in Detroit, and it just didn't work out. He became physically abusive and hit her. She left him the next day and went home and immediately filed for a divorce. Around the time that Florie got her divorce, her sisters were living in Washington, D.C. They sent for her, and Florie moved there."

When Robinson came home on his first leave from cadet training, he found out that she was in Washington, got her address, wrote her and they began corresponding. She was living with her sisters before she and Robinson got married and was working at the Pentagon. A few months later, in September or October of 1943, as Robinson was on his way overseas from Selfridge Field and Oscoda, heading to Hampton Roads, Virginia, he came through Washington, D.C., and spent some time with Florie. It was then that they became very close. From then on, they wrote almost daily while he was overseas. When Robinson came back from abroad and after he had recuperated in the hospital, he had thirty days of leave. Ten days were spent in Richmond, Virginia, going through the process of reassignment. Richmond isn't far from Washington, D.C., so he kept running up to Washington to see her. Soon Florie Frederick and Curtis Robinson got engaged.

"Florie and I were married while I was a flight instructor at Tuskegee Army Air Field," says Robinson of their wedding. "She was living in Washington until our wedding date. Then, I sent for her. On the initial wedding date, our day arrived, but the Chaplin had to travel to a funeral service for one of the pilots who had gotten killed. That forced us to reschedule our wedding date because of the scheduling conflict. We set another date for our wedding. The date came, something came up and we had to change it, too."

"It looked like every time we set a date, something would happen. Florie didn't appreciate the change of dates, got annoyed and was disappointed at how things were unfolding. I think she began wondering if I was stalling. But we finally got the date right and were married on April 25, 1945, at my aunt and uncle's home in Tuskegee with only a few of my friends present. Florie didn't have any friends down there – she had not previously been to Alabama - and it was still wartime so traveling long distances was difficult, which was probably fortunate given the change of dates and the inconvenience it might have caused traveling guests. We had ten days for a honeymoon, so we went to Orangeburg and spent most of the time there so that she could meet my family. Soon we set up housekeeping in a new development near Tuskegee Army Air Field in the fall of 1945. In the fall of 1946, during her seventh or eighth month of pregnancy, Florie went back to Washington to be with her sisters and have our baby."

Shortly before the Robinson's baby was to be born, the Air Corps started to close down Tuskegee Army Air Field. Robinson was transferred to Lockbourne Field in Columbus, Ohio, and their baby, a girl named Linda, was born while he was there. Robinson was a base technical inspector at Lockbourne making use of his chemistry background. It was a technical position and also a temporary one. After being a pilot and a flight instructor, Robinson was no longer doing any flying at Lockbourne. Colonel Davis was in charge, and the airmen were doing more restrictive military type things. On Saturdays, they had to be in parades, and it was hard for them to leave the base. Finally Curtis Robinson decided to leave the Army Air Corps. He was a married man with a family and more responsibilities. He got out of service shortly thereafter in January of 1947.

Right after Robinson left the Air Corps and settled in Washington, D.C., with his new wife, he and Florie lived briefly in Northeast, D.C., with Florie's sister, Allie Frederick James, and her husband Shepherd James. It was an area caught in change. Blacks were beginning to move into that part of the city which was the first neighborhood in the city to turn predominantly black. There were still significant numbers of whites there, but they were beginning to move out to areas like Riverdale in Prince George's County, Maryland, and other border towns just over the district line to buy homes. Areas like Silver Spring in Montgomery County, Maryland, began to grow. After staying with the Jameses a few months, the Robinsons bought a house in Northwest Washington, D.C., on Lamont Street.

Linda Robinson, Curtis and Florie's daughter, was born two months before Robinson left service, on November 11, 1946, at Walter Reed Army Hospital in Washington, D.C. She was a beautiful baby with pretty twinkling brown eyes, lovely soft black hair, and the cutest smile. They were very excited and joyous about her. She was alert from the very beginning and smiled and giggled a lot, and was a happy baby.

But by the time she was two or three months old, the couple began to notice that Linda was still very inactive. The only thing she could do was lie on her back; she never tried to sit up or rollover. They hoped that it was just that she was a late-bloomer and would come around. After six months things still had not improved for Linda and the Robinsons were extremely worried. Their daughter wasn't doing anything active, but she had an alert mind and cheerful disposition. The only thing they could get out of her, though, was smiles. The couple began talking to doctors and questioning them about her condition. They knew that there was something wrong, but they couldn't figure out what it was. She wasn't growing and couldn't sit up or stand up – couldn't do anything.

Whenever they visited doctors and left unclear about their daughter's condition, the Robinsons would try to find someone else and continually sought out more doctors. "Then alarming things began happening suddenly," Robinson says. "I remember we were playing with her. She was laughing and giggling, and then, all of a sudden she started to turn blue and began crying. We had to rush her to the hospital, and this happened scores of times before she turned three; sometimes they would give her oxygen."

Florie was frightened and felt almost helpless. Her heart was tortured and her young mother's love was cruelly played upon as she did all she could to find out what was wrong with her baby, but continued to come up with nothing. CC and she seemed to be going in circles. It was supposed to be a joyous time for her; everything should have been perfect. The beauty of her baby's room that she had so tenderly and thoughtfully appointed with colors and stuffed animals that created an air of merriment, mocked her. Her resolute style of dispatching and dealing with problems surrendered to sadness, her beauty glowed through anxiety, her countenance gave away to worry, and her confidence battled uncertainty and doubt. She questioned the whole dilemma - What on earth could she do to help her daughter? Why was this happening to her? She had never done bad things or had never hurt anyone – and she prayed. With all her heart and soul, she prayed.

Curtis and Florie would take their daughter to the emergency room at Children's Hospital in Washington, D.C., and the doctors would examine her and send her home but made no diagnosis of her condition whatsoever. If she was very ill, they would keep her at the hospital a while and then send her home. The Robinsons decided that a private doctor might be better, so they took her to a physician by the name of Dr. Owen who was a pediatrician in Northwest Washington. He examined her, looked in her eyes and said to the Robinsons, "Your baby has a heart condition; you should take her to Children's Hospital." They told him that they had already taken her there on several occasions. He wrote out his diagnosis and gave it to the Robinsons to give to medical personnel at the hospital, and the Robinsons took it and their daughter back to Children's.

Sure enough, Children's Hospital concluded that Linda Robinson indeed had a heart condition. Thereafter, they paid more attention to her medical problems than before. But still they said that there was nothing they could do about it. The hospital finally suggested that the Robinsons get an oxygen tent since giving her oxygen is what they were doing. The Robinsons bought an oxygen tank and bottles of oxygen for the house. "Whenever she had any problems, we would use them," says Robinson. "The hospital didn't offer any explanations as to what the problem may have been. They didn't suggest any specialists and never recommended alternative treatments. Their only suggestion was that Florie and I just take Linda home and care for her as best we could. And that's what we did."

It was a terrible strain on them, especially for Florie since Robinson was working day and night plus attending school at that time. Florie would see her daughter struggle most of the day. She worried that she would have a bad attack that would be fatal. She felt guilty that somehow she was letting her daughter down. And she endured it for quite some time. Linda was two years old before she could sit up on her own. Once she began to sit up, she started to have heart attacks periodically, and the couple would have to rush her to the hospital. The staff at Children's would keep her in the hospital for two or three days, giving her oxygen as needed. But they didn't do much more than that. The Robinsons would take her home, and a month later they'd have to rush her back to the hospital. So it went for months and then a couple of years.

Robinson had not previously encountered a problem for which his faith and determination had failed to help him conquer. But the situation with his beloved daughter, Linda, was different. He and Florie weren't sure what to do to help her and they were running out of places to turn. Then by pure chance, or providence, they read an article in the newspaper about two doctors at Johns Hopkins Hospital in Baltimore, Maryland, who had done research on "blue babies." The symptoms described in the article were very much like Linda's. The couple decided to go to Hopkins on their own, with no doctor's recommendation at all. It is incomprehensible to Robinson that they found out this information themselves and had to seek their own appointment since, as he surmised, "Children's seemed not to have known what the medical developments were in the area of 'blue babies' at that time; it's as if they weren't keeping up. I'm quite sure there were many articles in medical journals about these two medical researchers at Johns Hopkins. Florie and I found out about them in a newspaper article we read, so I don't know why Children's wouldn't have known about 'blue babies' or the doctors at Hopkins."

Curtis and Florie Robinson arrived at Johns Hopkins early one summer morning in 1949. They showed up without a reference or even an appointment. The hospital wanted a referral, but they didn't have one. The Robinsons were desperate; they had no other alternative, so they waited all day. Finally at day's end, two physicians at Johns Hopkins Hospital, Dr. Alfred Blalock, chief of surgery at the hospital, and Dr. Helen Taussig, a pediatric cardiologist, examined her. The Robinsons were informed that their daughter had a three chambered heart and that they would have to perform surgery, but that they had never performed the type of operation that they had in mind for Linda. Dr. Blalock told them that Linda was different from all other blue babies he had seen, and that he would have to devise a special operation for her. They didn't have anything that they could do immediately, but he promised that they would call the Robinsons.

While much of this was going on, the Robinson's second child, a son, Curtis Christopher Robinson Jr., was born on September 9, 1949, at D.C. General Hospital. Their son, whom the family calls Chris, was born the day after his mother's birthday, September 8th. The Robinson brought him home and almost from the very beginning they were able to see that, unlike Linda, he was a very active baby with lots of energy and was a head bumper in his crib.

Johns Hopkins soon contacted the Robinsons to schedule surgery for Linda. Finally, years of searching for a solution for their daughter had led the Robinsons to the foremost experts in the world on the treatment of the Tetralogy of Fallot, or the 'blue baby' syndrome. As preparations were being made for surgery, Robinson thought it strange that the black man assisting the doctors seemed so critical to the proceedings. He appeared to be as vital as the doctors. Of their first meeting Robinson recalled, "I didn't know who he was or where he came from, but they always wanted him there. They operated on his schedule, and the doctors wouldn't perform the surgery without his being by their side." The doctor's assistant who seemed so important to the operation was a man named Vivien Thomas. He was not a doctor but rather a technician who worked with Dr. Blalock. He designed procedures and programs for patients – for heart surgery. Thomas designed a procedure for the Robinson's daughter, a procedure whereby they took a blood vessel from her leg, and since she wasn't getting proper aeration to her lungs, they sent blood back to the lungs a second time with the use of that transplanted blood vessel. Mr. Thomas would go on to have a career in the medical field as illustrious and successful as that of Tuskegee Airmen.

The trio of Drs. Blalock and Taussig and Vivian Thomas had been performing operations for the condition that Linda had, just forty miles away from the Robinson's home in Washington, D.C., and they had been doing so since 1944. Dr. Helen Taussig had been hired to run Hopkins' pediatric cardiac clinic in 1930, was one of the first experts to recognize that the 'blue baby' syndrome stemmed from a lack of blood flow to the lungs and was adept at making the diagnoses. Dr. Blalock was the surgeon-in-chief, and professor and director of the department of surgery at Johns Hopkins hospital and medical school, respectively, since 1941. He headed the operation. Vivien Thomas, who was Dr. Blalock's highly respected technician for more than thirty years, supervised the medical laboratory at Hopkins for thirty-five years, and was an instructor in the medical school as well. He would stand behind Dr. Blalock as he operated and offer suggestions on the surgical techniques to use. After having performed their third successful surgery for the 'blue baby' condition in 1945, with their first operation having occurred on November 29, 1944, their work was published in the Journal of the American Medical Association.

After the surgery was completed, Linda began to grow so rapidly that it seemed miraculous. Within six weeks of her surgery she was standing up; within three months she took her first steps, and within six months she was walking. Her progress was so pronounced that Florie and Curtis knew everything would work out fine for their daughter. By the time she was six years old, Linda was able to go to school and managed to start with her class. Physically she caught up with her own age group. She had a good mind, was always talking, and she did very well in school. In fact, as she got older, she would correct adults' grammar sometimes. But she was always fragile. She couldn't run fast like other children, she wasn't as strong as they were physically, and she couldn't keep up with them. But with her active mind and sweet little girl's disposition, she got along very well socially and no longer needed much medication. She was a child who loved people, and people loved her.

Linda grew into her big sister role with great fondness for little Chris and began to keep an eye on her little brother. Once Chris started walking, he would climb out of the crib at night and she would yell, "He's out of the crib, Chris is out!" In response to her outcries, Florie or Curtis would go in and find him still in his crib lying down, very still like nothing had happened. Finally, on one particular night, Florie left the children's room like she was returning to bed after having been alerted by Linda and checking on Chris. But instead of returning to their bedroom, she stayed by the children's door. Chris looked around after his mother left his room, and seeing no one nearby, he climbed out again. Florie peeped in on him; he looked up and spotted her watching him and ran and jumped back into the crib. So they purchased a bed for him after that, knowing they weren't going to be able to keep him in his crib. Robinson says, "He was hard to train. He was so active that he always stayed in some sort of trouble."

Linda Robinson had adjusted very well and had no problems for several years after her surgery. She was a diligent mother's helper at home and a talkative passenger when she often rode with her father. All the neighbors thought her to be the cutest little social butterfly. And on those soft, carefree Washington spring days, she would frolic along the block playing with her parents and brother. She had a lot of spirit and didn't seem the worst for having suffered so severely during her infancy.

But eventually she outgrew the vein that had been transplanted during the operation. She began to have problems breathing again starting around nine years old in 1956. Linda's episodes had happened because she wasn't getting enough oxygen to her blood. The operation that had served her so well the past few years had involved the doctors taking a vein out of her leg and using it to connect the pulmonary artery to the subclavian artery in a manner that rerouted blood to her lungs a second time and provided more oxygen, since her blood wasn't receiving enough oxygen the first time. She was doing fine until she outgrew the vein. D. C. General Hospital scheduled her for surgery to perform a similar operation in 1956.

Curtis Robinson spent most of the evening before the operation with his daughter. After the family had dinner, he took her to D.C. General while Florie stayed home with Chris. The two of them rode while Linda talked constantly, as usual. Once in her room, her father stayed as long as the doctors allowed as he played games and read to her so she would get a good night's rest. And then he tried to leave. "I remember when she was in the hospital the last time," he begins, "the very last time I was with her the evening before the second operation. As I was leaving the two of us must have walked back and forth from her room to the elevator five times. She would walk me to the elevators, and I would tell her she had to go back to the room. But she would not go back to her room without me; she would insist that I walk her back to her room. I would walk her back to her room, tuck her in, but she didn't want me to leave her and she would turn around and walk me back to the elevators again. We walked back and forth and back and forth; I finally made her stay in her room."

"The next morning they operated on Linda, but she didn't make it. That evening before her surgery was the last time I saw her alive. She was ten years old. For me, the loss of my child was the most painful moment in my life."

"Everyday I had with my daughter was like sunshine. When she wasn't in pain, she radiated joy and happiness; she just glowed. I was the person she seemed to love most; I could do no wrong in her eyes. She used to ride with me when I made deliveries for my pharmacy during my first six or seven years. I could pull out into traffic, and whatever I did while driving, even if I made a mistake or something that was met with a honking horn, I could be wrong but she would say, 'Daddy, he was wrong. He shouldn't be so mean' I could do no wrong by her. Losing her breaks my heart even now."

Florie Robinson, too, was devastated over the loss of her precious daughter and angry about the recurring suffering Linda had endured. The last few years had been a roller coaster. First she had lived in sorrow as she watched her child suffer, then in desperation as they had tried ceaselessly to find out what was wrong; then she was full of hope after meeting the trio who would save her daughter. Now she felt that life had tricked her cruelly. So much of what she loved was gone. And as badly as she felt about Children's care, she was as angry at the Army Air Corps. She even suspected that the military might have somehow been responsible for her daughter's health. But Curtis Robinson accepted the tragedy that they were forced to endure as part of life. It was a fact, though, that quite a few of the Tuskegee pilots had kids with numerous health problems. Robinson shares, "Oh, there were so many of them – so many. Most of the kids that were born like that are now dead. The only one living that I'm aware of is Leonard Jackson's child. She is about fifty-four or fifty-five years old. She has never been able to work, and she's in a nursing home now. But it seemed like so many Tuskegee Airmen's children experienced that."

Florie knew that, too, which is why she was so angry and suspicious. Also, she had grown up in South Carolina, and had seen and believed that she couldn't put anything past whites. She thought it was much more than a coincidence that so many airmen's children seemed to have serious medical problems. She couldn't prove it but she was convinced that those maladies were connected to their father's service in the military.

Robinson figured that the frequency of incidences of Tuskegee Airmen's children's health problems was not much more than you would expect in the general population in the late 1940s and the 1950s. But Robinson concedes, "Whether or not it was truly representative of what was happening in the general population, I don't know. But I do know that an awful lot of my friends had children born with some type of deformity. We never really focused on it and I never discussed it with any of the guys. I don't know whether it was one of those things that we would have had undue concerns about if we had thought more about it, or not. The military hadn't done anything to us, I don't think, that they didn't do to other pilots as well, with the exception of segregation and the race thing. The only thing that I can say about myself is that the Army gave me an awful lot of shots - vaccinations. Every time we moved, I was taking a series of shots. I didn't think they were helpful, or necessary. For instance, I got a series of shots when I went into service. Then when I went to Selfridge Field, I got another series of inoculations. Leaving Selfridge and going to the port of embarkation I got more shots. There, I decided enough is enough. I didn't think I needed all of that. Three series of shots within the matter of a year; I don't know what effect that might have had. They gave me tetanus shots, other shots like smallpox and so forth, diphtheria and a series of regular shots probably some of which you would have taken as a baby. We did run into civilian populations with illnesses in some of our tour areas that called for inoculation, that's true. In places like Africa you would encounter the possibility of being exposed to different type of problems such as malaria. But I think that the military was too cautious and gave out too many shots, at least for my liking."

Little Chris also felt the pain of losing his sister. This happened when he was about seven years old. Chris and Linda had been very close. It was difficult for him to comprehend her death; he didn't understand why she wasn't coming back and he brooded for quite a while after she died. There were games that they had played at night, she read to him and helped teach him to read, and they shared all kinds of secrets together. At their ages, she had still been much the big sister and leader. And like a lot of little brothers and sisters, they were best friends.

Early in life Chris was very good in academics. Later when he was in the fourth grade, he began having difficulties. He was doing sixth grade math but he was reading at a third grade level. His teachers recommended that the Robinsons take him to a particular specialist which they did. "I guess he was one of the first kids diagnosed as having ADD – Attention Deficit Disorder," says Robinson. "In some things he was brilliant, but others he grasped very slowly. Chris visited the specialist for two weeks and the suggestion was that we send him to Georgetown Day School. It's an excellent private school and the specialist who made the recommendation felt that Georgetown Day could correct some of his problems." That's where he went to elementary school. It was quite a distance from their home. Robinson would take him over there every morning. It was a long drive since they were living in a different part of the city. Chris and he would get up early in the morning to make the trip. Then Robinson would come back across town and open his store.

Georgetown Day was a predominantly white school; there were two other black kids in his class. But the staff at Georgetown Day treated him very well, and everyone seemed to like him. Practically all of Washington, D.C.'s schools were segregated then but Robinson thinks, "not necessarily because of local law. One school in Adams Morgan was integrated around 1954, but the pattern of housing in the city was also segregated, and the composition of the schools followed that of housing. Whoever lived in the same neighborhoods went to the same schools." And Chris appeared to have adjusted to an integrated classroom environment.

After a year and a half of commuting across town every morning, Robinson decided he would get a place closer to his business. An attorney he knew had a house on Alabama Avenue that he wanted to rent, about a block from Robinson's pharmacy. So Robinson rented out their house on Lamont Street and the family moved into the house on Alabama Avenue. But after renting for about three years, Robinson decided to buy a home not far from Alabama Avenue in a newer area of the city, the Hillcrest section of Southeast Washington, in the summer of 1962. This was a very busy time for Robinson. He had opened his second very successful pharmacy, had real estate interests, a new home, and was providing a secure life for his family.

They must have been in their new home for two or three

months when it dawned on Robinson that he and Chris hadn't done anything together involving just the two of them for a long time. So for the first Christmas in their new home when Chris was thirteen years old, they went to find a Christmas tree on some property Robinson owned in the country in Pomonkey, Maryland. They went there seeking the perfect Christmas tree. They talked all the way down, searched for the tree they wanted, found it, cut it, and loaded it into the van. All the while Robinson showed his son things about nature, plants and wildlife, and they headed back home. That night, as they were putting up the tree, Chris told his father it was the best time he had ever had. Robinsons says, "I was shocked. I didn't know he enjoyed it that much, and it was just the two of us. It showed me that you never know about kids, about what impresses or pleases them because it was such a simple day out."

Robinson was closer to Chris than his father had been with him. His father hadn't been very close to any of his children, but they all loved each other. Robinson and his son found time to do things together; he supported him and encouraged him to strive, saying, "My expectations for him were that he would go to college and take an academic route in life as I had done. He went to Claflin College for about a year and left. Then he took a few courses at the University of the District of Columbia, and that was the extent of it. But I don't think I can fully know how deeply his sister's death affected him. I tried to let him be himself and never tried to influence Chris to take an interest in aviation but thought he might have taken an interest in the business."

Development had just begun in large sections of their neighborhood when they moved in. Hillcrest is a beautiful, suburban-like neighborhood of oak and maple tree-lined streets, hilled yards with natural stone retaining walls, brick and slate colonials and cape-cod houses. The neighborhood was all-white when the Robinsons arrived and continues to be a very desirable neighborhood. It sits atop one of the highest plateaus in the city, on sloping hills. J Edgar Hoover once lived in the area. He wasn't living there when the Robinsons moved into the neighborhood, however. "When I went into the service, the house Hoover lived in was there, and so were a few other houses on Branch Avenue," says Robinson of his knowledge of the history of the area, "but there weren't many. Most of the families who lived there then are all gone. A few whites remain on our block, mostly those without school age kids stayed."

The demographics of Washington, D.C., changed dramatically after the Brown vs. Topeka, Kansas decision as the white exodus accelerated. During that decade Washington, D.C., lost 300,000 whites and, conversely, gained 300,000 blacks. Further exoduses would occur after the March on Washington in 1963, and later, after passage of the Civil Rights Act of 1965– helped in no small way by local banking and real estate interests busily engaging in "block busting" and making huge profits. Curtis and Florie Robinson were the first black family to move onto their street and also the first black family to reside in the general vicinity of the Hillcrest area. After they had been in their new home about six months, "for sale" signs began to appear up and down the street and all over the neighborhood. When Robinson moved in, the neighbor next door, who was a retired policeman, stayed about six months and moved." Robinson was working such long hours that he hadn't time to be disturbed by the "for sale" signs going up in the neighborhood. He saw them when he was going to work or returning home, but he had many other things on his mind. "I didn't have a lot of contact with the neighbors," he says, "I didn't see them at all, so I didn't know what was going on."

"Block busting," a favorite tool of the real estate and

banking industries at that time, was what was going on. "It seemed that real estate people began frightening whites with the notion that black people were moving in, and if they didn't sell their houses quickly, their property values would go down," is Robinson's assessment of the dynamics at work. "They enticed whites into thinking they could get cheaper homes and pay lower taxes in the suburbs. They could still sell their homes for huge gains to blacks since they were beginning their influx into the area and wanted them anyway, and the sellers could move on. The white homeowners and the real estate professionals understood - at least implicitly - that developers, working with banks, would not sell to blacks in some of the newly developed suburbs that whites were fast moving to, at least not during the early years, and whites wouldn't have to worry about having black neighbors."

"Many of the whites who lived in the Hillcrest area originally, paid very little for their homes," continued Robinson. "The guy that we bought from had the house built himself, so I know that he didn't pay that much for it. We found out about the area and house through a real estate agent who took us all around the neighborhood. We saw the house and liked it. They didn't even have a "for sale" sign in front of the house when we put a contract on it. The agent told us that the owner was asking $32,000 for it. I wasn't in that big a hurry to buy a house so I offered him the price I felt I was willing to pay - $26,000 - and I didn't think any more of it. But eventually he accepted, and I bought it at that price."

Soon after the Robinsons purchased their new house, the seller's son made a trip from New Jersey and visited Robinson at one of his stores. "He accused me of taking advantage of his father and wanted to buy the house back at the price we purchased it plus an additional $2,000," Robinson added, "but I wouldn't do it. I believe he wanted to buy it back and re-sell at a higher price than they had gotten out of me. Even the bank had offered to loan us $40,000 for the house, or more than fifty percent above the asking price. We didn't need the additional monthly expense and wanted as low a mortgage as possible, so we turned the bank down. At that point, I knew the house was worth more than I had paid for it. I have the feeling that the banks and real estate agents were working together to make money in Hillcrest. They worked aggressively to scare off whites to the suburbs, drove up the prices of houses in Hillcrest for incoming blacks when they could, and made more money in the process. The neighborhood changed, but it is even better now than it was when I first moved in. Almost all the neighbors who moved in have improved their homes. It was a loss to the people who moved out. It has always been a good, quiet neighborhood."

By 1970 almost all of Robinson's business ventures were doing very well. He began to spend more time with his wife. They took trips together and made weekend outings to New York to check out live performances. It soon got to the point that he could come home during the day, spend more time with his wife, watch television, read or relax while Florie would be doing housework. "I had so much free time that eventually Florie said, 'Why don't you get out and go do something?' Robinson says as he laughs. "So she bought me a set of golf clubs and said, 'Go play some golf. ' and I got into that. I got to be pretty good at it and shot between 79 and 82, while playing mostly with salespeople from the pharmaceutical companies. That time of my life was fun."

"But of all my fun moments in life, moments with the family were best. Our happiest moments together as a family were those occasions when we would go away together on trips. When our daughter was alive, we would take her down to South Carolina, and she would stay with my mother for a few weeks.

She was such a lovely child and everybody loved her very much. On other occasions the family would go to Atlantic City on vacation for a few days during the summer. Then there were times when we just had family picnics around Washington. We had a lot of happy moments together, but not enough of them."

"I think I was a pretty good father and did a good job. I may have been too easy with the kids. I certainly was much easier going with my children than my parents had been with us. I tried to stick to principles and teach my children what was right and what was wrong. Perhaps we did too good a job with Linda; she wouldn't do anything wrong. I remember when I worked at night in the government and used to get home about 12:30 or 1:00 A.M. Florie was a hard sleeper. One night, I had left my keys at work, couldn't get in, and tried to get my daughter to open the door. She said, 'Mama said not to open the door for anybody!' And she wouldn't let me in. I had to go over to a pay telephone and call and call until Florie finally woke-up to let me in."

"As a family, we were rather religious and we liked to go to church. We also had family prayers. And just as family has been the source of the greatest joys in my life, much the same for the saddest moments. I don't think I have ever had times any sadder than when my daughter died. And almost as sad was when my wife Florie died on September 8, 2000, which was also her birthday. She was the next to the last child in her family to be born; and she was also the next to the last of her siblings to pass. And, like all of her sisters, she died overnight in her sleep, peacefully."

Legacy of the Tuskegee Airmen

The 450 black pilots in the 332nd Fighter Group who served in overseas combat earned 850 medals. They lost 66 of their members. An additional 30 were prisoners of war. For every one of their planes the Germans shot down, the Tuskegee Airmen shot down four of theirs. The only time a destroyer was sunk with a machine gun during the war, it was done by Wendell Pruitt and Gwynne Pierson of the 99th Fighter Squadron. Captain Roscoe Brown, Lieutenant Earle Lane, and Flight Officer Charles V. Brantley were the first American pilots to shoot down German jets – one each - during the war, and they shot them down while flying propeller planes. Most important and impressive, these men flew more than 200 bomber escort missions and never lost a bomber that they escorted to enemy fire during World War II. Another group, the 477th Composite Fighter-Bomber Group, was also comprised of Tuskegee Airmen, but was never deployed. Each of these men who were pilots was supported by ten other civilian or military men and women on the ground, who were also usually black, and whose contributions should also be praised and included as part of their legacy.

Every pilot who entered the program had some previous

experiences with segregation and discrimination from Colonel Davis' well known silent treatment at West Point - he was shunned by his classmates for four years and not spoken to outside of the line of duty; he never had a roommate, took his meals in silence often going from table to table and enduring the indignity of being spurned at each table, combined with his experience of having had the Ku Klux Klan march with torches in front of his house as a little boy to express their anger at his father's status as a military officer - to Curtis Robinson's trip to report for duty and efforts by train company to hide him in his Pullman car. Also the way the young cadets and officers were initially segregated once they got to Tuskegee – dining halls and living quarters - and the way they lived in town. These men were treated terribly by the white citizens of Tuskegee and every one of them had mixed feelings about it. There was an instance in which one of their guys was forced to land his plane in a white farmer's field and was chased off by the farmer with his shotgun. They realized that was the type of experience they could expect to have with the town. But that was a factor that helped to bond them; they had no place else to go, no where to turn.

For a while, Tuskegee Army Air Field had routine segregation on the base. There was a white PX and a black PX. No white officers lived on the base; they all lived in town, but all the black officers were required to live on the base. Colonel Noel Parrish did away with all of that when he took command in February of 1943. Though he was a white Texan, he was a fair guy. At the time, he was single and he even dated a few of the black women down there, too. Once he became base commander, he brought in famous black entertainers and improved morale.

Perhaps years after their service, Lieutenant General Benjamin O. Davis, Jr. said it best of the young men he led so proudly: "I give full marks to the Tuskegee Airmen themselves. They bore the brunt of it all. However, they could not have achieved their glorious record without lots of help. That help came from Gen. Noel Parrish, who held in his hand the key decision that blacks could fly airplanes at a superior level of proficiency; it came from "Chief" Alfred Anderson and his corps of Primary Flying School instructors, who performed their mission in exemplary fashion throughout all the years of TAAF existence; it belonged to the hundreds of officers and airmen who did the support job at Tuskegee Army Air Field, without which our combat effort could not have gone forward. I must also mention with admiration, the wives of the Tuskegee Airmen who suffered the privations of Alabama while they rendered the necessary support which their husbands needed and enjoyed through the long years of World War II."

What came to be called the Tuskegee Experience began in the throes of hope, doubt, and suspicion. Some said it was a program designed to fail. For starters, the program was segregated. The training was conducted in the deep-South, in Alabama of all places! But others saw it as an opportunity to demonstrate that black Americans, too, could fly; that they were courageous and patriotic and that, if given a chance to succeed in the cockpits of sophisticated aircraft, they would do just that.

However they may have been regarded in the beginning, the excellence of the Tuskegee Airmen as a group during World War II is undisputed, unsurpassed, unmatched, and well documented. Theirs was a story of answering a roll-call for a challenge requiring them to prove their worth as human beings as much as pilots. Grandchildren of slaves, a group perennially deprived of opportunities, they answered the challenge to perform with intelligence, poise, and courage at the highest levels; and under the weight of a nation who's hateful and misguided attitudes, ironically, challenged them to prove that they deserved better than the country had historically given them. They were black men leading black men, with segregation having willed it so. More than cockpit wonders, many of them had been groomed for success all their lives. They were the offering of black America to the nation and the world for the cause of freedom, and this was the first chance they'd had to make an accurate accounting of who they really were and what they were capable of in a meaningful way.

Cadets arriving at Tuskegee were quintessentially the "talented tenth" of Dubois lore, assembled from far flung places within the nation, from the top schools, highly accomplished – doctors and lawyers - and among the nation's brightest young men. It was not what they got out of the program as much as what they brought to it that gives cause to speak of them. "As young black cadets, we just had this special chance – to fly – and many of us could do it," says Robinson of his and his peer's capabilities. "Some thought that this was their special thing; they had wanted to fly all their lives. I had two or three guys in my class like that. One guy was always flying while he was there. Even in pre-flight, he was like a little boy with a wagon. Unfortunately, he didn't make it. Some guys thought flying was in and of itself the end of the world. We were brimming with confidence. Many of us thought that most of the guys in training could succeed. But it was a tough challenge. You couldn't be a slacker and get by in the Tuskegee Pilot Training Program. You had to be on the ball."

Their war-time record and post war successes provide ample basis to conclude that the story of the Tuskegee Airmen is not one in which being a successful graduate of the program made them great pilots, or great men. It's just the opposite. Theirs is a story of outstanding young men having made the Tuskegee Army Air Field, Pilot Training Program successful, and the term "Tuskegee Airmen" renowned as a direct result of the caliber of each individual. Tuskegee Army Air Field was a magnet for some of the best educated, best prepared and most competitive young men in the nation and the black community; they were outstanding scholars and athletes.

To name a few of his friends Robinson begins: "I had a friend who was a star athlete at Northwestern University, Bernie Jefferson. He was an all-American football player there, where he was a running back."

"Then there was Wilmeth Sidat-Singh from Washington, D.C. He was an outstanding basketball player and an all America football player at Syracuse. He was a tough sportsman and an excellent athlete. I believe he was also a semi-pro basketball player with the Washington Bears. As a football player and a running back, he used to bulldoze over everybody. He would have been great in the pros, but professional football wasn't integrated then. He became a policeman here in Washington, and that is how he managed to come to Tuskegee, from Washington, D.C.'s police force. He was at Oscoda, Michigan, taking gunnery when his plane malfunctioned over Lake Michigan and he bailed out. He got hung up in the parachute when it hit the water and was drowned."

"Ira O'Neal was the only black who played for Arizona State University at that time. He was a running back and a wide receiver."

"Then there's John Mosley. He was an all-conference and all-America football player, and was an all-conference wrestler all four years while at Colorado State University. He was also an accomplished musician – a piano player and composer."

"Another guy, Charles Williams, as I recall, was a standout basketball player at UCLA."

"Ace Lawson, (his name was actually Herman Lawson,

but we called him Ace) was a lineman for Fresno State University. He was also the national collegiate light heavyweight boxing champion for two years, and a letterman in basketball and track. These guys were great athletes and scholars, as well. And there were several others."

Those who made it successfully through the program at Tuskegee demonstrated that when given an opportunity, blacks could produce and were capable of sustaining a high level of proficiency, success and achievement – even in flying sophisticated and technical airplanes operated under the high stress conditions of air warfare – just like whites and anybody else. The integration of the armed forces was accelerated as a result of what these men did. Two things happened in the Air Corps that shifted the military's mindset away from segregation.

First, soon after the war's end, skilled white personnel began leaving the Air Force while, at the same time, the black portion of the Air Force began to have surpluses of skilled people. The Air Corps needed to backfill some of the vacancies created by the departure of whites with skilled blacks. Lockbourne had an oversupply of key personnel, highly qualified individuals with good skills. Almost immediately they were sent to different units of the Air Force. Consequently, when the order to integrate came along, the Air Force integrated within days whereas the other military branches took two or three years.

The next thing is that a few years after the war, President Truman integrated all of the armed services. Tuskegee Army Air Field was already closed by then, and the personnel had been moved to Lockbourne Airfield. Godman Field was closed, and its personnel were also moved to Lockbourne. It had been the home of the 477 Composite Bomber Group. Lockbourne also absorbed portions of the 332nd but soon Lockbourne was closed. The military began to integrate right after the United States Air Force was established as a separate branch in 1947 even before Truman signed Executive Order Number 9981 in 1948.[x] The Air Force's experience was one whereby it recognized that the armed forces needed blacks as well as everybody else. With the break-up of Lockbourne, it meant that these guys were scattered all over the Air Force. Many of them, like Robinson, retired out of the service and looked for other opportunities.

Success continued to accompany these men, both the ones who stayed in service, and those who moved on. From the Tuskegee Airmen ranks emerged an honor-roll of leaders – military standouts: General Benjamin O. Davis, Jr., the first black Air Force General and General Daniel "Chappie" James, Jr., the first four-star General and other officers - politicians, judges, educators, doctors, air force pilots, clergymen, entrepreneurs and members of a host of other professions. William Coleman, former secretary of transportation during the Ford administration, was a Tuskegee Airman. Some who weren't pilots, like Coleman Young, a bombardier navigator and second lieutenant who was elected the mayor of Detroit in the 1970s and 1980s, and Percy Sutton, an intelligence officer, who became president of the Manhattan Borough, became politicians with national profiles. Sutton also established the first black radio station in New York City. There's also Charles Diggs, who became a Congressman from Michigan. A few more Tuskegee Airmen were elected to public office in state and local legislatures, and Robinson knew at least four who became judges.

One man, Charlie Plinton, bought an old plane and formed his own airline that flew from Jamaica to Guatemala as Robinson best recalls. Plinton had been one of the first black flight instructors at Tuskegee. He only had one plane so he'd fly over, come back, and fly over again. His airline wasn't very reliable. If he had trouble, he often would have to stay overnight somewhere to get it fixed, but at least he was making money. In 1957 he made history when he became the first black executive at a major airline after having been appointed executive assistant to the director of personnel at Trans World Airline. Eastern bought out his company later and made him a vice president. He was their first black vice-president and the highest ranking black executive in the industry. About five years after Plinton was hired, Eastern hired another gentleman by the name of Cox, who had been a Tuskegee Airman, to supervise the mechanical engineers. Then Eastern started hiring black pilots.

There were others who excelled in new careers in business and education. Elwood Driver became Vice Chairman of the National Transportation Safety Board. Lee Archer became a vice president of General Foods; his buddy, Dr. Roscoe Brown, Jr. served as president of Bronx Community College of City University of New York and started NYU's Institute for Afro-American Studies.

Several Tuskegee Airmen have written books about their "Tuskegee Experience," and many others have good stories to tell. It's worth mentioning a couple of them. The first has to do with scouts dispatched by the 99th Squadron in early September of 1943 to locate a site on the Italian mainland to be used to establish a base for the squadron - about the same time Robinson and his group was searching for the 99th. This was expected to be a relatively safe and easy affair following successful allied landings at Salerno. The scouts left Sicily and went ashore near Battapaglia. There they found themselves immediately under enemy fire, were forced to retreat and join British forces who equipped the pistol carrying pilots – who were now cast in the role of infantry men - with weapons suitable for intense ground fighting. After that encounter cleared, the patrol group continued to their second destination only to find it still in German hands. Provided with an alternate third site, they moved on and arrived there exhausted. Soon after they made camp, they were discovered by the Germans and came under constant enemy air-fire – bombing and strafing. They were pinned down for five days and nights. They feared for their lives all during their search until reunited with their squadron in Foggia in mid October, almost six weeks later.

Another story has to do with a fellow named Clarence W. Allen from Mobile, Alabama, who was shot down in Italy while the Allied army was advancing. After he ejected, he landed in mountainous terrain and while moving about spotted some messages lying around that were written in German, so he knew the Germans were close by. Surveying his surroundings, he saw two German sentries at the top of a hill. At about the same moment, the sentries saw him and ordered him to halt. He fled down a hillside to a wooded area, jumped into the brush, crawled about under the bushes and stayed there very still. The sentries came down, poked the bushes a little and made a half-hearted attempt to find him, then moved on. After they left, he took off. He went in the opposite direction and another wooded area where he thought he would sleep for the night. When he awoke the next morning, he was alarmed to find himself in a German occupied area where they were stirring about getting their gear together to move out. So he sneaked off along a mountain ridge, spotted a cave, and crawled far back into it and hid. As he was hiding, two Germans with machine guns came along, entered and set up their guns at the mouth of the cave; they never checked out the area in the cave behind them. Allen stayed hidden for about an hour. Finally the Germans moved on. They were being chased by a group of Japanese-American soldiers, some of them Japanese-American citizens who had been interred in America by the United States government after Japan attacked Pearl Harbor. When they arrived, Allen joined them and they got him back to allied lines.

Then there's the tale of a daring escape made by Charlie Hall, who was attacked alternately both by German planes and Allied planes after they both mistook him for the enemy during a mission in Italy. He was on a bomber escort mission and spotted enemy aircraft approaching the formation after the bombers had delivered their loads. He peeled off, headed for the approaching enemy aircraft, closed in on them with machine guns firing and shot one down; the others fled. His plane, low on fuel, was damaged in the exchange. As he headed back to rejoin the formation, a pair of enemy aircraft pursued him, firing and closing in on him. Charlie couldn't outrun them so he maneuvered his plane around and charged at them head-on with his fifty millimeter machine guns blazing. They dispersed and he managed to escape and head back to the formation. When the formation spotted him coming up on them, a couple of those aircraft mistook him for an enemy plane and went after him. He fled again, this time away from friendly forces.

In making his escape, he came within sight of the German aircraft again, and they resumed their chase. He spotted two more planes off in the distance thinking that help was on the way. But it was two more German planes and now there were four of them chasing him. He was forced to use "evasive maneuvers" that he had instructed Robinson to use as he alternately attacked, dived, rolled, dodged, and fled. The Germans chased him but would back off as he maneuvered around to fight back. Then they would chase him again, almost toying with him – they knew their planes were faster. Charlie continued to fire and maneuver as he tried to fight his way toward Pantelleria where he knew he would find Allied planes.

As he neared Allied planes, they began to attack him yet again. After working his radio and advising the controller of his identification and the situation, he was allowed to approach the formation. After a twenty minute chase, he had made a daring escape while being greatly outnumbered and piloting a damaged plane that was terribly low on fuel – a credit to his considerable skills.

But for years much of the country knew nothing of these men and took little interest. In fact while Curtis Robinson was in the hospital in Charleston, S.C., recuperating from his accident, a public relations officer for the Air Corps, a young lady from Special Services, took him out. She interviewed him, took a handsome photograph of him, wrote a very nice article and sent both to his hometown newspaper in Orangeburg, South Carolina. "Well, what the paper printed when they got the Special Services write-up was a one liner," chuckles Robinson, "one sentence that said 'Curtis Robinson has returned home from Italy' - period. Talk about short, I'm telling you, no picture, no nothing. It was just a one-line story, a very short sentence."

None of the national news services or major papers picked up on any of their activity during the war. Only the black press did. The black press had the Airmen story publicized within the black community, but the regular newspapers carried nothing, absolutely nothing. Robinson tells of one particular case: "There was an instance when we were in combat in Anzio and shot down seventeen planes over a period of two or three days starting on January 27, 1944. Not one white reporter reported it. It wasn't in any of the papers in the States but it was a big thing. *Stars and Stripes*[xi] reported it, and several generals and dignitaries came around, but no white reporters. If it had been another squadron that had downed that many planes, it would have been in all the papers in the

States," observes Robinson. "It might not have been deliberate, but I believe we were just ignored. I don't think white reporters thought the Tuskegee pilots were doing anything worth writing about. They thought that we were just there. No one from the white press ever came around to interview anyone or investigate anything. I don't recall there ever being any white press around during the time I was in the service."

Had those men not formed the Tuskegee Airmen, Inc. organization, there would most likely not be very much information about them today. The organization was formed more then thirty years ago by a group in Washington, D.C., after a few preliminary meetings were held in other parts of the country. It was 1972 when someone came up with the idea of getting together all of the guys who were former Tuskegee Airmen. Letters were sent to all the former Tuskegee pilots all over the country, suggesting they meet in Detroit. As far as Robinson recalled, three former Airmen from Washington, D.C., went to the Detroit meeting: John Suggs, Eldridge Jackson and Willie Ashley. Ashley was one of the original Tuskegee Airmen who went over to Italy with Colonel Benjamin O. Davis, Jr. and the first group of pilots. That meeting in Detroit marked the beginning of formal efforts to create an organization.

The affair was a good start and everyone had a great time, but more work was required. Meeting participants asked Suggs to see if he could begin an organization in Washington, D.C. So upon his return to Washington, Suggs and Eldridge Jackson sent letters to all of the Tuskegee Airmen they knew in the area suggesting a meeting at a local church. About thirty people responded, and the Tuskegee Airmen, Inc. was established. Officers elected at that first meeting were: John Suggs - President or commander; Kenny White - Vice President; Harry Shepherd – Secretary and Curtis Robinson,

Treasurer. William Broadwater was the head of the board. These men got it operating and decided to have the first nationwide convention in Washington, D.C. They formalized the organizational structure - got their 501(c)(3) and 501 (c)(19) designation from the government - raised money, sent out invitations to every Tuskegee Airman they could think of, planned and held the first Tuskegee Airmen, Inc. convention.

Their convention, held on August 10th – 12th of 1973, was very well attended and extremely successful. They divided the country into three regions; East Coast, West Coast, and Central, although there were to be numerous chapters within these regions. Detroit, Chicago, Denver, and Kansas City, for example, would be part of the Central region; Philadelphia, Washington, Atlanta, and New York would be East Coast. The West Coast included Los Angeles, San Francisco, Sacramento, plus a few other cities. Spann Watson became president of the national chapter and under his leadership, the national organization received its 501(c)(3) designation on February 21, 1975. The registered address was Washington, D.C., though today it is Arlington, VA. The big turn-out was encouraging and was an auspicious beginning for the group.

To his credit, Spann Watson was also responsible for other important initiatives. He worked for the Federal Aviation Administration (FAA) for many years. The FAA held a meeting of all of the heads of the airlines in Washington, D.C., in the early 1960s, and the question came up as to why there were no black stewardesses working for any of those airlines. The industry's response was that they couldn't find any. They claimed that if they could find qualified blacks, they would hire them. Spann told them that he would find them some that they would be able to hire. He went to Howard University and other area colleges, identified and recruited some students, and groomed them for about a month with "charm school" training. Then he presented them to the airlines, and they were accepted. He was responsible for getting many blacks into the airline industry as stewardesses, and he eventually succeeded in getting a few black pilots hired, too.

That Washington, D.C., convention officially marked the beginning of Tuskegee Airmen, Inc. ®. The Washington Post sent a reporter and photographer to their 1973 convention. The organization established a National Scholarship Fund in 1978 that continues to provide annual scholarships to deserving and disadvantaged high school students dedicated to aviation or related areas such as aviation medicine, mathematics, engineering, etc. The scholarship has grown. It has an endowment that was approximately $2 million in 2004. The organization has provided more than $1 million in scholarships to more than 500 deserving youth - roughly, eighteen to twenty scholarships per year. Besides that, each chapter has an educational assistance fund that supplements scholarships by providing an additional $500 or $1,000 to buy books and miscellaneous items because, for some, the national chapter scholarship may not be sufficient.

Two years after the formation of Tuskegee Airmen, Inc. its members decided to establish a museum. Pilots began to send their flight clothing and war memorabilia to Detroit, Michigan where it's kept in two barracks at Fort Wayne. They are trying to preserve their history and legacy. The Tuskegee Airmen Inc. also began a tradition of annual achievement awards banquets that has given awards to the likes of General Daniel "Chappie" James, Jr., William A. Campbell who was one of the first airmen to receive two Distinguished Flying Crosses, was a Commander of the 99th Squadron, and the first black engaged in an aerial battle for the Air Corps; plus other notable personalities. They continue to present these awards each year.

The pilots of the 99th were special men who made such a

name for themselves in the war, that they were often sent into air battles where they were outnumbered three-to-one by the Germans. Early on they spent a lot of time training because the Air Corps didn't know what to do with them. Many of their pilots had well over a hundred hours in a plane before they went overseas. In 1943 Col. Davis estimated that some men had logged more than 250 hours in a P-40 before the time of their first combat assignment, the type of experienced new pilot that he characterized as "a hard man to find." Another consideration is that Tuskegee didn't have replacements to relieve pilots like other squadrons and groups. So many of them flew large numbers of sorties and soon acquired significant combat experience. That made them better than a lot of the German pilots they encountered. Also their extensive experience in sports certainly enhanced their eye and hand coordination, and it's possible that may have given them advantages against the Germans during dog-fights, too.

Perhaps John Suggs, first president of Tuskegee Airmen, Inc. best captures their spirit in his greetings for their third national reunion: "We were justly proud of ourselves, individually and collectively, for truly we were 'one-of-a-kind,' not through election of our own but through circumstances completely beyond our control. The unrelenting denial and complete suppression of opportunity, even to fight for our country, created within us the indomitable spirit of unity and the burning desire to succeed. When, at last, the breach was made, that potential - the theoretical power to accomplish became a reality, we moved! That forward movement – progress – has continued, albeit not as rapidly or consistently as we had hoped; but momentum is still present."

As for Robinson: "Being a Tuskegee Airman kept me going. It contributed to my being successful in life. Just knowing how much good all the other airmen were doing helped to keep me motivated. I can't think of any Airman I've known of who hasn't done something good, hasn't been successful at something once he got out of service. Meeting those guys and seeing what they were doing made me realize that I had to keep on doing the best I could at whatever I was doing. One thing, for sure, can be said about the guys at Tuskegee: the Army Air Corps got the best and brightest on the continent. They were really remarkable men. You can't imagine some of the guys who came to Tuskegee Army Air Field. The knowledge they had; how smart they were; they were absolutely outstanding! Some were positively brilliant! When it comes to the Tuskegee Airmen, let me tell you, it was something special to be among the best and brightest men from all the best schools in the United States and Canada. Everyone should have that kind of experience."

The Way I See It

"Pharmacist Fills Prescriptions and a Social Need"
by Marc Fisher

"Just for fun, I called one of the 48 CVS pharmacies in the District and asked if it would deliver a prescription. 'No, we don't do that," the nice pharmacist said. I checked the company's Web site, which offered to mail prescription items within 10 days, or, for a mere $16.95 "express" fee within six days.

'Then I stopped by Doc Robinson's basement on East Capitol Street N.E. Doc delivers. Six days a week, when he locks up the Robinson Apothecary, he drops off a few medicines at his customers' homes. 'I take it by when I close, and we sit and talk," he says. 'I might stay half an hour and visit."

'No charge." 'No, I couldn't charge," Doc says, 'Because I deliver at my convenience."

"The sign outside Doc's tiny entrance says just "Pharmacy." There's no light in the stairwell; "wouldn't want to bother the neighbors at night." No sprightly music whisks you through your shopping. No ads clutter the carved wooden doorway. No aisles of dry goods or notions block the way to the pharmacist's counter.

"No, there's nothing here but long and lean Curtis C. Robinson, 83 now, former Tuskegee Airman, veteran of 33 World War II combat missions over Italy, graduate of Howard University's School of Pharmacy, proud grandson of a slave who became a postmaster and a Methodist minister, stalwart survivor of the drugstore chains' war against independent pharmacies.

"Back in the '60s, Robinson owned [six] pharmacies in Washington. He was usually located in the same building, with a busy medical practice. He never did much with what's known in the trade as the front end – the cosmetics, toiletries and whatnot that now account for most drugstore profits. He just liked to fill prescriptions and advise customers on their drugs.

"At one time, I was doing a hundred prescriptions a day," Doc says. Now I look at television, fill 15 or 20 prescriptions and look at some more television which suits me fine. This is my life." The doctors, who worked upstairs in the three-story corner row-house, left a few years ago-one died, another found a new location. But Robinson stayed on, alone. He's especially alone since his wife, Florie, died [three] years ago. "Now I go home and look at more television," he says.

"Robinson Apothecary is an archive of customer records, a museum of office equipment of the past half-century, a stockroom with a specialty in geriatric drugs-not by choice or training so much as by the passage of time in the lives of a few hundred loyal customers. Robinson decided some years ago to refer new customer to his independent colleague down the block, Morton's.

"I don't carry any pediatric stuff anymore," Doc says.

"He's lucky to carry anything, given how the business has changed. 'When I graduated pharmacy school, it seemed like there was a drugstore on every corner,' Doc recalls. "Slowly but surely, the chains grew. At the independents, the senior was usually unable to get the junior to take over the store. Then Medicare and insurance companies took over and took the profits out of the pharmacy business. The only profits left were in the front end, and those independents that had no front end were out of business.

"Robinson's front end is a lawn. 'Only way I survive is no overhead," Doc says. He and a partner owned the building until they sold recently to a young couple who are returning the place to its original role as a single-family house. But the couple wants Robinson to stay, and Doc says, "I figure I have several more years.'

"The chains have forced most family-owned drugstores in the Washington area out of business, literally surrounding Mom and Pops with new branches, then buying their prescription files and sending neighborhood institutions off to an unsought retirement. Those who have managed to stick it out have banded together in buying groups to wheedle discounts from wholesalers; even so, the chains have a huge advantage in their contracts with managed-care companies and employers.

"But no chain can compete with what Robinson offers: 'People come from their doctor, and they want advice. I don't want to conflict with what the doctor says. But they seem to trust you more than they trust their doctor. Naturally. They've known Doc Robinson for 50 years, he comes to their house; he calls them to remind them if they need a refill. He's what we've lost, and we haven't the slightest idea how to get it back."

Though all of his classmates from pharmacy school have retired and are living a retired life, Robinson is the type of person who has an entrenched sense of purpose. It was a surprise to him to receive an award from the Howard University School of Pharmacy in 2003 for 51 years of service. They held a special program for him and presented him his award, of which he says, "I didn't realize that all of my pharmacy classmates were retired. There were more than forty of us in my graduating class. I believe only eight of us are still alive; I thought I had other classmates that were still in pharmacy, but I found out that I am the last one still working."

"Retirement is a part of life that I've never desired. I have to have something to do and pharmacy is something that I love, so I'll do it until I die. And I love people. That combination keeps me going. Besides, most of my customers are my friends, people that I've been dealing with for the last fifteen to forty years. Sometimes I'll leave the store in the evening, drop something off at one of my customers, sit down, have a cup of coffee, and talk for a while. It's nice to have customers like that. What I do is not work to me. It's a pleasure to be there. I started working as a young kid and, aside from the time I spent waiting to report to Tuskegee and the two weeks off after being refused an employment application at Eastern Airlines, I have been working ever since."

He was magnanimous towards his customers and all throughout his lifetime it has been easy for him to be thoughtful and considerate towards others. "A person has to be able to live right. If people see that you are living right, it carries a lot of weight," Robinson adds. He had an experience that bore that out, one that shocked, and surprised him more than thirty-five years ago. He needed some change and went to a store nearby to get it. A female customer of his was there cursing and confronting other customers and the merchant. She saw him and said, "Excuse me, Doc Robinson, excuse me," and she stopped immediately. There were many other people present that she had likely offended, but she picked him out to apologize to. "That shocked me because of the respect she showed me," he says of the incidence. "I believe she did it because I respected her. I always showed her respect. I respected all of my customers. As a result I've gotten along pretty well, and I don't think I have any enemies, at least none that I know of. Plus I never spoke badly of others and was always able to get along."

His family life and the way he was brought up laid the foundation for the person he became, the way he approached life, and sustained himself. With all his brothers as role models, there was little that his parents had to do or tell him. He saw what his brothers were doing, and he just fell in line, of which he says, "Nobody told me that I had to go to high school after I graduated from elementary school or college after I graduated from high school. I went over to Claflin on my own to see if I could get a job and pay for my high school education. I did the same thing when it was time to go to college. My grandfather, my parents, and brothers had already done those things."

And almost all Robinson's high school and college classmates did well in life, too, probably as well as they could for the times in which they lived. There was only so much that most blacks could realistically accomplish under "Jim Crow" rule and segregation. But his childhood friends succeeded. "The most successful friend financially would likely be Earl Middleton, who also was a cadet in the Tuskegee Pilot Training Program ahead of me. He washed out, and became a staff sergeant in the army," recounts Robinson. "He and another childhood friend, Eugene Montgomery, formed an insurance and real estate company together in Orangeburg. Their business grew to be large and successful. They separated and later Middleton became one of the biggest real estate developers there. He built two developments with forty-five homes in one and fifty-five in the other and made a ton of money. He was also elected as a state representative in the 1960s and served three terms. He was one of the few blacks in the state legislature at that time. He's been a millionaire down there for years."

"Two other Middleton brothers, Phillip and James, had much success after the war. One was a lieutenant assigned civil engineering duties and the other was a sergeant also in civil engineering. They held bachelor degrees in engineering. After their military service, they formed a construction company in California and did very well."

"Another classmate and friend was James Thomas, who is now Bishop James Thomas in the United Methodist Church. He was a class ahead of me. After college, he went into the ministry. Right after the war, three Methodist groups, the Methodist, Methodist Episcopal, and Methodist North combined and formed the United Methodist Church. Out of that group there were initially about thirteen bishops, nationwide. Bishop Thomas was the only black bishop in the group. There must be fifty now. He was located in the Midwest. Now he's down at Emory University, is retired, but he lectures there".

"There was Tommy Lee, who was half Chinese. His father was a full Chinese and his mother was black. When he first started school, his parents sent him to a white school which immediately sent him back to the black school. He was in the service with me at Tuskegee as a sergeant. After the war, he moved to California and landed a good job as an electrical engineer; he had majored in electronics at South Carolina State.".

"Another guy was Robert Spagna. After he graduated from elementary school, he went on to South Carolina State's high school and college. He took up architecture and became a very successful architect in Philadelphia."

"There's Dover Bowman. After high school, he went to embalming school, ended up owning several funeral homes, and was elected to the city council. They have a street named for him in Timmonsville, South Carolina. He died about ten years ago."

These men were all Robinson's childhood friends. There were only ten boys in his high school graduating class. Almost every one of them who either went to high school or college did well in life. And the schools he attended had dedicated teachers who dealt with overcrowding and still educated students well. He was fortunate to have lived in the shadows of the campuses of Claflin College and South Carolina State College. Schools were segregated, the races were segregated, and he had little contact with whites. According to Robinson, "Race relations were, 'don't you bother them and they might not bother you.' There were people being lynched and beaten, but it seemed to happen most often to people who worked around whites or interacted with them regularly, but not to anybody I knew, or from my neighborhood. The only real incidences I had with whites, with the exception of those I encountered when I worked in the drug store in Orangeburg, occurred after I entered the service. Otherwise, I just didn't have any real contact with whites."

"But while stationed in Tuskegee, Alabama, I had a different vantage point. When I was stationed at Tuskegee, during elections, all these white candidates came out on the stump campaigning. They would say, 'We're not going to let niggers vote, we're not going to let niggers fight and carry weapons,' and 'Niggers don't have radios so they won't know what's happening.' I had never seen or heard anything like that in my life, I never saw that happen in South Carolina. But in Georgia and Alabama, I'll tell you, that did happen."

By the end of World War II, Robinson could see small

changes in behavior – "a little more aggressiveness on the part of blacks and a little more stonewalling on the part of whites. It became a problem shortly after the war," says Robinson, "where a big standoff or a riot might occur at any time. The war had transformed hundreds of thousands of men into a fighting mode, an assertive mindset. It had reached a point where it was virtually impossible for the spirits of blacks to be destroyed and freedom to be delayed any longer. Since federal troops pulled out of the South in the nineteenth century, the South had been maintaining steady racial backsliding. Blacks occupied a world deprived by southern whites of occupational choices, participation in government, or public access and accommodation, and faced a cruel system backed by the courts and law enforcement."

"After the Brown decision, the big push for equality gained momentum, led by Dr. Martin Luther King who was a catalyst for positive changes. But when his charges tried to appeal to their government for relief, they were pummeled – they were viciously reminded that they had no government. I thought the Civil Rights Movement was the greatest thing going and I have nothing but admiration for Dr. King and all the people – the common people - in Birmingham, and Montgomery Alabama, for the sacrifices they made and dangers they faced in the furtherance of civil rights. I know how those people were treated and felt down there. When we were in the Tuskegee Pilot Training Program, our wives would go to Montgomery to shop and were forbidden to try on hats or shoes in the department stores because they were black. They were treated worse than second class citizens; yet their husbands were providing a service to their country."

When television arrived in the South to show the American public and the world exactly what was going on in Alabama and other southern states, the country began to act out of embarrassment. Gradually, around the time of Dr. King's "I Have a Dream" speech, Robinson could see things slowly begin to change. "Lyndon Johnson came along following the assassination of President Kennedy pushed through significant Civil Rights legislation, and the whole atmosphere began to change. When Stokely Carmichael[xii] started promoting the idea of 'black power,' in the late 1960s, I became concerned for that was almost the time things got really bad in my hometown. There was a sharp division between the two races still. During my youth, black kids in Orangeburg hung out around the college campuses, and white kids hung out downtown. But in 1968, area black college and high school students held a demonstration at the bowling alley downtown - mostly students from Claflin College and South Carolina State who wanted to bowl. The bowling alley was still segregated and they weren't allowed in. Crowds gathered around it. The state police and the National Guard showed up; the demonstration lasted four days. South Carolina highway patrolmen fired shotguns into a crowd of students and killed three, including a high school student, and wounded twenty-seven more.

Eventually, as a middle aged man, he could see race relations in the South and nation improve; a good thing from Robinson's perspective because his observation was that younger blacks were not going to tolerate old-school racism any longer. Television exposure that he and his fellow-pilots received in 1996 in a movie "Tuskegee Airmen" by HBO, gave pause for him to be slightly embarrassed when he visited a school in Washington, D.C., after the airing of the movie. He was speaking to a class with a white teacher who had shown the movie to her students; he was there answering questions when one little black girl asked him, "Why are white people so mean?" Robinson says, "I was shocked at first and tried to explain to her that all white people aren't mean. That sometimes, they just don't understand other people. After they meet people different from themselves and get to know them, they change. But," Robinson adds, "I tell you it was a shock that she had asked me that in front of the teacher. Kids today are far less likely to accept the type of racism that my generation put up with."

"As society has changed," Robinson adds, "it's become easier for strivers to achieve their goals. There are young blacks who have gone out and done things, gotten good jobs and have shown people what blacks can do. Then there's another group, particularly guys, who have held themselves back preferring to depend on society or women, and complaining about discrimination rather than really trying. That concerns me. They think the world owes them a living, and that's sad. There are too many of them doing that now. Their complaints about discrimination are valid to a point, but a lot of young black men have simply not taken it upon themselves to do everything they could to succeed. And then there is the number of young girls/young women becoming heads of households at a very young age. Without a man in the house, there is really no discipline or understanding of what should be done, particularly when rearing young boys. I cannot remember a single household in my community during my childhood that had children, that didn't originally have a man in the house. The man may have died and left a widow and a child, but otherwise there was always a man around. That made a difference."

"Many black kids today don't take full advantage of the opportunities available to them, particularly in urban neighborhoods. Some don't seem to see any advantage in trying to push ahead. In some city schools the smart kids are looked down on by the ones who don't study. They all could be smart, really, but some of these kids have no incentive. They just don't see themselves with big jobs or running corporations;

they don't make the connection between school and career. I wish they did. Students from families of some means usually have parents trying to motivate them, but they are also the ones who get all the material things they want. I was very conscious of that. Some parents who were deprived as kids want to give their kids things they never had and spoiled them - the clothes they wear; sneakers with star athlete names on them that cost a fortune. Our sneakers cost $1.50 and we wore them to keep from wearing our good shoes. Today kids want to wear $150 sneakers and other material things peddled by their role models. My philosophy is let them work for it. It has altered their value system. I had to pay for my high school and college education, and we shared everything; it was easy for us to do. If you come from a large family, there is no room for selfishness. Material things are great, but I'd rather have friends. As society continues to change, success will be within the reach of those who acquire and who strive to acquire as much knowledge as they can - educational, personal, professional, and otherwise."

Robinson adds that when he was in the second grade, a local firm gave each student in his class a foot long ruler. Across the front was 'The Golden Rule.' On the back it said 'Do unto others as you would have them to do unto you.' He emphasizes, "That was preached in my community. My parents preached it, the preachers preached it and it was something I grew up with and believed in. It was embedded in me, and it's still there; I still feel that way. The other important lesson was 'Love thy neighbor;' if you live by those rules you're bound to have a good life. And as I got older, I found out that the best happiness you can receive is when you make someone else happy. If you want to be happy, make those around you happy and it's a win-win for everybody"

Above all, Curtis Christopher Robinson learned to focus on maintaining consistency in his relationship with God by referencing his life's experiences. He says, "Life can sometimes be so worry free. And things can be going so well that you allow yourself to almost forget about God. Then something bad happens, and it brings you back to Him and you begin to pray and reconnect. That's a cycle that I imagine goes on throughout people's lives. Or at a certain age, you realize your own mortality and that you had better straighten out your relationship with God, your spiritual health. The older I get, the more I work on it. I say this because earlier I mentioned the incidence when I almost crashed. Things had been going beautifully. I was a young U.S. fighter pilot, educated, and doing well. I came within the breath of death. God came back into my life that day."

Then Robinson became busy with many other things. He flew more than thirty sorties in the war, became a flight instructor and delighted in his freedom and friendships. He remembers, "Everything was sailing so smoothly. I was having the greatest time of my life. On weekends, I could take a plane and fly all over the country, from city to city, and had friends in all the cities I visited. I would meet with my officer friends and have fun - Wednesday afternoon dances and Saturday evening affairs; I just had a great time. Everything was going so well that again, I almost forgot about God and my spiritual background. Florie and I got married and we had our baby, Linda, who was born very sick. Our prayers and efforts led us to the best specialists in the world who improved her life and almost performed a miracle – but our child died. That brought me back to where I should have been. My spiritual life picked up then, and I haven't lost it since."

"I know that my faith in God and myself provided me with the insight to find my strength and direction in life, and it is the reason I was able to succeed and to become a Tuskegee Airman."

APPENDIXES

Appendix A: Class 43-D-SE; April 20, 1943

By Curtis Robinson 12/31/04

Within my class, I was regarded as quite sociable. One of my classmates, Leonard Jackson, and I were thick as soup, best of friends and kept everyone else laughing. We always had a lot of fun. I think our fellow pilots saw us as good pilots, and we were both well liked. We could go to any party and have a lot of fun. I was always invited somewhere. I will always remember the men with whom I served and what follows is a brief recollection of my classmates. Their pictures are contained in the photo section. By reading from left to right, and starting with the bottom row:

Heber Houston went to Wayne State University in Detroit.

James Brothers was from Chicago and graduated from the University of Chicago. He was killed performing a diving maneuver during our transition period from the training planes to fighter planes.

Arnold Cisco was from Alton, Illinois, and attended the University of Chicago. He was killed in an air accident after he completed his tour of duty. It happened at Walterboro Army Air Field in South Carolina. He was at the end of the runway getting ready to take-off when an incoming plane accidentally landed on top of his plane.

Paul Adams from Greenville, South Carolina, graduated from South Carolina State. He was only about 5 feet 5 inches and was always crashing into something because the shorter guys couldn't see out of the planes as well as the taller ones. It's no problem if you're 6 feet tall, but at 5'5 it was difficult for him to see around corners. He had several accidents while at

Selfridge Field and became afraid to fly in combat. The Air Corps gave him a ground job, and that's what he did – provided ground support. It was rumored that he washed out two weeks before graduation. His father worked for Mendel Rivers, a Congressman from South Carolina. It was alleged that he called his father, his father called the Congressman, the Congressman called the base, and he was put back in and graduated along with us.

Billy Faulkner was from Nashville, Tennessee. His father was the Dean of Fisk University. I don't know how he made it. He always seemed to be struggling physically because he was quite anemic. He was shot down overseas.

Freddie Hutchins was from Donaldsonville, Georgia, and graduated from Tuskegee Institute. He had been taking flying lessons there before the Airman program began. In the dormitory, we had one phone in the back, and if it rang and someone other than Hutchinson answered, he would yell, 'Is it for me?' If the answer was 'No,' he'd yell back, 'Tell them that Hutch said Hello.' He loved to talk.

Wilson Eagleson was from Bloomington, Illinois. We called him "Sloppy Mack" because his clothes were never neatly on him; they were usually a mess. Someone was always on him about the way he dressed. He was what you would call "laid-back" - very "laid-back." He was an alumnus of West Virginia State College and was married. On the first Sunday of training at Selfridge, fellows who were married brought their wives to dinner. An announcer introduced each pilot and his wife. When the announcer got to Eagleson, he said, "Presenting Sloppy and Mrs. Mack."

Sidney Moseley was from Norfolk, Virginia. Moseley was a guy that had tremendous guts, but may have lacked sufficient skills for flying. I think the instructors may have let him through because he was so eager and courageous. He was killed in the P-40 fighter after failing to pull his plane out of a dive and crashing into the ground while we were in transition training.

Ulysses Taylor was from Kaufman, Texas, and was a very quiet man. His daughter was a news anchor on Washington D.C.'s Fox News 5 for awhile. His son graduated as a pilot from flight school and was killed in a flying accident. Both father and son are buried in Arlington Cemetery, but the senior Taylor died of natural causes.

Harold Sawyer was from Columbus, Ohio, and had graduated from Tuskegee Institute. He was a very nice, good looking guy, but very shy. The girls wanted him badly. I remember one summer on Tuskegee's campus, we were sitting down and these two girls came up. One of the girls asked, "Harold, when are you going to take me out?" Harold reached in his pocket, pulled out his cigarettes, took one out, lit it, leaned back and exhaled. As the smoke lingered and cleared the air, the girl asked, "Harold! When?" so he took another drag and then he said, "Soon." She asked, "Soon, Harold? What does that mean - this weekend, next weekend?" Harold replied, "Maybe." She asked, "What about this weekend, Harold?" He threw away the remainder of his cigarette, and I'm sitting there watching. He took out another one, lit it, blew out a puff of smoke and said, "I'm busy." I said, "I'm gone." I didn't want to see anymore, and I left them there. The mayor of his hometown declared January 22, 1945, as "Captain Harold Sawyer Day." He died of emphysema in 2002. He continued to smoke all those years.

Luke Weathers was from Memphis, Tennessee. He lives in Alexandria, Virginia, and went to Tennessee State College. When he returned from overseas, his hometown gave him a big parade and the local newspaper wrote a nice article about him.

Lewis C. Smith was from Los Angeles, California. We called him "Smirky" because of the smile he always had on his face. He was a linguist and had graduated from UCLA. After he left the service, he worked with the State Department for many years. He was stationed in Africa and in Laos during his tour with State. He died of cancer several years ago. He was fluent in Italian, Spanish and a few other languages. When we were in Italy, he spoke a lot of Italian and served as a translator for us while we were trying to find our squadron.

Leonard Jackson was my best friend in the service and one of the fellows who was shot down during a mission. But he survived it. He was from Fort Worth, Texas, had graduated from Tuskegee Institute where he had participated in their flying program and resumed flying with the Tuskegee Airmen Program. He was a great guy, and everybody liked him. He came out of the service right after I did, but he went back in. Another friend of ours, who was a class behind us, Albert Manning, also lived here in Washington, D.C. Jackson's wife was a friend of my wife and Manning's wife. They decided they would visit us. Jackson's wife flew to Washington, and he was to fly into Bolling Air Force Base from San Antonio. We were out at Bolling in Washington, D.C., waiting for him, but because of bad weather, Bolling was closed for the night and Jackson was rerouted to Harrisburg, Pennsylvania. But he didn't have sufficient fuel, his plane went down just short of the runway, and he was killed. His wife was with us when she got the news and was devastated, as we all were.

Vernon Haywood was from Raleigh, N.C., and graduated from Hampton Institute (HI), now Hampton University. He learned to fly in HI's flying program. He was a great guy and became our cadet chaplain. He married a really nice young lady named Melanie, right after graduation. She died about thirteen years later and he remarried a woman who looked just like her; she was nice, too. He died in 2002.

James Carter was from Winston Salem, N.C. His father was a physician who sent him to law school in Montreal, Canada at McGill University. He came in as a lawyer. His father was one of the founders of the trolley system in his hometown. I remember he used to get big checks from R.J. Reynolds because they leased some warehouses on property owned by his family. He had a half-sister, who was instructor of dance at Howard University. His family was very well-to-do.

Walter Foreman was from Washington, D.C. What stands out most in my mind about him is what he did in an incident involving his fiancé, who was in Washington, D.C. She had tuberculosis and was in Howard University's tuberculosis sanitarium. While we were at Oscoda, he found out that she was dying. He flew home the next day, married her, and stayed with her until she died – shortly thereafter.

Charles Bailey was from Punta Gorda, Florida. He graduated from Bethune-Cookman College, and if you said anything bad about Ms. Bethune, you had a fight on your hands. He was a very aggressive guy who went overseas a month before I did. He shot down a plane while we were on a mission together. When he returned from overseas, the city gave him a nice plaque commemorating his service. He opened a funeral home business in Blaine, Florida, and resided and taught school in Daytona Beach. He died about two years ago.

Charles Williams was from Lima, Ohio. He went to UCLA and was already in the service when he came into the program at Tuskegee. He had been a member of the Buffalo Soldiers. He was the oldest guy in our class and really lucked up by coming in there. He volunteered when he was twenty-five, but they didn't call him until he was almost twenty-seven. He was the commander of a B-25 unit. He got married while we were based at Selfridge Field. Later his wife died and he remarried. After he got out of the service, he took a job as the personnel officer for National Cash Register in Dayton, Ohio, and that's where he stayed until he retired.

Appendix B: Curtis Robinson's

Certificate of Induction

Into the Claflin University Hall of Fame

Certificate of Induction
Into The Claflin University Hall of Fame

This is to certify that

Curtis C. Robinson

was inducted into the Claflin University Hall of Fame
Friday, November 19, 2004
Jonas T. Kennedy Health and Physical Education Center
Claflin University
Orangeburg, South Carolina

International Alumni President

Vice President for Institutional Advancement

President of the University

In a fitting tribute to the special relationship shared between Curtis Robinson and Claflin University, he was inducted into the University's Hall of Fame on November 19, 2004.

Bibliography

Books

Homan, Lynn M. and Reilly, Thomas. *BLACK Knights The Story of the Tuskegee Airmen*

Cooper, Charlie & Ann. *Tuskegee's Heroes Featuring the Aviation Art of Ropy La Grone*

Cary, Francine Curro. *Washington Odyssey – A Multicultural History of the Nation's Capital; Smithsonian Books – Washington and London*

The Washington Post, *Washington Album, A Pictorial History of the Nation's Capitol*

Periodical and Newspapers

Fitchett, E. Horace (Dean, Claflin College, Orangeburg, S.C.) "The Robinson Family," February 17, 1944

Fisher, Marc. "Pharmacist Fill Prescriptions And a Social Need," The Washington Post, November 26, 2002

Miscellaneous

Brown, Judith. *Tuskegee Airmen Oral History Project,* National Park Service, October 3, 2002

Robinson, Thomas Archer. *The Robinson Family History*

FOOTNOTES

[i]Plessy vs.. Fergusson [163-US- 537,538] was a decision handed down by the Supreme Court in 1896 which sanctioned the practice of separate public facilities and accommodations in the US. It was the cornerstone of the "separate but equal" doctrine, and sanctioned racial segregation. Mr. Plessy, it was reported, was 7/8th white and 1/8th black, light complexioned, and could pass for white. He bought a first class train ticket, but was arrested for refusing to sit in the colored section. Mr. Plessy took his case to court and lost.

[ii]Booker T. Washington was an influential black educator and leader in the late nineteenth and early twentieth century. Born a slave in rural Virginia in 1856, Washington graduated from Hampton Institute and went on to establish Tuskegee Institute in 1881 as an industrial and agricultural institution for blacks. He was criticized by many black leaders of his era for advocating a position that accommodated racial segregation, a denial of voting rights, and other inequities deemed important to the black community.

[iii] The Reverend Jesse Jackson is founder of Operation PUSH (People United to Save Humanity), a human rights activist who was a field representative for the Congress on Racial Equality and the Southern Christian Leadership Conference – Dr. King's organization – during the 1960s, Rev. Jackson is a nationally renowned minister and was a Presidential candidate during the 1984 Presidential campaign.

[iv] The National Recovery Act was established by the National Industrial Recovery Act of 1933 to help the economic recovery of the United States after the Great Depression. This Act created the Public Works Administration, suspended many anti-trust laws, required companies to write industry-wide work codes, permitted the formation of labor unions and collective bargaining, and set aside funds to train teachers and youth.

[v] Buffalo Soldier was the name given to black soldiers of the 9th and 10th Calvary and 24th and 25th Infantry Regiments by the Cheyenne and Comanche Indians during the late 1860s. Black units were formed by Congressional legislation in 1866 following the involvement of almost 200,000 black Americans in the Union Army during the Civil War. Since white citizens in southern and eastern states did not want to see armed black soldiers in the areas where they resided, the soldiers were deployed in western frontier states: New Mexico, Arizona, Montana, the Dakotas, Texas, Nebraska, and Utah. The Buffalo Soldiers fought Mexican revolutionaries, hostile Indians and outlaws. These soldiers also strung telegraph lines, and built and repaired frontier outposts.

[vi] Army of the United States, as it relates to the United States Army, has been around for many years. During World War II there was such a high rate of draftees and the Army had grown so large that the military couldn't afford to give these draftees the same benefits that the regular army had. So the military essentially used the other unit for inductees who came in after a certain time. When the war was over, and veterans of the Army of the U.S. were discharged, it was with a "thank you" for being good soldiers. Veterans of the regular army received standard benefits.

[vii] Liberty ship was the name given to some U.S. Navy ships that were mass produced under

emergency conditions and very short intervals between 1942 and 1945. Characterized by a simple design and constructed to last about five years, approximately 2,750 liberty ships were built. They were pre-fabricated and mass produced quickly by welding the pre-fabricated sections together. It took approximately seventy days to construct a liberty ship; the record was four and one half days. The ships transported troops, dry cargo, munitions, machinery, food, tanks, and vehicles.

[viii] "Blue Baby" is a term used to describe a medical condition "Tretralogy of Fallot", a congenital heart condition by which sufficient blood does not flow into the lungs for proper oxygenation. As a result of cyanosis (deoxygenated blood) areas around the lips, fingers, and toes of babies with the condition appear blue, and a cyanotic cast to the skin can occur. Dr. Alfred Blalock a cardiologist, and Dr. Helen Taussig, a pediatrician, performed the first surgery to correct the Blue Baby condition at John Hopkins University Hospital on November 20th, 1944. When reporting on developments in Blue Baby treatment in February 17, 1947, The American Weekly stated: "Their lips are blue, and they can walk only a few feet without exhaustion. Doctors used to give them only a few tortured years to live. But now medicine can give hope…and more…for since November 20, 1944, Dr. Blalock, Professor of Surgery at John Hopkins University in Baltimore, has been conquering the 'blue' baby malady…]"

[ix] G.I. Bill of Rights can be regarded as legislation for veterans of World War II. It was signed by President Franklin Roosevelt on June 22, 1944, as the "Servicemen's Readjustment Act of 1944" and provided: education and training, loan guarantees for a home, farm or business; unemployment benefits of $20 a week for up to fifty-two weeks, job placement assistance, materials and supplies for Veteran Administration hospitals, and a military review of dishonorable discharges. The original program ended in July of 1956. In 1947, at its peak, veterans accounted for 49% of the nation's college enrollment. Eligibility requirements included: service of more than ninety days after September 16, 1940, and a release status of other than a dishonorable discharge. Veterans were allowed one year full time training, plus a period equal to their time served up to forty-eight months.

[x] Executive Order Number 9981 was issue by President Harry S. Truman on July 26, 1948 and it eliminated segregation in the armed services. It stated in part, "It is hereby declared to be the policy of the President that there shall be equality of treatment and opportunity of all of the United States Armed Forces without regard to race, color, religion, or national origin. This policy shall be put into effect as rapidly as possible, having due regard to the time required to effectuate any necessary changes without impairing efficiency or morale."

[xi] *Stars and Stripes* is the newspaper printed for the United States armed forces. It got its start as a newspaper for the Union Army during the Civil War. Publication was resumed for the armed services under General John Pershing from 1918 – 1919 in France during World War I. Its publication was again resumed during World War II, it has been published continuously since 1942 in Europe, since 1945 in the Pacific, and is sold at military facilities overseas.

[xii] Stokely Carmichael was a civil rights activist born in 1941. As a Howard University student, he became a member of the Student Nonviolent Coordinating Committee (SNCC) in 1961. He participated in Freedom Rides in the South and voter registration drives in Alabama in

1965 and Mississippi in 1966. By 1967 he had become disillusioned with this country's political system, the civil rights movement, and mainstream black leaders. He coined the term "black power," co-authored a book of that title in 1967, and became Prime Minister of the Black Panther Party in 1968. Stokely Carmichael was part of a budding group of black leaders that emphasized self defense in the face of violence, and rejected the "turn-the-other-cheek" notion underlying the traditional civil rights movement. He, H. Rap Brown and other emerging militant black activists were accused of inciting violence by the FBI and U.S. Government in the late 1960s and early 1970s as the Civil Rights movement became more militant.